INSIDE VIEWS FROM THE DISSOCIATED WORLDS OF EXTREME VIOLENCE
Human Beings as Merchandise

Gaby Breitenbach

Translated by Mary Jo Rabe

KARNAC

First published in German in 2011 as *Innenansichten dissoziierter Welten extremer Gewalt: Ware Mensch—die planvolle Spaltung der Persönlichkeit*

First published in English in 2015 by
Karnac Books Ltd
118 Finchley Road
London NW3 5HT

Copyright © 2011 Asanger Verlag GmbH Kröning, www.asanger.de

British Library Cataloguing in Publication Data

A C.I.P. for this book is available from the British Library

ISBN-13: 978-1-78220-245-5

Typeset by V Publishing Solutions Pvt Ltd., Chennai, India

Printed in Great Britain

www.karnacbooks.com

This book is first and foremost dedicated to my clients in gratitude for their trust and candor, with the hope that our work together will someday be so beneficial to them that they will be able to create for themselves a life that is genuinely worth living

CONTENTS

ACKNOWLEDGEMENTS

I have many people to thank. To thank for supporting my work, which made it at all possible, for sharing their insights with me, for standing by my side in word and deed, and also for their criticism. I have to thank them for giving me their trust and for letting me be a part of their lives, and not least for their courage in embarking on the journey with me.

And I have to thank many people for being there when I needed them most.

First and foremost I have to thank my clients who, coming out of a hell beyond all description, were still and continue to be willing to give it a go with me. I sincerely hope that they never have a reason to regret their decision to seek therapy and a different life.

I thank my husband Horst for bearing with me and my workload, and for actively supporting me in my work in such a loving way. I also thank him for entering my life and helping so many things in it take a turn for the better.

I thank my colleague Harald Requardt for making it possible for me to implement the values in our institute that are most important to me, and I thank him because I can discuss everything with him, even that which is unspeakable.

I thank Waltraud D. for her caring support and companionship and for apparently not keeling over about anything. Oh, if only I could clone you!

I thank my friends who have given me security and have always understood that I am sometimes almost a virtual reality to them, because I am always working. But you can be sure that I love you and that I exist!

I thank Marilyn van Derbur whose fondness for me warms me like a coat around my soul, who always accompanies me. We have shared much together professionally and personally and still do. It's good that you are there.

I thank Ellert Nijenhuis for writing a preface and for his commitment to research regarding dissociative people. I can only guess how much work this means.

I thank Luise Reddemann for her support and goodwill, which I can always rely on and for giving me a hand whenever I needed it. I want to at least mention how much I have learned from her practical work and how much I continue to learn.

I thank the lawyers "G.", "H.", and "Dr. M." for always being on hand with help and advice despite me always needing something special and unusual.

I thank the journalists Thomas F., Michael O., and Wolfgang H. for their dedication to the topics that are so near and dear to me.

I thank all the individual benefactors and the various fundraising campaigns for making money available for my clients over and over again, thereby making it possible for them to have a little more quality in their lives.

I thank all the unnamed quiet helpers, the colleagues, and the private individuals who have become involved in order to make it possible for my clients to have a better life. Above all I thank A.R. who as a former manager counseled many of my clients but also steadily supported them financially and personally and continues to do so. I don't even want to picture a world without him.

I want to thank Alison Miller for her loyalty and support, for her willingness to proofread the English version, and with deep admiration for her ability to put her work with those affected by mind control and ritual violence into a readable and structured form. And I want to thank her for her generosity in more than one respect. You are someone very special, Alison. What you did for me was much more than just proofreading. You helped me make concepts clear in English, you edited the book, and so much more … and you even stayed on my side and continued to work on the book when it was really not much fun at all. I have to thank you more than I can express, and I am still learning.

I want to thank Carol Rutz, representing all those affected by ritual violence and mind control, for your courage and willingness to share your knowledge with the public. What that costs someone who has suffered these things goes far beyond anyone's powers of imagination.

I thank Richard Kluft, whose explanations of hypnosis and dissociation have stood me well more than once, for his sense of humor along with the generosity with which he shares his knowledge, an indispensable source for my work. And, dear Rick, I have to apologize: in reading *Shelter from the Storm* I found that one of the therapeutic interventions that helped me so much, and that are so much part of that book, was created by you. You and the FAT-man (fractionated abreaction technique) helped me a lot in my work without my knowledge. I hope you accept my apology, that you find the book worth reading, and that you understand how many of my thoughts are based on or derived from that concept. And I have to say a special thank you to the FAT-man: Without you, my work would have been much more difficult and my clients' pain would have been much greater.

I thank Jennifer Freyd whose work gave me further insight into the destruction that betrayal leaves behind. Through her friendly, open manner in every encounter, she convinced me once again that brilliant scholarship and warmhearted humaneness aren't mutually exclusive, but rather complement each other.

And last but not least I thank all the readers who manage to use suggestions from this book for their work with highly dissociative clients, and I encourage them to travel this path together with me.

I want to end the book with this quote attributed to Confucius (2014): "It isn't enough to come to the banks of the river hoping to catch fish. You also have to bring along a net."

ABOUT THE AUTHOR

Gaby Breitenbach is a psychologist and psychological psychotherapist. Along with qualifications in working with clients who suffer from traumatic experiences, she is a systems therapist and behavior therapist. She began her professional career more than twenty-five years ago in a specialist hospital for adolescent drug addicts. It was there that she encountered the topic of extreme traumatization at a time when there was no official name for it. She got to know patients with dissociative disorders, including dissociative identity disorder, who described almost unbelievable experiences of violence. They presented with inner splitting that made their lives extraordinarily difficult. At a time when there were no therapy plans or publications in this area, Gaby Breitenbach embarked on a journey searching for a path through that harsh terrain.

Those first approaches evolved into the work at Villa Lindenfels, an institute for continuing education in systems therapy and trauma therapy, and a psychotherapeutic institute for treating traumatized patients. Villa Lindenfels, which Gaby Breitenbach leads together with her long-time friend and colleague Harald Requardt, celebrated its twentieth birthday in 2012.

With Harald Requardt, Gaby Breitenbach co-authored *Psychotherapie mit entmutigten Klienten* (*Psychotherapy with Dispirited Clients*) and *Komplex-systemische Traumatherapie und Traumapädagogik* (*Complex-systemic trauma therapy and trauma education*). She wrote *Vom Wert des Lebens* (*About the Value of Life*) in collaboration with Fabienne and Pierre Schneider. *Inside Views* is her first sole-authored book.

PREFACE

Many reasons could tempt us to leave this book unread. Deeply immersed in the comfortable beliefs that our "I", "me", "myself" are simply a given, largely stable, and quite secure, we are not happy at the thought of giving them up. However, the clinical reality and literature on trauma-related dissociation—one of the themes of Gaby Breitenbach's impressive work—tell us that one body can encompass more than just one self. This work also reveals that with exceptional torture and pain, even any sense of self can be temporarily lost—this means an exceptional agony, as some survivors convey to us.

It is hard to acknowledge the truth about our world and ourselves. With every philosophical and scientific revolution, we are shaken. The sun does not revolve around the earth (Copernicus), and we are far from being the center of the universe. We are unable to comprehend things in and of themselves; we are tied to the world as we can know it, that is in terms of time, space, and causality (Kant). Time and space are not fixed but relative (Einstein). Our self is a fragile, personal concept (Buddhism, contemporary neurophilosophy). And, at a more personal level, behind our self there can be yet another self, as Emily Dickinson (2007) describes in her poignant poem:

> One need not be a chamber to be haunted,
> One need not be a house;
> The brain has corridors surpassing
> Material place.
>
> Far safer, of a midnight meeting
> External ghost,
> Than an interior confronting
> That whiter host.
>
> Far safer through an Abbey gallop,
> The stones achase,
> Than, moonless, one's own self encounter
> In lonesome place.
>
> Ourself, behind ourself concealed,
> Should startle most;
> Assassin, hid in our apartment,
> Be horror's least.
>
> The prudent carries a revolver,
> He bolts the door,
> O'erlooking a superior spectre
> More near.

Dickinson is right, we prefer to shoot the truth rather than acknowledge it if it does not fit our core beliefs. "The truth which makes men free is for the most part the truth which men prefer not to hear," said the journalist and newspaper editor Herbert Agar (1943).

Another reason to put this book aside quickly concerns the need to hold on to the idea that dissociative disorders are nonsense, as some authors have argued, often without having ever studied even one patient with her accompanying distress. This idea makes its believers feel safe, because it leaves a complex and dark side of human existence concealed.

The ICD-10 (WHO, 1992) states that dissociative identity disorder (DID), the most complex dissociative disorder known, is rare. Many clinicians who accept the existence of dissociative disorders consider this statement to be correct. However, solid scientific investigations have demonstrated that the prevalence of DID is at least as common as the prevalence of schizophrenia. This rate is approximately one percent of the general population. The prevalence of dissociative disorders in psychiatric samples amounts to some ten percent.

The belief that diagnoses of dissociative disorders must be taken with a large grain of salt has been one reason that many clinicians and researchers avoid learning about them. This fact is not hard to establish. Type "dissociative identity disorder" in Google, and you will find 1,150,000 hits. Type "schizophrenia" and you get 27,200,000. Or try PubMed, a major search engine for scientific studies. You find 314 studies for dissociative identity disorder, and 102,681 for schizophrenia. Now look for the number of neuroimaging studies on DID and schizophrenia. The same skewed distribution pops up in seconds: nine for DID and 3261 for schizophrenia.

Is this disregard justified? Is Gaby Breitenbach a fool to invest her time, energy, and dedication in the description and treatment of disorders that do not exist, or that are, as quite a few professionals claim, due to suggestion, fantasy, and pretense? Are clinicians and scientists who ignore or reject dissociative disorders right? Careful clinical observation and research studies and science tell a different story. For example, Simone Reinders (2003, 2006), other colleagues, and I have documented that different types of dissociative parts of the personality in women with DID have different psychophysiological reactions and different patterns of brain activity when they listen to descriptions of the traumatic memories they themselves have reported. When they were presenting as their everyday life selves, these patients reacted to the trauma scripts as if they did not pertain to them at all. This subjective evaluation was associated with a lack of psychophysiological reactivity, and a pattern of brain activation that is similar to neural patterns in depersonalization disorder. But compared with the "I" who tried to cope with daily life, a different "I", who was fixated in traumatic memories, had a much higher heart rate and blood pressure, as well as an overactive sub-cortical "emotional brain" in response to the trauma scripts.

Skeptics of DID were not convinced that our studies demonstrate the reality of DID. In their opinion, high fantasy-prone women would be quite capable of simulating DID. This idea relates to their view that the disorder is not real but instead due to suggestion and fantasy (Giesbrecht, Lynn, Lilienfeld, & Merckelbach, 2008). "Give them descriptions of the major features of the so-called dissociative parts you studied, ask them to enact these 'parts', and they will have psychophysiological and neural activation patterns very similar to those of your patients," they claimed with confidence. This is exactly the experiment we recently performed (Reinders, Willemsen, Vos, Den Boer, & Nijenhuis, 2012). The findings are that neither high nor low fantasy-prone, mentally healthy women came close to the psychobiological activation patterns that characterized the women with authentic DID. The study demonstrates, for the first time, that the core features of different types of dissociative parts in DID cannot be explained by fantasy, suggestion, and role-playing. This should stimulate anyone who contends "I do not believe in DID" to think twice.

We also found that, contrary to what is commonly contended, women with DID are not highly fantasy-prone (Nijenhuis & Reinders, 2012). In fact, they are only slightly more fantasy-prone than mentally healthy women, and they are less fantasy-prone than women with borderline personality disorder. This finding should make a difference as well, because no authority has claimed to date that borderline personality disorder is due to high fantasy-proneness, suggestion, or role-playing.

There is thus every science-based reason to study Gaby Breitenbach's work, even though it may be frightening. The nineteenth-century philosopher Arthur Schopenhauer observed that all truth passes through three stages. First, it is ridiculed. Second, it is violently opposed. Third, it is accepted as being self-evident. Would this also apply to the dark side of human society, that we as members of this society would rather not know? What about reports of major and chronic emotional neglect, emotional abuse, physical maltreatment, and sexual abuse of children, all often inflicted by people who are supposed to love those children?

In 1975, a major psychiatric handbook stated as fact that incest happens to one child in a million (Henderson, 1975). When it became apparent that incest is a much more common phenomenon, this fact was first ridiculed, then violently opposed. Today, most sane people take it to be an evident, sad fact. Some would perhaps like to believe that chronic childhood traumatization only happens in the lower classes, and that intelligent people are unlikely to ruin their children's lives. The established fact is, however, that incest and other forms of abuse and neglect occur at all levels of society. We all witness how the church is now forced to face the facts of the sexual, physical, and emotional abuse of many children by numerous priests and other representatives of the church, and their major implications. We now also observe how the church has been forced to recognize its own dark role in covering up these facts for years, and how it struggles to accept responsibility. There is quite a difference between knowing and realizing the truth.

Has psychiatry become wiser over the years? Although there are certainly many positive developments, it is also true that even the simplest of trauma-related disorders are still massively under-diagnosed. Recognition of childhood traumatization and its implications in somatic health care is not particularly high either. The established fact is that the odds of developing a variety of "somatic" diseases are far higher when one has been exposed to childhood traumatization. But how many physicians know and realize this? Ignoring or rejecting such scientific facts out of hand is much more comforting than taking them in and becoming aware of their implications.

What applies to patients—knowing realities beneath the surface, getting in touch with the self behind the self—applies to us, to the perpetrators and their accomplices, to families with concealed darkness, to psychiatry, and to our society. Gaby Breitenbach shows us that there is, in addition to the now generally known childhood abuse and neglect, a dark world of organized crime against children, full of sadism, mind control, and who knows what else. Are we tempted to ridicule her words? Must we violently oppose the claim that some victims of these horrors have been trained, with the help of sophisticated psychological techniques, to run from people who want to help them, even though they long for such recognition and assistance, and to run harder, the closer they get to receiving this help?

It would be easy to say that this is all a lie, that we can safely keep Gaby Breitenbach's book closed. We might be tempted to believe she is confused and has been led astray by her clients. It would be quite possible to ridicule her words, or even Gaby Breitenbach herself. However, the troublesome fact is that there are individuals who are sharing their horrendous stories with clinicians who are willing to listen. When allowed the time they need to develop trust, there are individuals who will speak out. These are the individuals who find the courage to explore their hidden self behind their more superficial self, and to introduce us to a hidden world of lost human value and dignity. It would be so easy to say, "this cannot possibly be true".

However, there are known facts that stand in the way of such knee-jerk dismissal. For example, as Gaby Breitenbach describes, some of these individuals are highly intelligent, extremely sincere, and wise. They certainly do not fit the stereotype of the "hysterical, gullible" woman. Some of these patients' bodies show burn marks all over. One surgeon had to operate on a patient because she had mutilated herself so badly. He was not aware of the patient's life and her psychological condition. During the operation, he observed that underneath the fresh injury, there were scars related to burns that, in his professional opinion, must have occurred during the patient's early childhood. Experiencing major agony, in therapy the patient accessed the knowledge of some of her dissociated parts and told the complete story of how a group of people had inflicted these wounds on her on many different occasions; this group continues to pursue her to this day. We are all aware of the existence of massive organized child pornography, child prostitution, and traffic in children and women. We know human cruelty, organized crime, and abuse of power all too well. How likely is it that sadists, pedophiles, and criminals would not organize to satisfy their sick hunger for sex, power, and money, and take every measure to silence witnesses?

Gaby Breitenbach explains that we have a duty to provide appropriate treatment for individuals who show and tell us about this dark world. We must be brave, postpone judgment, and think things through deliberately and thoroughly. Reports of worlds we would rather ignore than recognize need to be heard, examined, and studied. Gaby Breitenbach has had the courage to speak. Are our heads and hearts brave enough to listen to her and to the patients she describes so well?

Ellert R. S. Nijenhuis, Ph.D.
Top Referent Trauma Center, Mental Health Care Drenthe,
Assen, Netherlands; co-director of Psychotraumatology
Institute Europe, Duisburg, Germany

FOREWORD

Like Gaby Breitenbach, my clinical work for the past 20 years has focused primarily on survivors of child abuse by organized perpetrator groups. I did not deliberately choose this specialty. I don't think any clinician would. I was working with children and teens, parents and families, when I discovered that some of my clients had been abused in horrendous ways by organized groups in which their entire families had been involved. I didn't want to know this, and it took me quite a while to come to grips with such a reality. The society in which we live encourages us to believe that the only sadistic child abusers are disturbed loners who abduct children from their safe and nurturing families. Children are to be alert for "stranger danger". If only this were the biggest danger to children. Far more common is the multigenerational abusive family, and the reality is that child abusers are frequently networked with other abusive families. When I finally faced reality, I could look back on my past clients and identify several who had very probably been abused by organized perpetrator groups.

I was also slow to recognize dissociation in my clients because, like most psychologists, I had received no education about dissociative disorders. We do not see "switches" between hidden parts of a person unless they are blatant. Few of us are attuned to dissociation and able to detect these subtle switches which mean that another part of the person has come forward or is listening. We are also very slow to recognize symptoms as indicative of trauma rather than of "mental illnesses".

Gaby Breitenbach's book addresses the reality of complex disso-ciative disorders, including "programmed" dissociation, in which the mind is deliberately split and different parts trained in different ways by sadistic perpetrators who know what they are doing. She addresses the fragmentation of memory in survivors, the result of the way in which the different levels of the brain work in life-threatening emergencies to separate sensory and emotional input from everyday consciousness. She describes several different types of dissociative structures, and sug-gests practical ways for therapists to work with each of these, as well as helpful guidelines for spouses and non-perpetrator family members of survivors.

Gaby's later chapters focus on a societal critique. I recognize how similar what she describes in Germany is to what I have observed here in North America. She points out that the same people often have power in both the known world and the "shadow world of organized violence". Organized perpetrator groups direct their members into pro-fessions such as psychiatry, politics, religion, child protection, and the law, in order to structure society in such a way as to discredit survivors of this abuse and to facilitate its continuance. She critiques the attempts to depict dissociation and fragmented remembering as lying, fabrica-tion, imagination, or fantasy, explaining that the very existence of dis-sociation and fragmentation of memory is evidence of severe childhood trauma.

Gaby acknowledges that effective therapy with survivors of this unimaginable abuse takes years, as it depends on a nurturing therapeu-tic relationship. In the world in which I work, institutions do not pro-vide more than brief therapy and medication, and individual survivors rarely have the financial resources to obtain the kind of help they need. It will be a long time before we have the kind of societal change that will enable survivors to heal and perpetrators to be brought to justice.

I believe there are two major obstacles to the change that is needed: first, that the organized perpetrator groups have considerable input into the societal institutions that deal with survivors, and second, that society itself is dissociative. Our Western world has its "apparently nor-mal personality" of democracy and social concern, but it also has its hidden aspects, what Gaby calls the "parallel world", which those of us who live in the normal world often do not want to acknowledge. The Nazis were able to take over much of Europe and run their death camps because of this societal dissociation. Neo-Nazis are just one of the several groups who now engage in mind control of young children, and it was imported Nazi scientists who taught mind control to the Americans. Other groups include occult religions, secret societies, and organized criminal groups who profit from child prostitution, child pornography, and child trafficking. Many people, including members of the helping professions, are afraid, and prefer to look on the "bright side" rather than to know that these evil groups continue to exist right within our supposedly enlightened and developed society.

I believe that this book will help bring the situation to light, and will make its readers, whether they are therapists, survivors, family members, or seekers of social justice, more aware of what is going on and what needs to be done about it.

Alison Miller
Canadian psychologist, author of Healing the Unimaginable:
Treating Ritual Abuse *and* Mind Control and Becoming
Yourself: Overcoming Mind Control and Ritual Abuse

WHO THIS BOOK IS FOR

First and foremost, this book is for therapists who work with clients suffering from dissociative disturbances after experiencing extreme and organized violence. My hope is that by describing varying perspectives, I will be able to contribute to developing a compendium of solutions to help these victims.

I would be happy if this book also proves to be readable and useful for clients and provides non-experts with an understanding of the structure and impact of organized violence.

People and contents described

I have tried to put a face on organized violence and to shine a spotlight on it from many different angles. Whereas many reference works include word-for-word, specific exercises and sources of assistance for the victim, I have deliberately refrained from doing so in this book. I have had to go through the painful experience of seeing good and helpful exercises and courses of action suddenly turn up again in a perverted form. Sometimes even a passing mention of a title of an exercise, for example "safe place", triggers painful processes in our clients.

The organized perpetrator groups have also added to their knowledge and seen to it that effective methods can no longer be pursued the same way as before. With respect to the perpetrators' courses of action, I have tried to limit the detailed descriptions as much as possible. The last thing I want is for this book to be a user's manual for sadistic violence. I want to make it possible for the reader to personally experience inside views of sadistic violence. One of the perspectives is of course that of the tormentor.

I have also disguised the experiences described by the clients by compiling these experiences like collages. I selected those elements which, based on my experience, are best suited to describe the clients' world of experience systematically. Under no circumstances should the descriptions of these experiences reveal the identity of the victims.

All the names used in this book come directly and exclusively from my imagination. Inner persons, alters, tormentors, and clients are never mentioned by their real names.

However, the parallel world I describe where human beings are systematically trained, tortured, and tormented is not a product of my imagination.

Various references to the United States in this book have to do with the fact that the prototypes of many current programs and conditioning methods originated with military research in the United States. This research in turn profited from the classification systems of Nazi medical experiments. Current organized violence extends the findings of that time continuously, according to their market demand.

With the reference to the roots of organized violence, however, I do not imply that this kind of violence is restricted to these countries. Sadism and organized violence know no boundaries, neither with respect to content nor to geography.

Multi-talking—the language of dissociation

The title, *Inside Views from the Dissociated Worlds of Extreme Violence*, may seem confusing at first. In this book many different dissociated worlds are addressed:

- The inside world of clients, containing the reality of the violence they experienced, which is shown in various dissociative phenomena.

- The reality of extreme violence that had to be split apart from consciousness and exists even though the consciousness knows nothing about it.
- The separation of this kind of violence from the normal world, because society's message is "that which we don't want to be true, cannot be true".
- The concealment of violence on the part of the perpetrators behind a veneer of decorum—inside there is violence; from the outside you can't detect it.

This extreme, organized violence does exist. And therefore the inside reality of those who have experienced it is also a reality, not only of memory but also a reality that can be experienced in a therapeutic setting.

A further distinctive feature of my language is that when I introduce my working theories, I deliberately speak in the subjunctive mood, that is in terms of possibilities. It's important for me to clarify the fact that with respect to theoretical differentiations I only make suggestions, whereas with respect to concrete therapeutic actions I do things in a certain way, or rather consider this way to be wise.

Inside views—a journey

This book is a journey. In various chapters I would like to invite the reader to observe the world of extreme violence from varying perspectives. This logic determines the order of the chapters.

In my view, Chapters Three and Eight are the ones that are the most difficult for non-psychologists to read. Nonetheless, naturally I still hope that all readers will be able to understand them. In my opinion, the other chapters are comprehensible even if the reader has not dealt with these questions previously and would appreciate an introduction to the topic of "extreme violence". At least that is what I very much hope.

SUMMARY OF CHAPTERS

Each chapter invites the reader to consider a particular perspective.

Chapter One: dissociation in everyday life; dissociation and programming

I invite you to get involved with differentiating various dissociation structures from a perspective of personal experience. I invite you to experience how dissociation is a question of circumstances and not a result of the client's "doing something wrong" or "being sick". Let me make it clear that dissociation can strike any of us and that it represents a fundamental possibility of what can happen to human beings. I will define a working model with seven different dissociation structures, that is, ways in which a mind can be structured in order of increasing dissociation.

Chapter Two: a working model demonstrated through case studies

In a few individual case vignettes, I would like to invite the reader to understand the perspective of the therapist and to see how the differing structures of dissociation show themselves in practice, how they arise, and the consequent difficulties in everyday life.

Chapter Three: practical conclusions for psychotherapy

With the examples of the vignettes from Chapter Two, but still from the point of view of the therapist, I show at which points approaches for solving the problems can be created, and which aspects have to be considered. Disgust as a catalyst for dissociation is regularly accompanied by guilt and shame in therapy—both aspects that the tormentors can avail themselves of systematically.

Since the explanation of the structures of dissociation is constructed on experiences of disgust, we deal with disgust, shame, and guilt in treating our clients. "What happens to me is my responsibility—that's the way I am."

Chapter Four: how distinctions in the internal and external worlds develop as a result of experiences

In this chapter it will become clear from the perspective of the therapist, how the structure of our internal world is connected with the structure of our external world. It's primarily about the question of how distinctions take on a greater significance and are maintained and which roles the systems of bonding and of curiosity have in the context of these experiences.

Chapter Five: inside views from a sadistic world

From the inside view of the person involved and from the therapist's point of view, I want to show here the nature of the hidden world of sadistic perpetrators. I shall try to communicate how their pitilessness (absence of empathy) was already learned in early childhood, and what happens between perpetrator and victim. As we more often encounter perpetrators who, behind the façade, reveal a neo-Nazi mindset in their staging and contemptuous treatment of the victims, this is also described in the example. The reader is invited to enter a world that would otherwise remain locked away. I believe it is indispensable for therapists to gain a perception of this shadow world.

Chapter Six: inside views from a survivor

This chapter invites you into the mindscape and the experiences of a client who endured extreme experiences of violence. At the time when she describes herself Nadja isn't aware of the contents of her dissociated worlds. She experiences herself as separated from the world, as cut off. She suffers, but she can't identify the origin of her suffering. Nadja's description is therefore from the viewpoint of a system that sees itself from the outside and attempts to describe what is going on inside. Nadja describes what she is able to perceive consciously from the perspective of an outsider.

Chapter Seven: death of an assassin

This chapter and the two preceding ones are not all parts of the story of the same survivor. Rather, each chapter provides a different perspective, to help the reader imagine how this world of violence is structured and how differently it is seen by someone with dissociated knowledge as opposed to someone with very detailed conscious knowledge of the crimes. The theme of the whole book is to invite the reader to look at these matters from various perspectives, giving examples.

Chapter Five provides a perspective to help the reader imagine the world of organized crime in which a victim grows up. Chapter Six shows the perspective of a survivor without any knowledge of the hidden and dissociated world. In this chapter the perspective is different. This woman knows about what happened to her and confronts her dying father in her own chosen way. It is like an inner dialogue while facing him.

Please keep in mind that this chapter might be triggering if you are a survivor yourself; and please, do not feel as a survivor, or assume as a therapist, that you have to confront the abuser. It is this woman's way; other people choose other ways.

Chapter Eight: about dissociative worlds

This chapter is concerned with the survivor's present-day immediate family. Sympathetic family members need support in dealing with dissociative partners. They face special difficulties, not only in the area of sexuality but also in the problems of everyday life. I will present options for supporting them in their understanding of dissociation and of the violence their family members experienced.

Chapter Nine: therapy to facilitate nurturing attachments

This chapter demonstrates how working models can help therapists to facilitate clients experiencing and learning from a nurturing relationship with a therapist so that they can establish healthy attachments with others. I will show some ways I believe to be helpful in developing a pathway to solutions. If healthy inner structures with respect to the client's inner essence are to develop, clients need support in order to learn: Who am I? What would I like to do? What is "mine", for me, in the truest sense of the word?

Chapter Ten: truth, lies, deception, fabrication?

This chapter is about doubt. When confronted with stories of extremely monstrous and inhuman abuses which have until now been hidden, not only the false memory movement but also our clients themselves, as well as the courts and society in general, ask whether these things can really be the truth. It is indeed possible that narcissistic and histrionic clients may well "adopt horror" in order to access longed-for care and attention. How we can distinguish the one from the other? This topic is a chapter of its own because within the framework of therapy it is such a frequent theme with clients.

Chapter Eleven: dissociation, imagination, and fantasy

Here the reader is invited to join me in neurobiological and epistemological speculation. What is the essence of dissociation? Which areas of the brain are affected and how much conscious activity of the human being can be expected at any one time? How conscious do you have to be in order to develop imagination, to be creative? My thoughts here are working models that should provide practical assistance, not ultimate truths about any topic.

Chapter Twelve: power and powerlessness

This central topic in the public eye and on the internal stage needs to be illuminated once again from a social perspective. From the viewpoint of the therapist, changes at many social levels are necessary in order to dismantle the societal structures which make the shadow world of organized violence powerful and which maintain this power. I agree with Salvador Minuchin (personal communication, 1994) that intervention on many varied levels is necessary and that therapists should definitely get involved in social activism for the benefit of their clients.

Chapter Thirteen: the language of violence

There is a language of violence within the inner world of our clients, as a result of a language of violence used in the world of violence where they grew up. But there is also a language of violence far beyond this narrow sphere, in the public eye, visible and respected. Language defines reality and language is power. This chapter aims to sensitize people to this fact and to set this perspective in relation to organized violence.

Chapter Fourteen: differences that make a difference

What specific aspects might therapists focus on so that clients who have been programed can discover an inner structure based on their own decisions and distinctions? Here I summarize and give an overview of the different kinds of distinctions that were described in the previous chapters.

Chapter Fifteen: prospects—so much is missing

A tentative but nevertheless optimistic conclusion from my own perspective as author and therapist.

INTRODUCTION

Night after night the men came out of the radiator. Every knock, every click announced their presence. I knew that they were men, and I knew that the fear they caused me night after night was crazy. They couldn't be where my feelings were certain that they were. As a ten-year-old child this fear had already become so overwhelming that I would flee to my mother's bed, either in conscious fear or while sleepwalking, to seek protection. It took more than forty years before my memory allowed me to see what, deep down, I never really forgot. The men didn't come out of the radiator; they came up from the basement boiler room, there were good reasons to fear their arrival, and at the same time for many years not to recognize how much reality belonged to this knowledge of the "men out of the radiator".

Dissociation is an option, a means to protect ourselves on the inside, when experiences threaten to overwhelm us. What we aren't capable of integrating, we split off into subconscious inner parts of our personality.

As long as we as an organism still have a variety of possibilities for reacting—when therefore no one ensures that certain splits develop—then it is our organism that determines the kind of survival response, the kind of dissociation. In the instant when a threat over-whelms our coping mechanisms, we have the possibility, inasmuch as the event only happens once, of protecting ourselves by separating what we observe from what we experience. This first possibility explains the increased occurrence of somatoform disorders as a result of untreated traumas.

In the case of extreme and repeated threats we split ourselves apart in a way that Nijenhuis and colleagues (2009) describe as structural disso-ciation. The self collapses, but how it collapses is determined to a great extent by our organism itself and its basic structure. The structure of the self is one part of the resulting effect not just the experience itself. This structural dissociation follows predetermined breaking points, which have already been established biologically. Going one step further, we are dealing with fragmentations whereby the human being who is threatening us wants to coerce a certain result, a certain condition that is useful to him. Within the framework of classical conditioning, people learn to behave in a foreseeable manner. This also always has an evo-lutionary value. What we experience over and over again teaches us that the best way to react is to submit to the will of the stronger. Once this happens, a previously neutral stimulus triggers certain behaviors automatically. These automatic reactions, or defense mechanisms, may be regarded as innate automatisms.

This can mean behaving compliantly in the presence of tormentors and their customers (those, for example, interested in sadistic violence or child prostitution) in order to limit the extent of your own suffer-ing; or it can mean hurting yourself before others punish you for your "misbehavior". Here the intentions of others are already integrated into your actions. It is clear in what direction your organism has to react due to its innate structure.

This is also true for the first programming steps. Unfortunately in professional literature the word "programming" is not treated with the required clarity so that you can recognize whether everyone is talking about the same thing. Often conditioning with complex origins, imple-mented through a sequence of steps, is already defined as a program. I consider a different terminology to be more helpful. I would only use the concept of "programs" where there is truly a complex sequence of behaviors affecting aspects of identity and where internal and external interaction with others is a part of the programming. This means that a reaction to a trigger such as a gesture or a noise would be conditioning. However, if a complete sequence of behavior follows the first reaction to a gesture, for example between multiple inner persons—that is to say, A gets a signal, then forces B to do something that makes C behave in a certain way until finally with the conclusive actions of D the complete program has run its course—then I would find the designation "programming" appropriate. Occasionally programs involve large groups of inner persons and span long sequences of action.

For the purpose of differentiation, I would like to introduce yet another concept, that of "inverse programming", which naturally must presume an inverse conditioning—in a certain program, conditioned internal personalities do things. Or to simplify, this is what happens: The actual options for behavior generated by the organism are systematically denied und eliminated (or more accurately, destroyed) and new specific behaviors are compelled. Basically you can say that the tormentors are playing God. They erase the old hard disk and create a new one of their own. That necessitates them also making sure that a person can no longer use her sensory organs adequately and make reasonable deductions from the sensations, but rather that the brain is trained with dysfunctional presuppositions, which make a normal life impossible. Alternate entities separate from a person's consciousness are created systematically and are substantially different from the core of the person in their words, actions, and perceptions.

Attempting to take possession of another person apparently generates a special feeling of power for the tormentor. Especially when he is successful at getting his victim to perform actions at the "push of a button" which she is forced to perceive as her own and which she can neither stop of her own accord nor reconcile with her own values. Eventually you have a completely fragmented personality, for the most part controllable by others through codes, and automated and dehumanized in the expression of her behavior. When we encounter people who have endured such continuing, systematic torture over the course of many years, it seems as if they aren't really there and as if they can't experience themselves consciously or perceive themselves as individuals at all.

In this book I would like to describe various "views from the inside": how survivors of extreme violence view themselves; how therapists view the inner world of their clients; and also how they view the outside parallel world of extreme violence.

When I mention this parallel world here, I mean organized, extreme violence, above all toward children (girls make up the majority of the victims) and women, who are forced to supply the market for sadism and sexual perversions. The designation "parallel world" takes into account the fact that this world exists without being visible to most people.

I want to point out connections between the *modi operandi* of certain kinds of extreme violence and certain patterns of dissociation. The better we understand how systematic dissociation is compelled, the better we understand how to make it possible for the victims to forge connections into which they can grow progressively and perceive their true inner structures commensurate with their inner core. Then what we call deprograming and deconditioning can also succeed better. I am completely aware that we can't eliminate thirty years of systematic, organized violence and that the scars of these experiences will also remain as losses that can't be recovered. Still, in the final analysis, every therapeutic intervention should be performed as precisely as possible in order to prevent as much further suffering as we can.

I'm talking about people who, for all intents and purposes, from the day they were born were denied the chance to control their own lives, to bond with others, and to pursue their own development. No horror film could allow itself to show what happened to these human beings in our midst.

It seems that such perpetrators presume to shape all of creation for their own purposes. With diverse knowledge of psychotherapy, techniques of hypnosis, use of drugs, neurobiology, and with sophisticated technology, a parallel world has come into being in which tortured human beings live, often invisible to us, who are no longer a part of our world with its potential to benefit humankind. The inner and outer reality that has been forced on these human beings makes it completely impossible for them to heal themselves under their own power even after escaping to this side of the world.

Inside views describes inside views of systems and inside views showing observer perspectives in and about these inner worlds and in and about the outer worlds. It describes encounters with a form of extreme violence which we wish wasn't a reality.

Still, this parallel shadow world is not an invention of therapists who get their thrills from visions of horror, and it is not the spawn of a perverse paranoia. It is the result of an increasing market for sadistic violence, which is often trivialized by the media and eventually thereby becomes socially acceptable. It is also the result of the increasing divide in society between those people without a chance who fall down out of society and those people who profit from society in a vastly above-average manner. Extreme violence can be found at both ends of the social scale. If the public, visible, often eruptive and disorganized extreme violence at the lower end of the social scale can be explained by a lack of participation in society, or as a way of reducing frustration, extreme violence exists as organized violence at the other end of the scale, in the upper social classes. Here the violence is not public; it is denied, hiding itself behind well-locked doors. It is often much more systematic and long lasting. When someone low down in the social order falls completely out of regular society, he doesn't feel obligated to obey its rules; and at the top of the social scale, the idea occasionally seems to prevail that someone can be a kind of superman who also is not obliged to obey any rules, for whom anything goes.

It took almost a hundred years after Janet's haunting description of symptoms caused by trauma before the existence of resulting posttraumatic dysfunctions entered the diagnostic manuals. For a long time the majority view in society was that posttraumatic disturbances could be attributed to excessive personal sensitivity and that experiences didn't leave lasting scars. Consequently it wasn't a huge step for consumers of violence, and violent tormentors, to tell themselves that their actions didn't result in significant damage to the victims.

Many consumers of ugly, pornographic products appease their consciences with the fact that these products can be bought legally and that there are so many consumers that it therefore has to be "normal". We are used to being voyeuristic observers of violence. We seldom ask what sort of a life a murder victim might have had, whose loss creates a huge hole in the world of those who loved him. But the details of his murder are brought to us in just as shrill and colorful a fashion as the details of the life story of his murderer. Often it is just a small step to feeling sorry for the murderers. Naturally no one turns out that way of his own free will but there is also such a thing as personal responsibility for choices and dealing with one's own life story.

We live in a society that is loyal to power. It's easier to come to a resolution that favors the perpetrator than it is to do justice to the victims—especially in cases of extreme violence. Giving testimony means being able to report, in detail and without distortion, consistently and in a logical narrative. A victim who has experienced extreme violence can't manage this, precisely because she has experienced such violence. This means, once again, being excluded from her rights, for example compensation for damages awarded through a court procedure. Possible reimbursement demands that the victim press charges and consequently that proof of damages can be lined up. However, someone who has fled from those who did violence to her, and whose safety depends on remaining anonymous, has to do without any such compensation. In Germany changing your name doesn't result in keeping this information from your next of kin. In order to get a new name and a new identity, charges have to be pressed. To attain some safety, the victim is therefore forced to reveal information. This endangers the safety she had attained through fleeing her situation. No doubt this was never the intention of the legislation; more likely no one gave any thought to those people who had become victims of extreme and organized violence. No one would have dared to imagine that this parallel world could exist.

The existence of an unbearable parallel world leads to the same phenomenon in society as in the inner psyche: Society dissociates—because that which we don't want to be true, we desperately believe cannot be true.

In his powerful work about Sebastian Castellio, Stefan Zweig (2003) wrote, "... and again and again a Castellio will rise up against every Calvin" [translated for this edition]. Dear Stefan Zweig, I can't even say how much I wish that you would turn out to be right with this courageous assumption. The people this book is about have been shattered by society. And I believe, as far as our knowledge leads us today, there are few chances that these people will ever be completely restored again. But when we understand their sufferings better, our possibilities for therapeutic activity will become greater and more efficient.

In *Inside Views* I would like to introduce, among other things, different working models of dissociation, some inspired by colleagues (when possible I will quote them to let the message come through in their own words) and some invented by myself, in order to contribute to a broader treatment base for dissociative dysfunction. At this point I have to thank all my clients whose trust has made it possible for me to understand their world a little better. And I would like to make this invisible parallel world a little more visible, to sharpen the perception for violence among us and thereby give a face to the victims and their suffering.

And because nothing happens if there isn't someone who dreams a dream, I would like to place my dream at the beginning. I dream that one day it will be possible to document this extreme violence toward human beings, primarily directed toward women and children, in such a way that the legal system can convict the tormentors for what they did in these crimes against humanity. The collage "Lobster Cream Soup with a Cloud of Cream" makes the existence of this inhuman parallel world behind the façade of society's decorum clear.

Figure 1. "Lobster Cream Soup with a Cloud of Cream".

CHAPTER ONE

Dissociation in everyday life; dissociation and programming

I invite you to get involved with differentiating various dissociation structures from a perspective of personal experience. I invite you to experience how dissociation is a question of circumstances and not a result of the client's "doing something wrong" or "being sick". Let me make it clear that dissociation can strike any of us and that it represents a fundamental possibility of what can happen to human beings. I will define a working model with seven different dissociation structures, that is, ways in which a mind can be structured in order of increasing dissociation.

The scope of concepts to be explained: attention, memory, and dissociation

The more complex the mechanisms of dissociation become, the more complex and better organized the violence imposed on the client, and the more planned and sophisticated the sadism we encounter in these imposed actions. This violence is no longer just directed towards the victim's body but rather deliberately aimed at the victim's cognitive and emotional potential. Eventually complete dehumanization prevails, compounded by the formidable influence the tormentors have on the victim, making the victim commit deeds against her will, and—this is the distinctive feature here—often without the victim's conscious self knowing what she has done.

The more organized and ritualized the violence, the more fragmented the victims and their experiences. This means that their chances of putting the events into a context, coming up with an adequate description, and thereby understanding who was responsible for each act, who wanted it, etc., simply don't exist. Whereas victims can't prepare themselves in any way for what will happen, the situation for tormentors is completely different. Tormentors generally have a network and can organize wide-ranging defensive strategies and future support. Since they know what they plan to do and what their victims might be capable of saying, should memories somehow ever again reach the conscious level, the tormentors can take all these possibilities into account. At this point it is a small step to discredit any of the victims' memories that may emerge.

I would like to illustrate this theoretical section with a personal example, for which I have to give some background information. At our institute the teaching therapists own personal ordeals, experiences that were hard to bear, as practice exercises for the participants in advanced training courses. We often say "That will be a practice exercise".

As a teaching therapist and advanced training teacher, for personal reasons my heart goes out to the clients who have become victims of such far-reaching, horrendous violence. And there is one thing that I have always attempted to prevent: No proponent of the "false memory movement" is ever to teach at our institute—for personal reasons as well as professional ones.

Sadism in word and deed is very familiar to me, as is the experience of how it feels, and how it is shown, when the dissociative barriers break down, and the buried, dissociative experiences emerge back into consciousness. No, it is not a pleasant experience, and perhaps I can be grateful, in theory, for the knowledge that explains a little of it. But first there is the oppressive shame that people who have undergone such experiences feel towards the memories of the experiences that suddenly reappear. They worry about possibly making false accusations, about whether they might have wanted the violence to happen. They register over and over again the fact that everyone is questioning them. They search for another explanation. They assume: "I am like what happened to me. It has to have something to do with me. It just can't be true, because it shouldn't be true. Maybe it is a kind of schizophrenia. Maybe I'm neurotic. Maybe my hormones are out of whack ..."

What escapes from this containment isn't anything elegant; it's nothing to be proud of, but rather something you want to get as far away from as possible. Bessel van der Kolk (1996) once said about trauma, "People desperately want not to have been traumatized. They would rather take a chance on any other explanation, even serious mental illness, than to accept having become the powerless victim of massive violence." Genuine experience forces us therefore to relive highly unpleasant feelings when the dissociative barriers break.

You can try a little experiment on yourself here. Think back for a moment to a shameful experience such as violence or sexual assault, and let your feelings from that time return as you relive them completely one more time. And now imagine telling someone about this experience who is then able to see you just as you were in that shameful condition. While you describe this experience, you are unable to leave. Does that feel good? Then assume also you were lucky and you only had a few annoying symptoms afterwards like fears that you couldn't understand. Just to get some explanation, would you want to be persuaded that your fears were the result of such a shameful experience?

Naturally there are also the narcissistic, histrionic, disturbed clients who try to cover up the distress of inner emptiness with stories they invent. But they only succeed because the stories aren't genuine and haven't been experienced. The clients have only thought up these stories to induce feelings in those listening to them. The clients themselves are far from connecting any feelings to these stories. And, also an important factor, these are stories that are told—and not experiences that first have to become stories, for example during the course of therapy. What emerges from dissociation is a fragmented, incomplete story, nonintegrated, traumatized material, highly emotional and indeed not yet a narrative that can be told and placed into a context of time.

This makes it relatively easy for a therapist to differentiate between the two kinds of clients. The therapist's own experiences, worked and thought through, provide additional assistance. The newest research in neurobiology, memory processes after trauma, and dissociation provides sufficient indications about how the human brain differs in the way it processes overwhelming material and how it processes material it has already come to terms with. And not only this! As Ellert Nijenhuis shows in his latest study (2012), even for highly suggestible people, it is not possible to simulate the neurobiological processes of dissociation. Or, expressed more simply: The brain does something different and you can see that too. Evidence from numerous, tightly controlled studies shows that it is simply impossible for people to talk you into remembering traumatic experiences that did not occur or for you to talk yourself into remembering such things.

People can talk you into accepting interpretations of events, speculation, and things that correspond to so-called reconstructive memory. If you hear over and over again how you loved to play with your toy dog when you were two years old, and your relatives regale you with sentimental descriptions of what the toy looked like and how you interacted with it, then eventually you will come to believe that this is a part of your personal history, but that is not the same thing as remembering. It's not your memory that is active here, but rather that of your relatives. What happens to you here is the same as when you imagine something.

When we urge a client to imagine a comforting scene for her inner child, to let the scene run through her brain like a movie again and again, she doesn't mistake this for a real event. Rather, the client can remember the story as a story she told, as imagination. We don't mistake this for memory.

Suggestion means, for example, that through an established pattern of "yes, yes, yes" that we all are familiar with from hypnosis, we develop a greater acceptance for each successive suggestion. For example:

> The therapist says, "Your name is Mr. Maier." The client says, "Yes."
> "You're forty years old." "Yes."
> "You have a child." "Yes."
> "And you would like to change a certain behavior of yours."

The client is much more likely to feel motivated to change than if the therapist instead merely blurts out, "Good morning, Mr. Maier. You're here to change your behavior."

Suggestion can also occur when it is unclear as to what a certain fragment of memory might mean, and you, the therapist, suggest that the client attach a certain meaning to it. This could happen, for example, when a drawing or a dream that at first seems to be ambiguous is evaluated as unequivocally referring to a certain incident. This, again, is nothing that we can confuse with memory.

Dissociation works quite differently. Here we split unbearable experiences into little fragments without coming to terms with them, and so we are at first unable to approach these experiences consciously or purposefully. When the same unbearable experiences are repeated, they create their own internal entities that can have, more or less, their own consciousness, a conception of themselves, and their own inter-actions with others. This occurs when our consciousness has to rec-ognize things but cannot bear to recognize them. However it is clear that absorption and selective perception are not dissociative processes. I need dissociation when a bearable organization of my memories is not possible in any other way. Then the experiences get split up and split apart from my consciousness.

Such fragmentation creates numerous problems in everyday life, as the following example shows: The patient, a well-educated, intel-ligent woman, asks during a therapy session, "Tell me, do I stink? And when you touch me, do you have feelings of disgust? Don't you have to throw up?" Responding to the next obvious question, she reports that she often wakes up in the morning and notices that her mouth is smeared with feces, which she must have eaten without consciously being aware of doing so. In further sessions, fragments of the scene can be put together to create a composite picture of the violence she has experienced. A similar situation occurs when, during flashbacks of smell, the patient is convinced (because she or rather her brain registers it this way) that she stinks terribly. Another time one of her inner parts reports that a different alternate part must have eaten spoiled food out of the garbage, and that this was truly disgusting. This report describes graphically how the other inner parts feel this disgust.

I personally see no reason to assume that this woman, who is a free-lance architect, would say such a thing just to make herself sound inter-esting. Her distress is visible during every detail of the descriptions she gives, regardless of whether she feels the disgust bodily as an inner per-son or emotional personality (EP) inside the system or as the apparently normal personality (ANP) or host in a state of waking consciousness. Dissociation is therefore not suppression, not a simple forgetfulness, but rather a unique way of dealing with extreme experiences and their resulting eruption into consciousness. There is research to prove that dissociation exists as a unique phenomenon.

Now it is only one more, small step to get to my story: I work with many clients who have experienced extreme violence. Fear, pain, shame, and disgust are especially useful tools for the tormentor to demonstrate how powerful his influence is over another human being. What great power you have, when you can force someone to eat feces whenever you demand it! How much power is involved when you can make the victims believe they do it of their own free will!

I myself have a personal life story that makes it possible for me to know that extreme violence exists and that dissociation as a phenomenon exists. Precisely for this reason I am one of the staunchest opponents of the movement that has embraced the concept of "false memory" (FM). I am aware that selective attention can lead us to make mistakes while storing memories, that while accessing memories our minds can play tricks on us (above all in reconstructive memory that of course is a combination of memory and creativity), and that mistakes can occur even in dissociative recall. I don't want to claim that recall is never mistaken, but rather that the so-called error the FM movement complains about not only does not exist, but on the contrary is based on deliberate deception by a special interest group. You could simply say FM is based on the claim that there is no such thing as dissociative memories and that the worse the memories, the less likely they are to be true.

FM claims that the worse the experience, the better the recall should be, and that there is no possibility of a missing memory returning later. If someone therefore experienced something terrible, then this terribleness should make her remember it especially well. They claim it is impossible for someone to come to remember things later, or for memories to emerge some time after the violence has occurred. Here they construct their evidence based on an illegitimate transfer of the results of research on the everyday phenomena of normal memories onto the stored memories of traumatic experiences. Of course, if we consider something to be especially important, we are better able to store it in our memory. But we also all know that under conditions of extreme fear we can't learn effectively and can't recall what is already stored in our memories.

However, when the experiences blast through the barriers of our fears, then it is emergency programs that kick in, not everyday psychological mechanisms. Then we move outside the limits of that to which we can adapt ourselves and we have to answer the situation with dissociation. Regarding this situation FM makes use of a trick in its argumentation. Just as with a magic trick, our attention gets diverted so that we don't see what is actually being done to us. I'd like to illustrate this with an example. We agree that being able to observe well and perceive well are fundamental prerequisites for good therapy. Then I ask the following of you: In order to taste the salinity of your skin, please rub a finger on a sheet of paper, and then lick a finger.

Did you lick the same finger? A proponent of FM would say this proves that you can't perceive well or that you can't listen well. Deductive reasoning proves that you would not do good therapy. It would, however, be more correct to say that I seduced you into believing the important criterion was the salinity of your skin and for inexplicable reasons it was necessary to rub your finger on a sheet of paper—in order to divert your attention away from the fact (because it was classified as unimportant) that I didn't necessarily rub and lick the same finger. Naturally this experiment is more impressive "live".

The original experiment comes from a doctor's little demonstration in a media lecture about the topic of observation. He had asked his students to do as he did, dip their finger in a glass of urine, and then lick their finger. Urine from diabetics would taste sweet. He dipped his index finger but licked his middle finger. At least he was kind enough to have apple juice in the glasses for the students and not urine.

I have intentionally chosen such a simple and unspectacular example because here you can observe the illegitimate generalizations of FM very well. Naturally the example says absolutely nothing about your therapeutic qualities—just like the FM set-up of an experiment in which a test person is persuaded that he got lost in a department store when he was two years old. Nothing about this claim has anything to do with a traumatic experience—and it has nothing to do with a stored traumatic memory. It is the same deception as the set-up of the experiment.

Now to the next part of the story. After getting a recommendation, I invited a speaker to design a seminar specifically about neurobiology and trauma. We had given him advance information and made it clear that we were specifically interested in the special conditions of traumatized memory proficiency as the topic for the seminar. We discussed in advance and in great detail what contents we expected. The speaker assured us of his expert knowledge and his willingness to give a lecture on this topic. With all the speakers who teach at our institute, it is customary for us as hosts to participate in the seminars. The speaker started by thoroughly and eloquently reciting general fundamentals of the neurobiology of normal memory proficiency, demonstrating his expert knowledge and respectability. He clearly knew his field and we then expected him to turn his attention to explanations of the specific situation of trauma after having explained the fundamentals of memory.

My expectation was that he would address the topic of traumatic memory and the contrast to non-traumatic memory. My question on this topic brought about a quite different answer. First he declined to answer, saying he hadn't familiarized himself with this aspect of the topic; later he said there were no reliable findings. From this field of general fundamentals the speaker switched (and I hope you recognize the trick from before) to the biology of memory (what sorts of memory there are, where they are localized, which brain structures are involved) and from there in a seamless transition to the psychology of perception, to optical illusions, selective perception, etc. I should have realized what was going on by then. However, my brain didn't sound an alarm but instead tried to call up calming patterns from the frontal lobes: "He was recommended to us; he will certainly still get to trauma; he's just being thorough", up to the thought that "he might have missed the point ..."

During my calming flights of fancy (the reality of the talk was already somewhere else), the speaker finally got to his actual topic. He showed a film that is popular among those who want to show how faulty memory proficiency works. It is of course important in the case of witnesses to a crime to discover what they really remember. In the film a group is playing basketball, and the spectators are urged to count the number of times the ball hits the floor. At the end of the film the viewers are shown that while they concentrated their attention on the contacts of the ball with the floor, a man in a gorilla suit walked through the group of ball players many times, unnoticed by the viewers. The fact that the viewers, focusing on the number of contacts between the ball and the floor (having been instructed that this was the important content to be observed), didn't notice the man in the gorilla suit, was extolled as proof by the speaker that "false memory" was a reality! In reality this film only proved the capacity of human beings for selective attention. However, it was cited as an example of faulty memory. Furthermore, the topic of dissociation was dismissed as fantasy and unproven claims. He asserted that people could be persuaded to falsely remember experiences of violence. Later I discovered he had been lecturing on this topic for years and that as proof of the respectability of his sources he didn't discuss the quality of the so-called studies[1] of "false memory", instead just mentioning the periodical in which they were published, according to the motto, "It has to be true because it was published in XY."

I immediately felt the stomach acid shoot up my esophagus; my vocal cords and larynx suddenly registered pain, and I was speechless.

It took more than ten days before I could speak normally again. At first I thought the only cause was suppressed rage and fury. In fact, many things were happening simultaneously. On the one hand, my organism shifted from a defense to an attack mode, which I, as the course instructor, was able to combine with cognitive corrections as the seminar progressed. On the other hand, though, a disgust that I was unable to suppress mushroomed, making me wake up with a start over and over again during the next few nights. This lasted until I realized that my body was clearly pointing to my own life story, as if it wanted to emphasize: "Dissociation exists." Without comprehending it completely at first, I had recognized the recurrence of a pattern of interaction from which much disgust had originated. Once that was clear to me, my discomfort began to decline.

For this reason I would like to identify a further phenomenon. When we seriously address memory fragments, when we come to understand what they belong to, then we are able to put them in a time frame after all and to organize them, to put them into a context and to integrate them. To begin with, we can help the organism to separate the now from the then, thereby reducing suffering. Each phase of working through the trauma starts by stressing the fact that the trauma is not now, and that we are not working with the trauma itself but with the traumatic memory. In order for us to be able to even choose such a course of action, we have to be in the happy position of having our present life offer us considerable stability or at least the beginning of stability through therapy.

Luise Reddemann (2001) says that in fifty percent of complex traumatizations such a course of action is not possible. According to my somewhat optimistic perception, this approach does succeed with some severely traumatized clients and patients, though only partially. I believe that we can be of assistance to more than fifty percent of the clients and patients who want to confront their traumas, if we adjust to their special needs.

A working model

Now I would like to turn to the topic of dissociation in my own way. In this connection I consciously want to build a bridge from the simple adaptation that everyday life demands of us up to the adaptation that exceeds the limits that we can deal with. I do not claim this is a scholarly model; rather it is one that has become a feasible working model in my therapeutic practice.

In order to survive, we have to adapt to the demands of our environment, no question about it. Dissociation could also be understood as a kind of adaptation to a traumatic experience. That also means that we can deal with normal problems and tasks without the necessity of dissociation—we can integrate even very unpleasant experiences within the limits of what we can come to terms with.

If we look at possible external demands, then we can build a bridge here from the adaptation everyday life demands of us up to a first, single trauma up to substantial and repeated stress and finally up to the complex traumas and their differing characteristics (see Figure 2).

The more complex the responses demanded of us by any situation (for example fear, disgust, pain, shame), the smaller becomes our freedom to be able to act according to our inner needs.

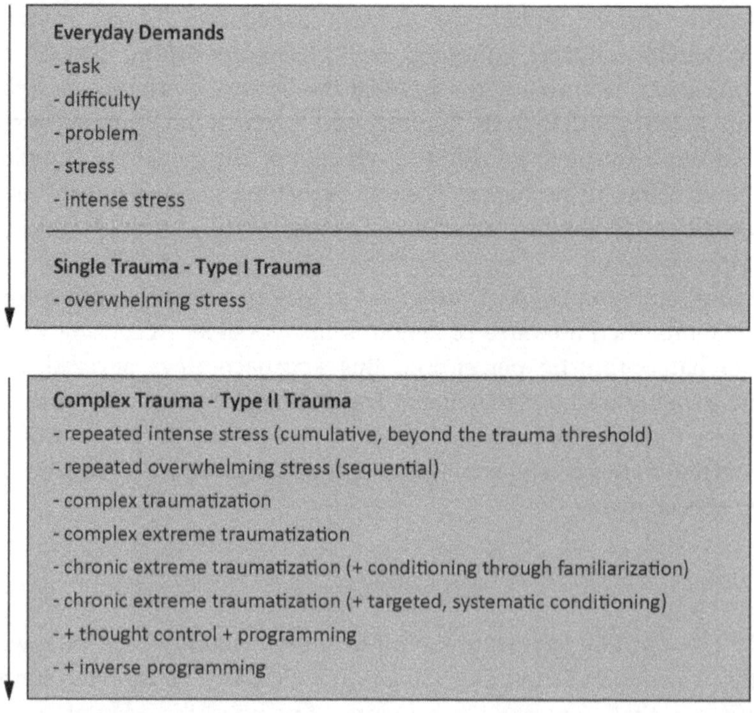

Everyday Demands
- task
- difficulty
- problem
- stress
- intense stress

Single Trauma - Type I Trauma
- overwhelming stress

Complex Trauma - Type II Trauma
- repeated intense stress (cumulative, beyond the trauma threshold)
- repeated overwhelming stress (sequential)
- complex traumatization
- complex extreme traumatization
- chronic extreme traumatization (+ conditioning through familiarization)
- chronic extreme traumatization (+ targeted, systematic conditioning)
- + thought control + programming
- + inverse programming

Figure 2. Possible adaptation demanded.

Accordingly, the situations that can hide behind the headings of the Figure 2 are also more complex (see Figure 3). At the same time, one has to consider that, depending on the inner configuration of the violence experienced (how serious the individual experience is, what is going on when the violence begins), there could be an alternate sequence of stages. This would naturally mean different overlaps (therefore the sequence is not mandatory and many events share certain aspects with each other and could therefore also be on the same level, depending on what is demanded by the situation). This is just a model.

The model on the next page (Figure 4) illustrates how the degree of demanded adaptation shifts increasingly in the direction of the limitations of adaptation. The easier the demanded adaptation is, the more varied the possible answers are and the greater are the degrees of freedom with which we can answer them. Challenging tasks are not the same as trauma. When faced with a difficulty in normal life—even a major hurdle—we generally know: "I can do that, so I'll choose the

- plan meals, go shopping
- accept criticism, criticize
- foreseeable events: retirement, children leaving home
- experiences such as a difficult separation, unemployment
- accidents, operations, serious illness
- natural catastrophes
- assault, burglary, witness to violence
- rape, kidnap victim

- life-threatening illness with relapse
- abuse and serious neglect
- serious domestic violence, sexual abuse
- child pornography, organized violence
- torture, imprisonment in a concentration camp, ritualized violence
- organized sadistic violence
- conditioning
- programming   } mind control
- inverse programming

Figure 3. Sequence of experiences according to degree of stress and level of adaptation demanded.

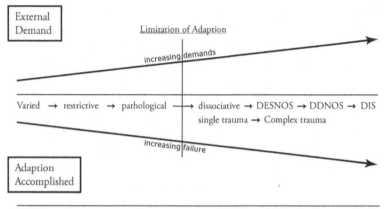

The extent of coming to terms with things in an integrated fashion declines.
Finally there is total fragmentation.

Figure 4. Demands and limitations of adaptation.

following way of dealing with it ..." We have a broad repertoire at our disposal.

If, over time, we continue to be successful performing a particular group of roles in order to respond to a demanded adaptation (for example the tough businesswoman who defies her boss), then our choice of role can get out of control—in the sense of a maladjustment (compulsively taking on the role of a rebel toward the boss). And as a final example, still within the framework of an adaptation which is not dissociative, out of habit we can slip into an angry or fearful ego state in which we react to a demand in a pathological manner. Without a doubt, though, we are still ourselves and we also experience our reaction as "I'm doing this".

If stress becomes overwhelming, it breaks through the limits of our adaptation, and then we slip into dissociative states. In my terminology I don't designate these states as ego states, in order to differentiate ego states from dissociative, split-off inner parts. For me ego states would be conditions that you can choose consciously, that you can also slip into, that the consciousness knows or that can be accessible through normal reflection, and that you can perceive as a part of yourself.

Task: These are the commonplace tasks, the ones that occur every day. I want to make myself some muesli with yogurt. I open the yogurt container and see mold on top of the yogurt. Disgusted, I throw the yogurt away. I decide to eat something else.

Task with increased difficulty: This is also still the realm of the commonplace, but it can become a little tricky. Same situation, but I don't notice the mold until I already have some of it in my stomach. If I am successful at forcing myself to vomit, the disgust will probably recede faster, especially if I permit myself to eat something fresh and pleasant-tasting afterwards. I would very likely deduce from this experience that I should look at the yogurt before I start eating it.

A more difficult problem still: A more complex situation, for example dealing with violence in marriage. And yet, even here I still have choices. True, I can't choose not to have any feelings of fear triggered when I confront certain situations, but I can decide whether I will flee, turn away, resist, fight, protest against the violence, etc. Even without resisting, I can choose the role of the helpless victim and tell the whole world what has been done to me. I can, however, also choose the role of a woman capable of defending herself, who makes it clear what someone is or is not permitted to do. I can file for divorce.

In dealing with problems and already challenging demands I can select a solution from my repertoire of roles, for example persisting in the role of the patient sufferer. Or, through its emotional quality the situation could persuade me to prefer to slip into an ego state or to let the ego state determine the solution. A decision at the level of an ego state, as I have defined it here, would also be possible for me.

The possibilities of choice here are already a little more restricted. It is possible for me to slip into certain states because certain stimulating constellations and/or situations from my childhood are familiar to me, and my organism might respond to them accordingly. I could, for example, react like a mad fiend or like a frightened child—that would depend on which inner entities, which inner parts had formed my history. Here it still would be as follows: I would know that I carry these ego states in me, wouldn't always make a conscious decision to remain in one of these states, but would consciously identify them as being parts of myself. Or in my own words: "I know there's an aspect of me that's a real stinker—I don't like it much, I'm not proud of it—but without a doubt it's a part of me, and I am aware of it." And this part of me would then not be of a dissociative nature, even if I didn't know at that particular moment how it happened to come into existence.

Finally, still in less than the highly traumatic level, when we get stuck in states or inappropriate roles, what we call personality disorders develop. We remain in a vicious cycle of inappropriate loops of responses, which play over and over again. This could mean that a young man with massive problems in making contact with people will always be disappointed when he meets new people, since for him every new contact has to immediately be something profound. What is more, he remains in his state of a rejected and unloved child who experiences rejection over and over again.

Outside of dissociative states, we can basically find the following possibilities for adaptation:

- competence, experience, situational solutions, creativity and imagination
- coping strategies, problem-solving strategies and skills
- choosing from existing roles
- engaging in ego states or slipping into them
- personality disorders as a result of roles incorrectly chosen or persistent, triggered ego states.

Our reactions can be depicted in the short term as situational solutions and in the long term as coping strategies and skills. Over time we can also use consciously adopted roles in order to deal with situations successfully. Roles here should be understood as consciously implemented containers of skills correlated with each other. We can adopt roles consciously and plan to use them; they are selectable, flexible, and consciously controllable. That means basically nothing more than that repeatedly occurring situations, or comparable situations, allow us to come up with helpful solutions successfully. We don't have to split off any memories; rather, we can successfully avail ourselves of our memory.

In contrast to roles, in ego states our possibilities for action are already somewhat restricted. We don't have only freely chosen states that allow us to adjust to a situation in an optimal fashion, but rather through a certain stimulus constellation, states that we were previously not entirely conscious of can be triggered, so to speak. In my understanding, an example for this would be the fully automatic rage reaction of borderline clients. Borderline clients have problems regulating their emotions. While expressing sadness may be difficult for them, expressing rage and anger often occurs too quickly as a result of misinterpreting a situation as an assumed attack. This condition is especially energized in situations of assumed or actual abandonment. Borderline clients know very well that they have the capacity to react in such a way, even if they don't happen to be in that condition at the moment. The client knows therefore: This is what I am capable of; this is how I behave sometimes. These parts are conscious parts of the ego and not really dissociated parts. Possibly the experience of how these inner parts originated or came into being is not consciously available to them, or at least not consciously associated with their out-of-control emotional states. In this sense, personality disorders, in the final analysis, would be a kind of faulty selection from solution strategies, which also could refer to roles or ego states. However, in this case we are definitely talking about fairly complete narratives that are stored in the memory.

When, as shown in Figure 4, overwhelming situations demolish the limits of our adaptation, we cross a boundary beyond which it is necessary to develop dissociative symptoms. Depending on the extent of this overwhelming situation, all that we can do is to experience aspects of the situation as fragments and save them in our memories. We no longer have any conscious freedom of choice concerning which parts of our personality we split off and which we don't, but rather, within a fraction of a second, our organism activates its emergency program.

The first response in terms of dissociative responses to that which is overpowering would be a posttraumatic stress reaction. So, within dissociative structures of coming to terms with an overwhelming situation, you could differentiate as per Figure 5 on the next page.

In terms of Bennet Braun's (1998) BASK model I would like to explain the previously described structures of dissociation in more detail as follows. With his BASK model, Braun referred to the components of a complete narrative. It's common knowledge that the process of storing the memories of an experience as a chronologically correct and complete narrative doesn't work in the case of traumatic experiences. In the model by Reinders et al (2006), these structures of scattered, partial memories can be subdivided into the ostensibly "normal personality" and the "emotional personality" or can be portrayed as shown in the following working model with respect to a break in the narrative.

Structures of dissociation with increasing fragmentation

The qualities of the BASK model are **B**ehavior, **A**ffect, **S**ensation, and **K**nowledge.

PTSD

Posttraumatic Stress Disorder

Dissociation refers to that which was experienced and observed

Internal experience, experiencing and observing the body

DESNOS

Disorder of Extreme Stress, Not Otherwise Specified

The levels of dissociation reveal themselves as: predetermined breaking points

in terms of structural dissociation / functional dissociation

---

DDNOS

Dissociative Disorder Not Otherwise Specified

Dissociation reveals itself in the development of inner specialists

(the principle of structural dissociation continues to be valid),

and there are conditioned inner parts with their own self-images.

DID

Dissociative Identity Disorder

Reactive-DID: Inner parts who result from repetitive overwhelming situations, with communication inside and with the outer world, as a reaction based on their own inner structure.

Created-DID: Programmed inner parts whose inner communication and communication with the outside world is a result of deliberate and planned splitting of the person's core by perpetrators .

Inverse conditioning and/or programmed parts/inner persons with their own self-images and internal and external predetermined communication

Figure 5. Breakdown of dissociative coping structures.

The first split in the narrative

In my view, the first split would occur in separating that which was experienced from that which was observed. In the charts below, the parts the person consciously experiences are on a white background and the inner parts that are just observed are on a gray one.

In this way there would be at least one fragmentation. With respect to disgust as a part of an experience, this would mean, for example:

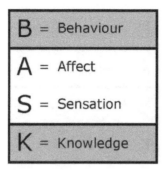

Figure 6. First split.

Either *I experience something as disgusting* or *I observe it and judge it to be disgusting*—but both things don't happen at the same time. Either I feel the disgust of an earlier situation or I know about it. For example after rapes, some women report conditions in which they would feel themselves to be completely disgusting and wouldn't be able to touch themselves. They report other situations in which it is possible for them to touch themselves and look at the situation matter-of-factly from a bird's eye perspective with no emotional participation, just reviewing what happened. While they are in the state of feeling, the knowledge about the "why" of their feelings is, at first, just not there.

A further split would occur on the boundary between the development of a posttraumatic stress disorder (PTSD) and a disorder of extreme stress, not otherwise specified (DESNOS). Now the affect from experiencing disgust is split off from the sensation, for example of having to vomit, that, in the final analysis, makes it possible for disgust to be experienced. This means that I need a further differentiation in our BASK model here.

The second split in the narrative

Figure 7 (overleaf) displays a trisection of the narrative. Feeling and experiencing are now independent qualities that are separated from each other. With respect to this split, I also find it important that the necessity of a further separation from qualities of experience comes from the organism itself and is not systematically induced from the outside. We can picture it as follows: Now the body and therefore the somatoform

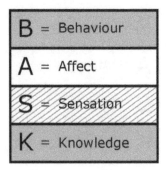

Figure 7. Second split.

dissociation, that is, the dissociation at the level of the body, provides a further possibility for splitting.

In the fragmented narrative there is now a separation of

- the sensation memory (the body's memory) from the
- cognitive memory (knowledge) and the memory of behavior (observation) as well as from
- the inner feelings (affect).

I think that this kind of description can provide an explanation for why so many victims of abuse complain about pronounced somatic problems (for example, pain) even though there is no existing body correlate that can be detected at the time of their complaints. Many fears of suffocating or of being strangled, are, in the final analysis, nothing other than the body's memory, for example of an oral rape. Van der Kolk (1996) describes this as "the body keeping score" which means that the body's memories are retained undistorted as long as we are not able to understand and integrate them. The body can't reflect on the experiences it has stored: it can't evaluate them; it can only preserve them.

It's good to reconstruct how the victim, through the mechanism of introjecting and merging with the tormentor, that is, assuming his viewpoint, accepts what the tormentor ascribes to her as her own self-description, and finally how the tormentor's attributed perception (for example, that she is disgusting or ridiculous or ugly) can arise when the victim observes her own body. If the victim has dissociated the fact of her having become a victim, she completely lacks an understanding of which mechanisms here are truly operative, and we will more likely receive from her only varying pseudo-rational explanations for why she sees herself as she does.

The third split in the narrative

If now further splits are necessary in order to make survival possible, there is not only a horizontal separation from the qualities of the experience, but rather the individual aspects are divided vertically into still smaller units. When certain threatening constellations repeat, the organism responds with the dissociative answer that it has learned.

A lattice structure arises which breaks up the individual qualities of the narrative further.

The crosshatch lines can be understood as differentiations, as separations between the individual fragments.

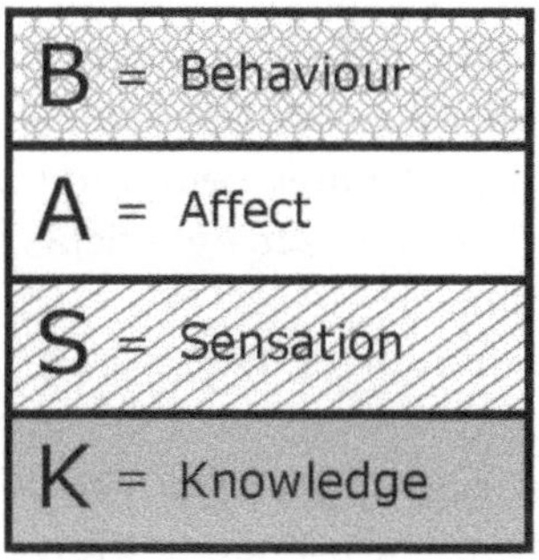

Figure 8. Third split.

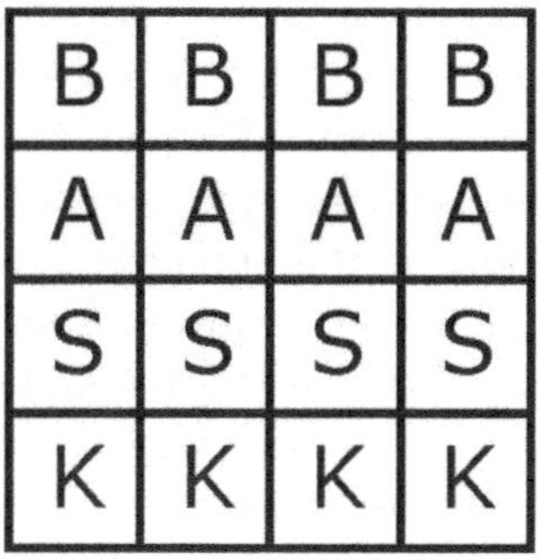

Figure 9. The third split, also in the vertical direction.

A person moves from DESNOS to dissociative disorder not otherwise specified (DDNOS) when repeated experiences of severe violence create "inner specialists". The simplest form of such a specialist on this lattice structure would be different parts of the person who hold different parts of the narrative. Inner parts of the person arise, who "know" that the situation requires their appearance. As Ellert Nijenhuis describes structural dissociation in *The Haunted Self* (van der Hart, Nijenhuis, & Steele, 2006), in order to survive, inner parts for defense, attachment, and submission come into being. The basis for their functioning is that they perceive their functions separately from each other.

In my understanding, these survival specialists can be described as split parts with a certain inner structure. The "how" of the disintegration follows the established paths of the organism, the predetermined breaking points. Survival is accomplished through splitting into separate inner parts. To quote a client: "Only when no one is there, when no one helps, when no one loves you, and you would have to die otherwise, because the body, the soul can't endure, then you split yourself apart and create a new space for your body." If you otherwise can't escape to the outside, then the only way left is to the inside. This way follows established paths, and implements important functions—if necessary also in separate "worlds", separate fields of actions, habitats for alters, created in the brain.

The so-called pseudo-narratives that arise are no longer narratives of complete events that were experienced, but rather one could call them inner narratives with survival functions. The true narratives are split apart, taken out of context. The pseudo-narratives are like markers that can activate these survival functions in a split second.

This kind of splitting happens in a suspenseful situation that elicits many different emotional reactions. Normally, when we are able to behave and perceive in an integrated way, feelings are necessary for orientation so that we can survive. Disgust, for example, would be a hint to refrain from doing something, to distance ourselves from something, not to eat something. In this situation, however, it is exactly the opposite: Survival demands that we put feelings of disgust aside. Survival has a higher priority than reacting adequately to disgust. Here we have to split ourselves apart—because such actions aren't provided for in our organism. For example: During sexual abuse at home, a child has learned to provide good oral sexual satisfaction—and therefore to survive. In order to "do her job" she has to be able to ignore feelings of disgust and her own gag reflex. If the tormentor demands it, which makes it essential for the child's survival, the child will act as if she enjoys the act. In reality she is exclusively obeying the necessities of survival.

This example also shows that the tormentor's rationalizations conform to this script. At the beginning there is often ostensible caring behavior on the part of the tormentor: for example to provide sex education; or because the child needs to experience physical love; or because of a supposed misbehavior of the victim that the tormentor has to punish (so that from the view of the tormentor sexual abuse is a necessary part of child-rearing); or the contention that the victim wants it (in which case the tormentor would just be fulfilling the wish of the child). The tormentor continually denies responsibility for the deed and his own self-interest. The child who submits in order to survive finds herself again in a situation in which she more or less has to grin and bear it—behavior that is then construed as being of her own free will or subsequently put into the context of a reward: "You did it for the reward" or "You showed your consent because you didn't fight back". Finally this also ultimately turns into the perversion: "You are my property, and I can do whatever I want to you."

The confusion for the victim doesn't just come from the dissociative disorder; rather, it is already there from the beginning of the torment, from the manmade disaster of violence inflicted deliberately by another human being.

The fourth split in the narrative

With the fourth split the structure increases further with the dimensions of depth. Then further levels of depth and splits of the lattice accrue.

Here the internal specialists develop something that you could call personality. The first inner persons come into being. Since further parts of the original self are being split off, the client, whose personality is often designated the host personality, is robbed of the greater part of her capacity for emotions. It would be presumptuous to assume that the other previously described splits didn't have an influence on what the client felt and experienced, but here it is more extensive. If this happens, it produces the DDNOS type of disturbed and split self.

At the beginning of therapy DDNOS patients are often convinced that they have no time gaps. They believe that they are in possession

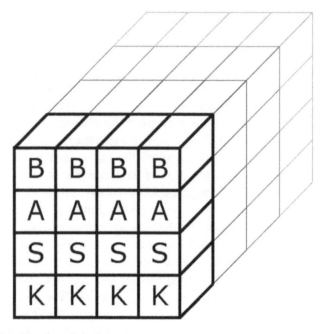

Figure 10. The fourth split.

of a complete autobiography. Their inner parts aren't visible to them in their everyday lives, and genuine time gaps, which can sometimes last for days, are attributed to other causes (medications, drinking, illness). Some of these patients have the impression that they have no inner parts. Other patients absolutely recognize different inner parts, but they attach no importance to them. What all such clients have in common is that, in retrospect, they describe their lives as not very spirited, as not very joyous. The clinical picture of DDNOS demands well-defined inner parts that can successfully take on certain activities under certain circumstances, completely separated from the consciousness of the host personality.

Here dissociation had to make sense for survival. If a constant, alert consciousness was necessary and/or the traumatizing didn't begin in early childhood—this can be the case, for example, when adults experience imprisonment in a concentration camp—then the DESNOS disorders are more likely to occur. They can include pronounced dissociation which, however, then appears less as parts of the personality but instead as containment for experiences.

What is typical for DDNOS is growing up in parallel worlds. The patient sees herself consciously in a good home and school environment—it's her dissociated inner parts that endure brutal violence. Since feelings contain a potential for triggering violence, they are often unconsciously avoided when she is in the public eye. Indeed, if anything, these patients are also rather restricted with respect to the number and intensity of their friendships or acquaintanceships. In the final analysis, they seem quite isolated, as if they had no desire for contacts; they are withdrawn and shy and sometimes also give the impression of being arrogant as they retreat from others.

The drawing (Figure 11) illustrates such a view of oneself. Lonely, frozen, joyless. It's all there, only no human contact.

Figure 11. A childhood.

What might be hiding behind what is shown in public emerges slowly. That can happen within the framework of a therapeutic setting or it can also emerge on its own, as the victim grows older. For example: The conscious patient believes at first that she is in possession of a complete and continuous life story. She alternates mistaking emerging horrors, nightmares, images, and messages from her inner world for evidence of a developing mental illness, while wondering on the other hand, when feelings emerge and her body reacts to them, whether these experiences have something true about them. At a conscious level, for example, the patient knows that during sexual activity she panics and does everything she can to prevent feelings of lust or pleasure, because lust and mortal fear somehow belong together. Slowly but surely, a scene emerges, composed of experiences from many inner parts. As the following description indicates, the tormentor's actions have consciously taken advantage of separate inner parts that were created systematically. Perpetrators are aware of these inner parts and know how to produce them and use them.

Because of a forced act of violence committed by Margit, who is told she could through this act take a step toward cleaning her black soul, Petra, who suddenly wakes up with a tool in her hand, feels the obligation to assume the responsibility for Margit's deed, of which she however knows nothing. Petra, however, has no way of putting up a fight against several adult men, and endures their extremely brutal rapes, which disgust her. Nonetheless, she does experience an orgasm, whereby, as the violence increases, Mardita finally takes over. She is visibly sexually excited by the combination of lust and violence and takes over when the other personalities can't continue. For the client, the affected inner parts realizing it first, an inner image arises that creates the impression of being berated as an oversexed nymphomaniac, which seems more than justified, and the patient feels above all disgust for herself. This separates the inner parts from one another and from the consciousness of the patient. Through the actions demanded in the scene, there is no way to avoid inner parts coming into being that already have a notion of what they themselves are. Mardita inevitably thinks that brutal sex is desirable. Margit would like to be sweet and kind, and finally Petra can endure pain up to a certain point. All three inner parts assume that they are autonomous persons who can act independently of each other. The front person, that is, the part who handles everyday life, knows that it has to be over quickly if she allows herself to have sex, so that Mardita has no opportunity to push to the forefront and to perform those acts which the client finds disgusting. However, it may well be that the client first feels the need for speed without even knowing anything specific about the existence of Mardita. At any rate, she only senses that it will be absolutely disgusting if she allows herself too much time during sex.

The goal is clear. The inner parts experience themselves as guilty and entangled in what happens, which they attribute to being their own nature. Thereby tendencies of shame and withdrawal are connected to each other, which prevent integration. These inner split parts manage to evade the knowledge and control of the patient successfully.

The fifth split in the narrative

Here the tormentors out-and-out train the inner parts for certain behaviors. In this area, for example, you would include training regarding disgusting situations, for some parts to feel extreme disgust and other parts not to feel any disgust at all. With systematic violence, inner parts arise which then have to be trained systematically. It's a matter of conditioning, not by establishing habits, but by forcing patterns of behavior systematically through training which can then be triggered by the tormentors just as systematically. In order to survive, the individual inner part learns to overcome the boundaries of feelings of disgust through various stages of enduring disgusting things, like eating spoiled food, garbage, feces, and creepy-crawlies (reptiles or insects).

I don't want to delve into these disgusting things any further, but I want to ask you to pause and imagine: What would you be willing to eat, in order to be let out of a box buried underground (where you are buried alive) again? What would you be willing to do to be allowed to breathe again or to be freed from a tub of icy water? What would you be willing to do, to stop electric shocks being applied to your sensitive body parts?

With the fifth split the structure is increased by a further depth dimension. Pseudo-narratives arise which are trained systematically.

You see for yourself: Under these circumstances we don't need to make decisions because we have no choice. There is no decision to be made—not even the one of dying. The perpetrators have long since taken over this decision. The tormentors have already decided everything that makes a relevant difference to us in the world. They

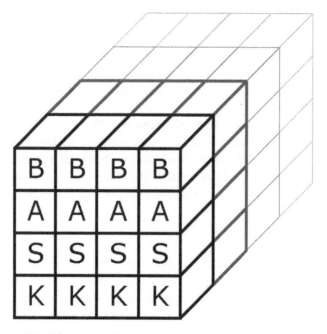

Figure 12. The fifth split.

determine what we have to learn and do in order to survive; they make the rules. They define which differences we are to perceive and which we are to ignore.

If we are to survive, we have to share the consensual reality of the tormentor and split ourselves up—in the way that the tormentor forces us to do. There is no alternative. And we learn to perform the required behavior when triggered by the stimulus. This and nothing else is the conditioning of inner parts as mentioned above. The required behavior of the victim, demanded by the perpetrators, takes place over and over again, triggered by the conditioned stimulus. This particular trigger pulls up the respective inner person, who then, in order to survive, has no choice other than to do what is demanded of her. A trained knee-jerk behavior and no conscious decision!

Only through an arduous process can the patient recognize that through planned, systematic violence the first inner parts were created which, easily controllable with a certain stimulus (or multiple stimuli), showed clearly defined, automatic patterns of behavior. Even in the split inner parts, actions leave traces in the episodic memory, and this seduces the patient into thinking the behavior comes intentionally from her: "I did it, I see myself doing it, then it must be the case that I wanted to do it." The patient is unaware of the violence that led to the splits and that conditioned her ("I had made a mistake ..."), as are the inner persons. "I act—therefore I am: I am what I do."

The additional efforts of the tormentors to determine the context (for example, to show where I see myself doing something; evidence that shows what kind of person I am by the things I do) go a long way toward making me experience the situation in a personal way, as being my own fault, as being solely my responsibility. This also creates the prerequisites for deliberately creating inner parts or, in my words, inner persons, from inner conditions and personality states.

The sixth split in the narrative

With the sixth split in the narrative the structure adds at least one more depth dimension. Pseudo-narratives come into being as well as connections of interaction that are trained consciously. Conditionings are interconnected.

"Programming" is a further dimension of the split. I define programming as intentional planned splitting of an inner system for the purpose of creating clearly defined inner persons who discover themselves on differing levels of the system[2] and who are in contact with each other as defined by the tormentor. Everything is determined by the tormentor: Who (inside) knows whom? Who speaks whose language? Who fulfills which function? It is not individuals who are created, but a system that is useful and applicable in multiple ways and is not restricted to a certain tormentor's field of influence. This system is structured externally and therefore easily controllable from the outside. It is possible to know from outside the victim which output will result from which input.

The programming follows in the direction of that which the organism itself has developed as a response—if defense were to be demanded, then the *how* and the *when* to defend (under which circumstances) would be especially arranged. But the response would continue to be, on its own merits, defense. Inner persons would feel guilty and responsible and would possibly even say that they had wanted a disgusting or evil act. But if they are asked to describe how they know that they enjoyed it, they have no answer. They describe themselves at first in terms of

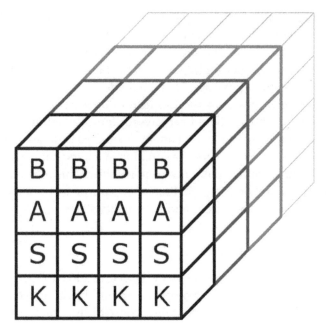

Figure 13. The sixth split.

the act, as "That's what I am—as you can see", but the act itself in all its detail can only be described as fulfilling a task.

A special characteristic of programming, as opposed to just conditioning, seems to me to be that the inner parts involved are blind to these aspects at first (and that can encompass a long period of time). They believe they are acting according to their own rules and don't recognize their submission to the will of another person. What happens totally within the programming itself eludes their consciousness. So they lack a meaningful framework that would enable them to understand why these acts and views simply cannot come directly from the core of their true selves.

A further aspect of seeing and comprehending that I am acting according to the intentions of another person, has to do with the fact that it seems completely unbearable to us as human beings (and also as fragmented parts of personalities, or inner persons) to be controlled by the wishes of another person. Human beings don't want to have ever experienced such things or to still be in such a situation. This feeling is shared by inner persons.

The seventh split in the narrative

With the seventh split the structure adds at least one further depth dimension. Before establishing pseudo narratives, there are effective additional attempts at erasing the person's existing views of the world. Pseudo narratives and interactive connections arise that are trained systematically. Inverse conditionings are interconnected.

Inverse programming would be the complete destruction of your own personal "hard disk" in certain areas of functioning. Basically, you could say that the tormentors have created a new human being. Everything is deleted that defined this human being at her birth, her capacity to form attachments, her predispositions. Everything that this organism would do as its own reaction is switched to the opposite. Here, language and actions are consciously and systematically distorted. In the end, the result is a well-controllable, perversely aligned system that deploys a monstrous, destructive momentum the closer we therapists get to it. And, not coincidentally, the deeper we penetrate, the more disgusting and evil things we are deluged with—interpersonally and with descriptions. What was done is often of such hideousness that many therapists have difficulties when they encounter these descriptions with their clients. The clients then have the longest way back into human society, if in fact they ever succeed. Because at the point when they begin to make their way back, they themselves are completely overwhelmed by their previous actions. It was expected of them to act like dehumanized monsters without their having a possibility of

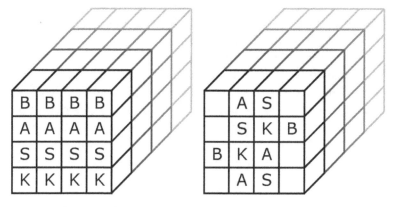

Figure 14. The seventh split.

exerting any influence or making any changes. There simply weren't any adequate experiences that would have corrected things.

I'm not talking about people who do abominable things from a sadistic perspective, because of a supposed insult or to satisfy their narcissism, because they have divided the world up into masters and servants and therefore believe that they don't have to follow any of society's rules. I am talking about those people, who, deformed through unspeakable tortures, split apart, and disenfranchised, look back on a life story of horror—when the dissociative barriers break and they become conscious of their true life story.

Then such clients present us with existential questions: "When you see yourself—how you killed another human being in such a heinous way and did such terrible things to his body, and if this human being, whom someone was doing terrible things to, was your own flesh and blood, and if you have seen the superior grin on your face, meaning that you therefore have to know that you enjoyed it—how would you be able to continue living? And if you were able to, would you even want to?"

In dealing with people who suffer from the consequences of programming and inverse programming, it is necessary to consider that we are confronted not only with people who have been split apart to fit into a world of sadism and disenfranchisement, but also with people who had the opportunity taken away from them to make meaningful decisions on this side of the world, far away from the desires and acts of sadistic groups and tormentors. Many of their possibilities for communicating have been limited; many of their possibilities of perception have been reduced to a black-and-white level. Through these circumstances, important frames of reference for human relationships, for an understanding of social interactions, are missing.

This can mean at first not finding your place anywhere in the world and feeling hopelessly lost, separated from other human beings, without a right to live. There are paths from which there is no way back. But sometimes it's possible to build a bridge to a different and more humane country. This can only work if we therapists are willing to enter the country of inhumanity and torture without forgetting that we are guests in a world of memories that our clients or patients haven't freely chosen.

In my opinion, the advantage to thinking in terms of narratives and their fragmentation is in creating a therapeutic setting that can concern itself with completing the narrative. We can ask ourselves, therefore, what is missing, what keeps the narrative from being complete. In the presence of learned pseudo narratives, we can formulate invitations into a more human country. It's about understanding which aspects of the life of the client are missing, which areas of experience and interaction, and which areas of relationships, need to be reopened by psychotherapy.

With regard to the structures I call pseudo narratives, I picture them as an arbitrary number of parts that can be combined with each other. They don't need to come from the same depth level (although they may) and they don't have to construct a complete BASK model with their combined fragments. Individual elements can be represented multiple times. And of course, these pseudo narratives will also become more and more complex.

CHAPTER TWO

A working model demonstrated through case studies

In a few individual case vignettes, I would like to invite the reader to understand the perspective of the therapist and to see how the differing structures of dissociation show themselves in practice, how they arise, and which hardships they mean in everyday life.

"My disgust is me"—dissociation using the example of disgust

The decision to use the example of feelings of disgust in order to illustrate the individual increments of dissociation more precisely comes from the experience that disgust is especially suited to compel dissociation and that it provides many sadists with a special thrill; it enables them to feel superior to and have power over the victims in a special way.

Separation between what is experienced and what is observed

Example: Ms. Aller

As a child, the patient experiences brutal sexual abuse from her grandfather. The grandfather himself triggers disgust through the kind of sexuality he imposes on her, through his smell, and through the acts themselves. Naturally it is without question that she also has the accompanying feelings of fear or accompanying pain—for the moment I want to put that aside. The grandfather therefore does something disgusting—which the patient can't escape from. The only chance she has left is to cope with the situation by splitting herself apart.

This split is aided by a further circumstance. The patient is very over-weight as a child. At that time, in contact with classmates, in pre-school, and on the street she is constantly bombarded with ridicule and scorn—she is described as disgustingly fat.

Through this split, the original situation is removed from its context and the arbitrary act of violence on the part of the grandfather gets a new meaningful context: "I don't deserve any better. This is only hap-pening to me because I am so disgusting." In this way, disgust becomes a personal experience, something that belongs to her identity. Disgust is a part of her. This explains why, on the one hand, the patient ulti-mately continues to think of herself as disgusting and fat, and contin-ues to see herself that way even though as an adult woman she is slim and very attractive. Her brain trained itself to know: "I am disgusting. I am fat." Her eyes don't see, rather her brain confirms its implied self-perception.

This supposed "knowledge" confirms itself later once again when she discovers her boyfriend in her bed with one of her girlfriends—and yet continues to sleep in the same bed after separating from her boyfriend, as if she wanted to punish herself. She believes "This only happens to me because I am disgusting." Just as her grandfather wasn't at fault in the past, now her boyfriend has no responsibility.

The implied premise, "If I am not beautiful when I'm overweight, no one needs to treat me with respect", is something the patient doesn't question. In the same way, benevolent acknowledgment from her envi-ronment is of no use to her. So the circumstance that the size of clothing she chooses in the store is much too large for her or that her girlfriends give her compliments on her appearance in the swimming pool doesn't make it possible for her to truly put the facts into a new context.

She can't make use of this correction for herself. Disgust is where it doesn't belong, and it is missing where it actually should be. For this reason she misses out on the chance to channel meaningful behavior from her feelings.

And this is naturally not only the case when dealing with feelings of disgust, but rather a fundamental state. Dissociations that are forced on us over a long period, separate us from our feelings, our mental processes, our experiences, and finally from ourselves.

Separation from the body's memory and from experiencing feelings

Here there is a further separation between the body's memories and inner feelings. In this way especially pronounced somatoform dissociations arise. We often first find this kind of split with DESNOS clients. They show further splits as seen in case study three.

Example: Ms. Berger

In therapy sessions Ms. Berger talks about situations in which for her—completely unmotivated and not appropriate to the situation, for example in the therapeutic setting—there is suddenly a disgusting smell in her nose, a bad taste in her mouth. She feels nauseated. At first she can't make any connection to the oral rapes she experienced as a child. In another one of the inner parts of her consciousness she is able to report what her father did to her, in a businesslike, objective manner without any emotional involvement. A further inner part can describe the disgusting experience and the inner feelings connected to it.

Ms. Berger is surprised. She did notice once, when she visited her dying father, that she was disgusted when he tried to touch her, but she saw herself as a horrible girl, not a good daughter. Another inner part finds itself disgusting and describes itself sometimes as indiscriminately promiscuous with respect to sexual partners and practices, which are actually abhorrent to Ms. Berger.

Ms. Berger needs to fill in the gaps of the true narrative in order to make it possible for her to see things differently. It's like putting a puzzle together; a few pieces fit, but you can't see or understand the complete picture. The pieces are all there, but they show up at different places and at different times.

Separation between observation and evaluation

Example: Ms. Ciller

At the beginning of therapy Ms. Ciller presents herself exclusively as the victim. She has a distinct alcohol dependency problem, which, however, she denies. For years she has been married to a sick man who has taken early retirement and is unable to work. Although it would be possible to make his illness a little more bearable by following a specific, strict diet, they eat and drink as though he were completely healthy. She has a degree in biology but only works as a salesperson and cleaner. She has never tried to get into an academic career. With her educational background, she would have had the chance to make a good living for her family.

The only son of the family stagnates at home. For years he has completely neglected his personal hygiene, and hasn't even brushed his teeth. He downright stinks; for all practical purposes his clothes are never freshly washed. He is thirty-nine years old and completely helpless.

Ms. Ciller is also in no way attractively groomed and reeks of alcohol even from a distance.

Within the framework of sexual violence from her parents, Ms. Ciller eventually became a co-tormentor. She joined in with her parents completely and assumed their model of perversion. When she describes how her son never washes or brushes his teeth, she has no problem with the fact that he stinks and that she herself exudes a massive stench.

Everything disgusting about her family is split off and blamed on the outside world. Everyone else is responsible. Ms. Ciller herself takes no responsibility. "If someone would just help us, then ..." Here dissociation is due to accountability. Variables in context, which would indicate a different interpretation of reality, are immediately split off.

We can assume that Ms. Ciller has learned to experience this kind of split as appropriate and can only endure her world as a victim, by consciously only perceiving that section of the world compatible with her view. She doesn't consciously deceive those around her about her true situation; rather she describes that which she believes to be the truth.

Naturally she wasn't born a tormentor, and she herself has had many distressing experiences during her life. These experiences are just as split from her awareness as is her own accountability. Her genuine life story as a victim is no longer part of her awareness. In the here and now she presents herself as a victim of others and of circumstances. In this way she presents a narcissistic view of herself. No one suffers as much as she does. In the here and now when she has the opportunity, she behaves like a tormentor; one, however, who is limited because of various external circumstances and only experiences herself in a restricted fashion and feels she can't behave in any other way. She really doesn't perceive her behavior as that of a tormentor at any time or place. Her concept of herself is completely different. She doesn't perceive the genuine victim story or the genuine tormentor story. What remains is a reduced segment in which she herself is exclusively a helpless victim.

Transferred to a four-field diagram it could look like this:

Genuine victim's story genuine helplessness, weakness, pain	Blaming others for her lack of possibilities and lack of success, invented victim story
Genuine tormentor side with all its advantages her own failure	Making light of her tormentor side, exaggerating her unfulfilled possibilities; reports about her own important successes can be "borrowed" successes

The gray side would be split off from the consciousness, and is absolutely not accessible. The manner of self-presentation would suggest that the one making the presentation believes it herself.

DDNOS—dissociative disorder, not otherwise specified

Where DDNOS develops, we are in an area where constant repetition ensures that repetitive habits of behavior and experience come into existence. Often we encounter systems and families in which violence has its own tradition. Certain modes already exist which a tormentor can utilize. The goal isn't to create a certain inner split personality, but instead, from the perspective of the tormentor, to create a condition that can be maintained.

Example: Ms. Deckert

The brutal abusive father makes it clear to the child over and over again that the child's suffering will only stop when the child responds with feigned desire to the disgusting sexual practices which she finds especially abhorrent; it will only stop when a recognizable orgasm takes place. In this way the child learns faster and faster, almost automatically, to respond to overwhelming disgust with desire. Through this bodily response, it will later be impossible for the child to put this behavior into the context of "not me". In the child's episodic memory there are multiple narratives stored that seem to say: "Look at me, how disgust makes me horny."

When, additionally, as a result, she seeks sexual partners as an adult with whom she indulges in disgusting sexual practices or when she experiences "normal" sex as boring, then it becomes clear why Ms. Deckert perceives herself as perverse. "It shouldn't make me horny, but it does."

The more she has such experiences, the more impossible it becomes to believe the explanation that this all comes from the outside. When, for example, she has the experience of looking at disgusting pornography, thinking she should find it disgusting, but instead feeling sexual arousal as a response, she is at first convinced that she is perverse. The tormentor and the initial situation are no longer present in her new narrative.

Actually, what happens is as follows. Through the necessary dissociation, the original context of the brutal father who forces the connection of desire with disgust as a survival method on her is split off from consciousness. In the memories of inner persons that become conscious there are only pictures and actions that seem to show: "When disgusting things happen, it makes me very horny. This is what I demand." Ms. Deckert has the feeling that this is a part of her.

Ms. Deckert has to learn that it's not about a part of her that defines her, but rather that there is a split-off inner part in her that knows something about what she experienced. She has to get into contact with this inner part.

The examples in the following sections aren't labeled with a concrete case study but rather with a structural one. I would like to make clear how we encounter such clients in therapy. To provide a concrete case study each time would exceed the framework of description.

DDNOS, DID and conditioning

Now we are dealing with specifically trained inner parts. The tormentors haven't just worked with setting goals to make certain things possible; instead, inner parts have been systematically created, often with names given them by the tormentors, and these parts perform specific functions when the right buttons are pushed. In contrast to programming, the creation of this inner world and the way the inner parts "work together" is left up to the victim as an organism.

Since the victim is conditioned over various steps she generally needs to keep the specialized inner parts separate from each other. Ultimately, one can say that through this step-by-step training, each of these specifically trained inner parts develops an image of a self and a separate personality. Often enough this image means: "This isn't my body; I have nothing to do with the others."

Because inner parts conditioned through disgusting experiences are experienced as especially aversive, naturally the client's front person has a phobia of these inner parts; and these inner parts, conditioned to disgust, out of their own shame, also have a phobia toward the other inner parts and toward the client's front person.

For the tormentor, the attraction is that these inner parts, whose names and functions are known, can be activated at the push of a button by anyone who knows the code. It's about the marketplace for sadism, about satisfying the customers' desires, and about certain functions that should be available on demand, like from a machine. What is unique is that at first the client only has the impression, perhaps because of strange symptoms, that something isn't quite right. The disgust brought on by these symptoms is primarily experienced by the inner parts. "I'm perverse, a piece of shit." The presenting person herself can't make any sense out of it all and naturally finds herself disgusting when she is standing in front of a garbage pail and feels hopelessly compelled to eat the bugs circling the container.

These "disgust trainings" which determine the creation of specific inner parts, consist of a sequence of behaviors. What all the steps have in common is that doing something disgusting is required in order to survive. The demands become more and more massive until finally they become something impossible to do under normal circumstances. One variation makes the survival of a different person dependent on the behavior of the inner part: "If you don't function, then X will die, etc." So, in addition to the threat "You will stay buried if you don't lick up the last bit of the disgusting substance" there are even more confusing scenarios.

In addition for supposedly good functioning there is a reward (which then logically creates the context of "You did it for the reward.") after which you move, for example, up one step on the ladder. But this step can be taken away later if you no longer function correctly. For example, it can be an animal that you grew fond of, which then is destroyed "because you didn't do something right ...". At the end of such a chain of linked events, you are then confronted with "After all that you have done, you can only stay with us—we are the only ones able to tolerate you, even though you are so terrible ... Be grateful to us because we are so kind to you."

When, as in the example of Ms. Ehrenfeld, we have the situation of blatant training in disgusting experiences, by which an inner part with her own name, who shows herself as something completely perverse, is created by means of the method described above, then we have at least two levels on which disgust arises. One level is a client who feels extreme disgust for her own body and describes it in words that leave the outside observer at a loss because the visible reality offers no confirmation of such a label except perhaps for the symptoms of her waking up smeared with feces, which at least provides a situational explanation. The other level is a clearly disoriented inner part who knows how she learned to do this but who has forgotten that it had a meaning. The client and the inner part don't know each other and have no relationship to each other. This is the only way to make sure that the client won't be able to talk about what was done to her.

And this means she also can't explain to herself the things that happen, except that it is because of her, of the way she is. If she begins to remember the disgusting and perverse things that were done to her, then at first she will suspect that only such a disgusting person as herself could entertain such fantasies.

DID and programming

As I work with extremely traumatized people, it is important to me to differentiate between conditioning and programming. Conditioning, just like programming, creates certain inner parts, very specifically with depths of dissociation, details of creation, gender, specific functions, etc. Then, however, there is a second step, establishing the interaction between the individual inner parts. Whereas the creation of such an inner part runs through different steps and shows downright training, in programming there is further practice, like different roles systematically practiced in a theatre play. The interaction among the personalities is rehearsed just like on the stage.

What is different from a performance by actors on the stage is that a programed person must not forget that every step, every supposed mistake, can cost them or someone else their life or health. This is as valid for individual conditioning as it is for any non-functioning within the framework of a performance. The perpetrators demonstrate to the victim that no faults are allowed and every one of them will be punished. It is no coincidence that this programming contains any number of near-death experiences as part and parcel of it.

On a small scale we can view such a scene of programming performed on an inner part that we will call Tanja. As an individual being, Tanja first learns to run through training for disgust until she is able, without hesitation, in a dissociated state, to eat parts of a cadaver.

A further step in the conditioning would be that of a princess. The princess is the sexual object of the main tormentor and learns to "appreciate" especially disgusting sexual practices. "My daddy made me a woman; that was the most wonderful day of my life." As a princess she is narcissistic, in love with herself, and indifferent to the sufferings of others. "Only good girls become princesses."

Still another conditioning would be that of the slave. Her task is to endure extreme injuries and not show any reaction and also to endure disgusting things, including begging for mercy or thanking the tormenter for the abuse. And to complete this very small system, yet another inner part would be conditioned, Nadja, who isn't good enough to be tortured by the main tormentor and has to endure performing disgusting practices with other men in public. Her task is to suffer visibly from feelings of disgust.

And for them to practice the interaction, it's only necessary, for practical purposes, just as in a theatre play, for the child to take on each role once, in a situation in which the other roles are played by other children. Here they rehearse how each one reacts to things; they learn how to comment on each action. Each (real-body) child may play the princess while another real-body child plays the slave. Then the roles are reversed. When two (real-body) children engage in these role plays, it teaches each inner part that it is only that role, that the person in the other role is external. Each inner person is unaware that the other role also exists—in the same body.

In the description it becomes clear that Ms. Gronau has an inner system that she isn't aware of. This system assumes that each inner part exists independently and has its own body. And, depending on the role, the disgust is either denied and raised to a desired and beautiful feeling (as with the princess); reduced (as in Tanja who learns to do everything without showing any feelings or as in the slave, who experiences it as "That's how I am; that's what I want; that's what I'll do"); or always present as with little Nadja (where the tormentor gets his special thrills from her suffering from disgust so much that she always wants to throw up).

What we experience as therapists will depend on which inner parts we first come into contact with and how well they, in turn, are capable of describing to us their roles in the performance and the conditions surrounding the task. Generally this work for the client always begins in dissociation and is only later, and then only partially, a part of the conscious description in the therapeutic setting. Since the inner parts are ashamed and also trained not to be allowed to show themselves or are convinced of their own importance and greatness, we only achieve good access to them very slowly.

But even people who are not dissociative certainly recognize that a princess would rather not give up her role and a Tanja doesn't want to give up her possessions. Each inner part has her own personality, a view of herself, even though that view has been trained through many interactions and not freely chosen. It is now our task to approach these inner parts and not judge them. Here also, however, the relationship is what's important and not the technique.

DID and inverse programming

When we talk about how disgust, for example, appears within the framework of inverse programming, then we are talking about dissociative systems that have several levels. The inner persons on any particular level of such a system have different values from the inner persons on other levels, for example regarding right and wrong, or truth and falsehood. We are talking about organized, ritualized violence where people are dehumanized in deliberately created programming. The market is worldwide—the demand is huge.

You could say level one is a kind of "white" system. In its values it relates most closely to what we know about ourselves, what the expectations are in public. Because of the splits that still take place on the system level and because of the similarities to inner splits that take place with borderline patients, I also sometimes call this level the borderline level. Integrations are relatively easy to achieve, and we encounter the disgust on this level, for example, in the knowledge that certain experiences were disgusting and that, for example, there are inner persons that can finance an education for another life through sadomasochistic sexual practices (that function chiefly in submission and domination). These inner persons would almost never describe it as being a wonderful or good experience. Naturally this can occur as a message showing loyalty to the tormentor, but not really with a connection to any experience. That is, the inner person can certainly express herself to the effect that everything's great, that she doesn't mind, but when confronted with the consequences of this claim, it becomes clear very quickly: She learned to say it that way, to call it that way. Her true feelings and values are quite different.

Level two would be a kind of dark system that shows, relatively precisely, what kind of value system the perpetrators lived by. Here there are inner persons who have certain specific tasks and for whom the question of what the disgust means is never asked. They do what they're told and never question anything that comes from the tormentors. They can swallow living mice and it doesn't bother them at all. Kill, slaughter, eat—it doesn't make any difference. You do what you're told. It is beyond the level of trained soldiers.

Finally, level three would be where everything that ever made the person human is completely annihilated. It's the level of the most extreme betrayal. If at level one there is still a possibility of a relationship with a normal human being, and at level two still the possibility of a relationship with the tormentor, at level three there is absolutely no connection remaining. This level is pure betrayal and fragmentation. The hard disk of the victim has been completely erased and reprogramed—often with subprograms. This is the level of the most extreme resistance to change.

At first nothing is felt here—these are robots at work. They are also capable of programming others. Disgust only exists in transference or as a genuine disgust among observers. Level three is the complete denial of relationships or interests.

Both motivational[1] systems do maximal damage. That's what makes this level so easy to control from the outside. Via multiple types of therapy and at the cost of consciously risking injury to ourselves, we can finally come to find some convergence in this area.

Level three is absolutely merciless and at first doesn't include the capacity to reflect, not about feelings, not about personal motivation. If we want to work here, we need ideas that will eventually make an emotional connection possible. We must ask ourselves as therapists over and over again which of the client's possibilities of perception are the least damaged.

And we need to be able to anticipate the extreme hatred, the attempts at fragmentation, and all the horrible relationship reality we experience in clients with whom we have especially intensive contact. Fully automatic destruction can be encountered in the garb of a client who looks like the person we know and for whom we advocate with such dedication, but acts in a manner full of hatred.

If we don't have this firm and supportive relationship, then we won't reach the clients at the third level and won't be able to help them integrate their parts. The cost of such a relationship is also that personal injury, humiliation, accusations, and insinuations as well as betrayal or the allegation of betrayal will enter into the therapy relationship. Our efforts will be reassessed, given different meanings; apparent events that never occurred in that way will suddenly arise, such as distortions of what happened in therapy and new scenarios that make the therapist appear sadistic; there may be accusations directed toward the therapist from actually benevolent and seemingly securely attached inner parts.

It would be dishonest to say that this can be handled by any therapist because she is a professional. It hurts to be attacked, and you need to have a relationship for the therapy to work, you cannot just end it when you are hurt. So far I have only encountered very few therapists who have entered as deeply into this level of programming to the extent that I consciously do at this time with some clients. (Such therapists may of course exist, but I have never heard of them.) I know, therefore, that it involves recognizing your personal limits very well and being able to endure enormous distress.

And it hurts to see that clients at such moments also recognize what is happening through no fault of their own and what is destroying so much that would be necessary for survival. They can hardly bear the destruction that the tormentors have created and which is deployed as planned. I'm not just talking about dark inner parts, because you can always find a way to wheel and deal with them at levels one or two. I mean the completely dehumanized inner persons—victims of pure annihilation.

The programs have their own barbed hooks, and these clients are worth so much to the tormentors that for the clients there is no place left to flee to. They are under constant observation and we can only decide whether to make the effort or to give up on them.

Here, therefore, we struggle against perpetrators who will stop at nothing to hinder all of our work and relationships, who will stop at nothing to create new programs and trigger them in order to make any of our clients' recovery impossible, because these clients are living witnesses to a parallel world of immeasurable horror.

It isn't all that unusual for clients to be made to fear that their presence alone will endanger the therapist, that it would be their fault if the therapist died. As illnesses, deaths in the family, and similar catastrophes at the same time are mysteriously defined as being the result or the fault of the existence of the client, it is especially important for the therapist to be clear and unambiguous in explaining such things. If I (the therapist) am sick, if I myself have worries, I need to make this transparent and to make it clear that this has nothing to do with the client. It is important not to give details but to give just enough information that if the client notices I am tired or upset, she will know there is a reason that does not involve her. If she becomes aware of details of the therapist's worries, the client is likely to attempt to get involved and reverse the roles. It's sufficient to say: "I look tired today. I've had personal problems and that's why I slept badly. It's not your fault."

A further point to be considered is what the tormentors are telling the victimized client regarding what will happen to her if she doesn't make sure that the therapy ends. It's important to clarify which inner programs and conditioning will be set loose if the victim disobeys the tormentor. The barbed hooks of programs or conditions must first be deactivated because not all self-inflicted injuries end up being harmless. In addition, you absolutely have to know whether the client or any of her inner parts still meet up with the tormentors (or are forced to) or if the tormentors have access to the client's residence, because in that case the tormentors' threats aren't simply empty threats but can cost the client her life.

In my practice the multiple safeguards have proven their worth in protecting the therapist and the client by means of various safety nets. The clearer it is for the tormentor that he can no longer achieve any silence through violence, that information in all its details already has been shared and that each and every attack, no matter on whom, would reveal the tormentor's guilt, the faster any danger to anyone's life is eliminated.

The tormentors of course don't stop at threatening consequences for the client and therapist. Such threats wear themselves out. If for the twentieth time, I return from a weekend vacation in which my death had been predicted, then the weapon has become dull. The next step is almost always making the client doubt the therapist. If the therapist knows her way around and is competent, then this will be used to claim the therapist is on the side of the tormentors. This can mean that methods used or therapy materials will be seen or understood by the client in this context. Or the client will be persuaded that the therapist only knows so much because she is in cahoots with the tormentor.

Some perpetrators go even further and produce material (such as digitally altered pictures) that shows the therapist in this context. For the client, who has a hard time trusting anyone anyway, this is a hard test. It doesn't help for the therapist to feel insulted; the only thing that helps is psychoeducation and explanations for the client.

It was especially stressful for one client—at least during her therapy—worrying that the tormentors would train one inner part to attack and kill the therapist. Knowing that terrible things had been done in her life under dissociation, she really despaired about the possibility. She wasn't sure whether the inner part was at all controllable or able to be influenced. I was very certain that I had such a firm relationship to the client's system that I would help and that the danger wasn't that great. Still it was necessary to create a framework and to take further measures to show the client unambiguously that even a fully automated inner part couldn't harm me. It wasn't enough to assure her that nothing bad would happen; instead I had to document which measures would be taken to assure my safety, even directly during a therapy session, if necessary.

With these clients we should keep in mind that because of their inner structures, they are not capable of keeping the relationship stable. In addition, it is very difficult for them to rely on the relationship. They need more than the verbal assurance that we will get involved, that they are important to us. They need concrete objects (such as a stone, a shell, a stuffed animal) through which the relationship can express itself.

Considering the environment of organized violence, these concrete things should above all be selected so that they are unique in a certain way, but on the other hand replaceable. Tormentors who know how stabilizing such objects can be will try to destroy them or to take them away. Then it is important to build further bridges. I always find it helpful to replace something that was destroyed with something even nicer.

Last but not least, we should give some thought to the fact that tormentors also read our professional literature and that among the tormentors there are also professional therapists. When we give instructions about which exercises are helpful, we have to assume that they will also be used to achieve the opposite effect. An independent individual modification or exercise construction achieves security and safety. Even if some tormentors seem superficially a little slow on the uptake, it is usually important not to underestimate the intelligence of tormentors who can create and run programs.

It's not difficult to discover which values any particular therapist tries to impart, which essences and possibilities for protection the tormentors then can attempt to poison, reversing the whole vocabulary for help and affection. We have to be resourceful and imaginative when we see that our well-meant suggestions are met with fear and resistance by the client.

It is therefore a further important step in therapy to observe very carefully the reactions of our clients to certain words, suggestions, and exercises—sometimes the tormentors haven't left much upon which repair and rehabilitation could begin. This can lead to long and tenacious discussions in therapy about the meaning of words. Clients find it very difficult to bear when they discover that their perceptions don't reflect reality but rather distort or reverse the meanings of what therapy has to offer. Much work is necessary so that the merciless black-and-white view of the world that they have acquired can be changed appropriately. Often enough, in the background a kind of "black" scanner is running which calls our efforts at discovering reality in the outside world betrayal and deceit, thus burdening the therapy relationship immeasurably.

The client's healing is about taking back possession of the world as a place where she can live, where she has a right to her life and a right to a quality of life. The radius that our most tortured clients initially can claim for themselves is very restricted. Often enough at first, having survived only leads to stagnation because positively experienced feelings are missing or are connected with life-endangering actions or prohibitions. These feelings themselves can unleash conditioning—a vicious circle in the seemingly endless horror and the inability to escape from it. She, whose right has been denied to decide whether she wants to live or die or to even have the possibility of deciding, has a hard time imagining that there could be anything like a future worth living.

CHAPTER THREE

Practical conclusions for psychotherapy

With the examples of the vignettes from Chapter Two, but still from the point of view of the therapist, I show at which points approaches for solving the problems can be created, and which aspects have to be considered. Disgust as a catalyst for dissociation is regularly accompanied by guilt and shame in therapy—both aspects that the tormentors can avail themselves of systematically.

Since the explanation of the structures of dissociation is constructed on experiences of disgust, we deal with disgust, shame, and guilt in treating our clients. "What happens to me is my responsibility—that's the way I am."

Ms. Aller

What are the important criteria in order to work with clients like Ms. Aller, who have to overcome the separation between her emotional experience and her awareness of the events to which it should be connected? The top priority is the therapeutic relationship. Human beings with traumatic experiences that have caused dissociation are very dependent on experiencing a clear and safe attachment in a therapeutic setting. Only in this way can they enter new realms of experience, doing new things, finding out new things, and regaining curiosity about the world.

Ms. Aller has to experience the therapeutic relationship in such a way that she doesn't experience any fake sparing of her feelings. All feedback, whether positive or critical, has to be sufficiently placed into context. It is very important to prevent Ms. Aller from carrying out her own contextualization according to her inner trauma scripts.

To begin with, Ms. Aller needs to receive feedback about her behavior over and over again, for example her avoidance of eye contact and her body posture. Her posture essentially prevents a view of her body and thereby the mental processes connected with it ("I should stay away from others, no one will be able to tolerate me, I am ugly ..."). We would want to reactivate and confirm the knowledge that she actually should have (which Ms. Aller wasn't allowed to have in her consciousness as a child), that characterizes her traumatic experiences as an injustice. And we would subject our own behavior to an analysis by the patient. The patient should learn to be able to rely on a relationship again.

Which criteria can she draw upon to determine whether she can risk getting involved in a relationship? How can she test us to see if we mean well by her?

• Does she assume that we will give her authentic feedback?
• Does she experience any expression of disgust in our behavior (a feeling that is known to be hard to suppress) and if not, how does she explain this lack on our part?

We would connect our behavior with our mental processes (because we are this way and think this way, that's why we act this way) and give her criteria for the observation of our behavior and the conclusion ("What makes you think that ...? What could be helpful criteria to find out, or to base any conclusions on?"). And ultimately via psychoeducation we would reconnect the original situations to the original narrative. To this end we would want to use work with the inner parts as a helpful instrument, among other things. We could make use of a bulletin board showing the relationships in the family or of sand tray animals.

With the help of these techniques we could make it clear to Ms. Aller how disgust became an inner part of her "self" and where it really belongs—not to herself but to her grandfather's deeds. The therapist would therefore, so to speak, tell the story in a new way, and in this way make it clear to Ms. Aller that she had no means of resisting her grandfather successfully so that only fleeing to the inside and splitting herself off became possible.

This inner part (which retained the memory of the experience with the grandfather) would have, for all practical purposes, remained stuck in time. This part would need help so that it understands that its inner working model of that time was necessary in order to make survival possible, but does not constitute an adequate image of the situation.

In such a situation both working models from Brisch's (2010) attachment theory can be used for the client as explanatory models. Brisch assumes that a child in a traumatic situation develops two working models in order to find a way to deal with the world:

• In consciousness, for a start, a working model would develop that allows me (the child) to continue to imagine that I have a loving and caring caregiver (on whom I depend for survival). This allows me to reinterpret the situation: This is happening because I am wrong, bad, or disgusting, and if I learn to be better, not disgusting, etc., then there will be a possibility for me to be cared for. In consciousness the situation changes from one of hopelessness into one of guilt.

• Split off from this conscious explanation, internally a working model would survive whereby the situation is as it objectively is: A caregiver who is merciless, leaving me without protection and with no prospect of change. This knowledge has to remain far removed from consciousness.

Only with increasing independence can the victim be encouraged through therapy to confront this experienced reality. It would be helpful to point out that because of the violence she experienced and thereby the attachment she was denied, she only had the possibility of trying, above all, to hang on to the attachment, at the expense of questioning the behavior—which, however, meant that the possibility of any questioning was eliminated. Anyone who has to maintain a bond at all costs may not and cannot question the caregiver and his behavior. Ms. Aller must learn to understand that as a child she assumed the view of her grandfather and was therefore able to behave in such a way so that the attachment to him remained intact, accepting that the price for this was that it wasn't possible for her to explore the world and question her grandfather's behavior.

Because the patient perceives herself as horrible and viciously disgusting, looking at comparable situations will also be helpful: If a child is overweight, does this mean that it is OK if she is raped? On the inside and on the outside new internal and external stories can slowly arise. As benevolent bonds are realized in therapy, and we help the patient, so to speak, come to a new view of the world at certain points and encourage orientation and a new understanding, she can understand why things developed as they did. And with much internal work she can eventually admit to the little, injured, inner part: "Bad things were done to you and you deserve comfort."

To accomplish this, a benevolent examination of the stories she tells and the fragments she remembers, precisely from the point of view of the client, is necessary. For example: "But I was truly disgusting—he didn't do these things to others—my girlfriends don't get cheated on by their boyfriends—this must all have something to do with me ..." Patience is necessary. Even with such examples, we are working with a model developed by the client for her very survival—and no one gives that up quickly or frivolously.

Ms. Berger

In the case of Ms. Berger, whose psychological and physical experiences add yet another level of splits, the work with the inner parts will have to be expanded significantly. We will integrate many inner parts into the work, including various inner pieces of split-off information. When we have accomplished enough stabilization in therapy so that the material that has arisen can be "contained" adequately, we will then begin to try to complete the picture of this fragmented narrative.

In order to create possibilities for Ms. Berger to approach herself differently and to experience curiosity, desire, and courage, certain exercises might be helpful, for example an exercise of thankfulness for her own body or the cleansing exercise demonstrated by Richard Kluft in a workshop in 1998, a kind of cleansing ritual in order to wash away feelings of disgust.

Another possibility is externalizing disgust. When an experience such as the feeling of disgust is seen as separate from the self, a former "disgusting" client (a client looking on herself as "I am disgusting") becomes capable of experiencing disgust as a feeling again. If she can perceive her disgust, then she has to be more than the disgust. Ultimately, and this would follow here, all the possibilities of new observation, including the observation exercise created by Luise Reddemann (2001), can be helpful in such a situation. Unpleasant and aversive feelings on the level of the body also can slowly ease. Only when Ms. Berger can recognize what actually belongs where, can she also distance herself from stories in the final analysis and calm herself more quickly when new material pops up: "This is from the time when I was five years old. It is understandable that it pops up at this point, but today I am no longer five ..." She can develop concrete narratives, stories to be told. In this way the information becomes easier to put into a time frame and ultimately it also becomes possible for her to assign responsibility where it ultimately belongs. Ms. Berger has to learn to give up the responsibility that she took on because of the necessary but incorrect contextualization.

Ms. Ciller

In contrast to Ms. Berger, with Ms. Ciller who still exhibits inner parts loyal to the tormentors in her everyday behavior, in the beginning there has to be a gentle but clear confrontation to help her understand her own patterns of behavior, the results they create in others, and how they developed as a result of being a victim. It is like assisting her to look in a mirror and helping her to deal with her shame and fear. It is necessary for you as a therapist to pretend you do not see what is going on, and accept any behavior as okay as long as it is a result of trauma. Initially Ms. Ciller provokes both transference disgust and real disgust. You need to destroy the context and ultimately creating a new context. It's about examining the initial narrative that was offered, and the question should be asked, "If you expect someone to put up with something, then how is it supposed to be that person's fault?"

Ms. Ciller's splitting, in contrast to the previous example, goes in the opposite direction. In her family, everything that is disgusting gets split off and assigned to others outside her family. Those others are responsible—the Ciller family has no responsibility. "If someone would only help us, then everything would be different." Ms. Ciller's actions are clearly within the context of "It's everybody else's fault" and are stored in her memory in such an episodic fashion. She already split things off when implementing each deed, as a prerequisite for being at all capable of doing such things. "I only do it because the others are so disgusting and deserve it ..." For Ms. Ciller a confrontation with the genuine narrative is necessary, in order to change her view of herself and the world and to get her to accept her actual guilt instead of denying it.

A first therapeutic step in the right direction would be a confrontation with the following fact: The others don't reject her son Fritz because they are mean, but rather because they find him disgusting. Their rejection is therefore substantiated. Fritz does things that make others flee in disgust. It isn't the others who deny him his well-deserved appreciation.

With both confrontations the therapist will need to do some persuasion: Ms. Berger has to be encouraged to see things today as they really are (so that she can encounter the trauma without fearing that she can't bear it). Ms. Ciller has to exchange her narcissistically shaped, noble egoism as a victim for a less than clean slate. She will only succeed in this if she also has something to gain.

Ms. Deckert

In the case of Ms. Deckert, through the splits an inner part has arisen which has, for the most part, isolated the initial experiences and kept them apart from her consciousness. Looking at her pattern of behavior, we must first search to find where the initial experience began.

"Is someone born this way?" As we are already maneuvering in an area in which the perpetrators have invested a great deal of planning and single-mindedness, we have to ask ourselves over and over again with respect to her way of thinking, where this really comes from, whether it is really about what the patient chose to do herself, of her own free will. We need much psychoeducation, and we ourselves need to find a way to truly like these fiercely rejected inner parts, in order to make a case for these inner parts with the client.

"The child had no chance; its organism was programmed for survival—it could only do what was conducive for survival." "At that time the child was betrayed—does the child deserve to be in such a situation again today?" "This inner part took it upon itself to endure this experience and this blame—whereby the other inner parts and the consciousness were protected. Did it ever get any appreciation for this?"

Exercises could follow that make it possible for a truce to exist between the body and the parts, which then could give up ways of behavior that always confirm the patient's disgust at herself. One example would be that Ms. Deckert, among other things, in addition to genuinely disgusting sexual practices, had to perform sexually on a garbage dump. Every time this was triggered, although she didn't register this at first, after she came home she began to compulsively clean things. When it became clear to her in therapy, that in this way she just gave the tormentor room for action, she was able to stop these actions from one day to another: "I'm not going to give him more room in my life. I'm here; I'm okay, and he isn't going to get me to fanatically clean everything—after all, he is the disgusting one."

She learned to get herself quite consciously into an inner dialogue in which she informed the tormentor unambiguously in the case of her compulsion to clean: "You disgusting swine! You will never manage to have any power over me." She enjoyed it more and more when she could return the disgust to him. "Of all the things that are disgusting about you, not a single one can be cleaned. With you the disgusting things are all on the inside."

There is also a good possibility for inviting this inner part that has accepted disgust as a part of itself onto the inner stage and telling the story once again together with the part that has rejected the disgust. In addition to the previously mentioned techniques of psychoeducation and creating new contexts, we have to work with this inner part so that, as much as possible, the client can develop a condition of mutual consciousness between herself and her inner part.

It's typical for DDNOS clients to believe that they know their complete story and to interpret emerging symptoms as proof that "I am a perverse person right now" because the earlier frame of reference is completely dissociated. Reconstructing this frame of reference is the task of psychotherapy. This necessitates a compassionate explanation for seemingly inexplicable things like "Why didn't I fight back? After all, I was already seven."

Through the splits and often through the active "assistance" of the perpetrators many clients have the impression that tormentors and victims had equal initial possibilities at their command—therefore resisting would have been child's play, you would have just had to want to. If the tormentor also managed to verbalize the opinion, for example in the case of Ms. Deckert, with comments on her forced orgasm that she was a "horny nymphomaniac", who liked it better the more disgusting it was, then this repeated feedback eventually became a part of her self-image. Here too we have to go back to the beginning of the story, and analyze it step by step. Our motto has to be: What had to happen so that a situation arose in which a child asked for or seemed to enjoy having to do something disgusting?

For therapy it is a great help if a client is able to approach this initially split-off inner part with respect. For this purpose pictures from the past (if they are available) are a big help. In time it becomes easier to really see what is shown in the pictures: A child who was tortured, not an adult whose own desires were realized in this situation. There is an adult whose goals were accomplished in the picture, but he can't be seen. What you see is the child. A partial interview, in the sense of working on the inner stage, is a good possibility.

For this kind of split, what Marilyn van Derbur (2003) has described is a good example: A split between a day child and a night child. Only in this way was it possible to hide from her consciousness what happened in her relationship with her father. Working through this was only possible when both parts approached each other and the client's consciousness finally recognized that a parallel world existed beside the public world.

Further examples

In the case of Ms. Ehrenfeld, as therapists we have to create a relationship with our client and through this relationship also get permission to contact the inner parts. For contact with the inner parts we woo them just as we wooed the client, with a great deal of psychoeducation. The teaching is: "This is how violence functions." Here we suggest over and over again that that which we see will make sense, even if the client can't recognize it right at this moment. Basically, we work on two stages: on the inner stage at first, often behind the dissociative barrier so that the client's main adult self at first isn't present (can't consciously follow what is happening)—and then with the main person, where we try to increasingly encourage a convergence between the experiences on the inside and the client's consciousness. It is our responsibility as therapists to weigh carefully how the patient should access the information received from the dissociated inner people.

This connection between the parallel worlds also has to take place for the client later in the outside world. Many clients, even when they begin to work with the traumatization and have broken the dissociation, try to be just as productive as they were back in the times without this additional burden. They have to learn to allow themselves to perceive themselves as burdened and to allow themselves relief—even at the cost of no longer being categorized by others as able to withstand unlimited stress.

When disgust is present in the entire system and doesn't just affect one inner part, then naturally "small experiments" can be carried out very carefully with the inner parts and with the client: "How long can you stand to have your finger stroke your hand before the disgust becomes completely unbearable?" "Which sentences arise here, where do they come from?" Increasingly you can encourage the client to make the exception "I am touching myself" a little more the rule.

In my experience, it's not helpful to pass on every gruesome detail that we learn from the dissociated parts of our clients to them in an unfiltered fashion but rather only to make enough of a connection possible that the edges of horror, the extent and important central experiences of the client become known by the main person. And naturally the information has to be sufficient so that the client can basically integrate the trauma and ultimately allow herself to see her life experiences as factual. Not every detail with regard to contents, but the structure has to be known.

The relationship of the psychotherapist to the client and to the inner parts of the client is the basis for the client and the inner parts to be able to enter into a constructive relationship with one another. Often the inner parts and the client on the outside share a catastrophic view of themselves but are willing to show mercy to all others. In this way the inner part XY may be convinced that it is just as abnormal as the experiences that it was forced to endure; other inner parts can question this view. They can assure XY that they perceive it differently. Its knowledge about these other parts, which have already worked through their own horrible experiences, could be used in the process. It would see them not as perpetrators but rather as victims. "I'm sure that Tim and Margot know that it wasn't the fault of inner part XY, that in fact others were responsible for what happened. Isn't that right?" "Do you see, inner part XY, that Tim and Margot know that I was right, that it isn't your fault?"

These are often longer sequences in which the system reciprocates and absolves itself of any guilt. Here it's always important to me that the inner parts support putting things into the correct context. This doesn't have to occur in spoken language but can happen with pictures, figures, drawings, using clay for sculpture, with elements of body therapy, hoops, objects, and so on, and also in work with flip charts and chalkboards.

What is important is that we don't force anything on clients just because it seems suitable to us. One client had had the experience of always having a stuffed animal pressed into her hands after especially gruesome and disgusting incidents and at times during these incidents. Everything soft and cuddly was tainted with such an overwhelming disgust that while working through memories of disgusting incidents we had to revert to hard and seemingly non-comforting items as encouraging objects for stabilizing support. Only in this way could we make sure that the client worked through disgust from the old incidents and not from current triggers.

When we now come into the area of programming, in which also the respective relationships of inner parts to one another was dictated, we have to have a great deal of compassionate understanding for how the client's inner system became that which it is now. How did the inner parts learn to see one another reciprocally? How can we advocate for each of the other parts with each inner part? How can they achieve an understanding of the inner distress, how can they take in the perspective of each of the others, and how can we communicate to them that all this is happening in one body?

We need a proper map to help us understand who interacts with whom and how. Which inner parts share the same language space, the same interaction space? And ultimately, which I consider to be very helpful, we have to seek the individual stories of conditioning and programming and transfer everything onto a composite map, a kind of timeline for the formation of the individual inner parts in the life of the patient.

An "inner guideline" would be: No inner part chose to be where it is and whoever endures the disgust or did disgusting things contributed to the other inner parts' not having to do this. Dissociation is then reinterpreted as a kind of mutual protection, and in the way I as a therapist construct mutually appreciative relationships and explore the stories, I provide a model for how they can interact with one another. I therefore advance mutual understanding and emphasize regularly that under such circumstances, I would have behaved exactly the same way.

For all intents and purposes the techniques don't differ from each other, but we have to do many things frequently and thereby keep an eye on which inner part we can demand things of and how it can be supported so that a good inner cooperation arises. What is important is that a mutual compassionate understanding arises: "This is how it looks through your glasses, and every pair of glasses is only one part of the whole."

Here is one example from an actual task with an inner part programmed with a great deal of disgust, which experienced itself as completely perverted and repulsive. After many sessions it became clear to the inner part that what happened was actually not its responsibility and said nothing about it, although it was convicted in the "court" of the tormentor. Rather than being relieved, it was, as we so often experience with relatives of psychopaths, stunned and appalled. It would have preferred to be dead rather than know that such disgusting and dreadful things happen, and indeed happen unjustly. The inner part would have found it bearable if it had all been its fault. The fact that people were senselessly tortured and died for no reason was more than it could bear. Here much inner consolation is needed for the inner parts. Consolation through the therapist and advocating for understanding from the client, who, when she emerges from the dissociation, will still have to deal with a portion of the feelings of the inner part and will have to understand these feelings, in order to make sense out of them.

Much psychoeducation and repeated psychoeducation will be necessary in order to make understanding possible on all levels and to achieve a kind of cooperation instead of dissociation. At the same time, this shows once again the importance of the therapeutic relationship. Only when this relationship is absolutely intact will it be possible in time for the relationship to overcome the extreme storms of misunderstandings. Many inner persons continue at first to live in the previous time. If something doesn't work for them (for example, preventing garbage from being eaten), this can create its own context of: The therapist will abandon us, he will be angry with us, we will be punished … And it doesn't help in the slightest that the therapist has explained this over and over again. What is necessary is much and varied repetition and compassionate correction. If you are dealing with a client who has experienced very potent rituals to implant beliefs, healing therapeutic rituals and positive symbols, chosen by the client himself, can be valuable assistants in the process.

When we encounter the topic of disgust, we must not be surprised that we need many hours in order to achieve internally a somewhat enduring change in even one inner person. If you make it clear to yourself how many hours of extreme violence and conditioning these clients have experienced, then this is the price that has to be paid for success. A dissociative client who has developed her dissociation as a result of violence but not of programming can, of course, be treated faster. Her cooperation simply has much more to do with her own self than in this case.

My suggestions for working with such clients are very labor intensive. I can only afford them on the basis of mixed financing in the context of an institution, with a willingness, financially as well as time-wise, to go beyond the limits. This also means not allowing any gaps to arise in the course of treatment and to make some things possible through donations and personal commitment. This is not a suggestion for colleagues who are forced to work within the framework of what health insurance will pay for and who have to see that every hour is financed.

If we want to take a further step, then we arrive ultimately at inverse programming. This is actually a one-way street, a path with no return. My attempts to achieve something here also mean that it is necessary to personally participate actively and, to a great extent, this means being subjected to unfair attacks, deceit, and lies, to become the target of betrayal, the further the relationship develops. Normally this happens outside the client's system and is caused by the perpetrators, but here it almost always happens within the system; it is implemented almost automatically.

And yet my experience has been that if we hang in there, if we allow our feelings to be released and become visible, if we place vast amounts of humaneness against inhumanity, then what happens is that this constant drip is able to hollow out the largest stone. Since levels one and two can be integrated considerably faster, with increasing work the possibilities for inner support will become greater. Working through disgust on level two and later on level three (where it can only develop when feelings come into being) results in the emergence of massive feelings of guilt and shame, the feeling of being a monster and not having a right to live. And without a doubt, the deeds are so monstrous that it is difficult to imagine how anyone could continue to live with the memories of them. Many and varied forms of reinforcement and support are necessary.

In conclusion, in my therapeutic work I make myself as a human being completely and clearly visible, and also with respect to my inner structures, my values, and their consequences. I try, therefore, in my interactions and within myself to offer a model and again and again to combine it with: "In your case it was so because the world was the way it was, and you understand me right now in this way because you have learned to see the world in this way. I would like to invite you to my side of the world, where things function differently." Anyone who gets involved to this extent doesn't just make herself vulnerable; she will be hurt, almost inevitably. Systems clash that previously had no contact with each other, and sometimes struggles cannot be avoided.

I see it as the task of the therapist to approach clients in such a way that they have a chance to connect with us. We have to learn to adapt what we offer to fit their needs and not the other way around.

To quote from therapy with a client who was forced to commit deadly violence to her own child and had no possibility of a worthy burial of the child's corpse: "How can you see me other than as a monster—it was my hands, it is my fault, blood is sticking to my hands?" My answer: "For me to get the impression that it was your intention, everything would have had to convince me that it was your free will to do things or to refuse to do them, and at no time would so much violence have been necessary. If this was already a part of you, then they wouldn't have had to torture you—and if it was your nature, then why would you suffer so much now, when you are confronted with it? Why can't you then feel any joy or even indifference right now?"

I then regularly repeat what I know about what led up to such an incident, providing psychoeducation about violence and consciousness. Too much violence turns consciousness off—in this case it was deliberately shut down and deliberately made able to be manipulated. What happened then reflected that which the tormentor considered desirable, not what the client would have wanted from her point of view. What makes it possible for the client to form a relationship at all and to achieve a relationship with herself are her feelings and the capacity for forming relationships as well as the relationship that the therapist can offer her.

A first step into a new freedom is accomplished when, at the very least, the decision about life or death is no longer in the hands of the tormentors. Only with this basic human freedom are further steps at all conceivable and ultimately intentionally feasible.

This makes sense in the context of this most extreme of all experiences of violence and dehumanization. If the client's organism with its drive for "survival at all costs" first ensured that she would have to endure so much without having the opportunity to simply choose to die, in the further course of action it was the perpetrators who determined that whether the victim lived or died depended on their discretion. It is not unusual to encounter victims who can't even count the number of resuscitations they went through and tell us moving stories about the offers they made their tormentors, just to be allowed to die.

One former patient committed suicide a few years after she had to discontinue her therapy with me because she moved away. She had a burning desire for justice for her sufferings, an apology from her parents, and an admission of the injustice that was done to her by the perpetrators involved, but these things did not occur. At the end of her journey she felt it wasn't possible to live in a world in which such a correction didn't occur. In contrast to her situation as a child and as an adolescent, she then had the means and the possibility to successfully end her life.

This is the ultimate human right, even though we as therapists always hope that our work will enable human beings not to have to make use of it.

How distinctions in the internal and external worlds develop as a result of experiences

In this chapter it will become clear from the perspective of the therapist, how the structure of our internal world is connected with the structure of our external world. It's primarily about the question of how distinctions take on a greater significance and are maintained and which roles the systems of bonding and of curiosity have in the context of these experiences.

Normal human development, growing up healthy, to maturity, means that at the beginning of our lives we experience reassurance from the outside, and orientation from the outside. And in a kind of long-term experiment we learn to make the important decisions and note the distinctions in our world. In time we learn to be self-effective once we understand how this world works and what we have to do in order to be successful in it. Our inside world can orient itself toward what proves to be helpful for our survival and wellbeing in the outside world. In the first interactions with our primary attachment figures we also learn to understand how human beings function in the world, how social interactions function, and how we can understand them. Finally we learn to master the language of our surroundings, mimicking, gesticulating, and ultimately verbalizing.

As attachment researchers have pointed out over and over again, we must first have a secure bond before we can search for new experiences in the world. To achieve this bond we need attachment figures who answer our cries and our laughter correctly, who encounter us with interest and care, and who let us know in so many ways that we are "valid" and that our needs are reasonable. Through certain communications we need to be able to make people aware of us and to have our needs satisfied. We have a right to live, and it is good that we exist. If everything goes well, then someone takes our hand and shows us the world. Then we have a reason to be curious about the world around us.

As a general rule, decisions and distinctions we have made along our sensory-motor journey lead to varied patterns of interactions between people and environment being stored in our minds. After new information has received its emotional meaning in the amygdala, it is forwarded to the hippocampus, a brain structure within the limbic system, which is itself structured by experiences. The hippocampus is an important structure for learning and memory because although it is still beneath the level of the cerebral cortex, for all practical purposes it structures the foundations of our internal world. When information from sensory and emotional channels reaches the hippocampus, it becomes associated with a specific time and place. It becomes available for comparison with other information that is already stored in the cerebral cortex. Often dissociative people do not know that something they are re-experiencing in the present actually belongs to the past, because the elements of that experience have not reached the hippocampus. If everything goes the way it is supposed to, ultimately a suitable "hard disk" for a human being arises spontaneously through the encounters of human being and environment, making it possible for this human being to move around her familiar world as a welcome guest.

During a workshop in 1987 in California, the researcher Heinz von Foerster expressed it in this way: "Only those questions which are in principle undecidable, we can decide." In order for us to find our way in the world we have to give ourselves the right to live with presuppositions, to use decisions made on a single occasion as a basis for how the world is, so that we don't have to keep calculating everything over and over again. In this way we develop habits of seeing, hearing, and smelling. At all levels of our senses we figure out important components from the world around us and thereby have the advantage of being able to reduce their complexity. In this way we can let ourselves tolerate inconsistencies. We don't have to take everything so literally.

In a reliable world and coming from a world of secure attachments, we can count on finding a mutually consensual world in our cultural environment. We can assume the right to make personal decisions and distinctions in this world according to our values. We can define what we consider to be important.

People with a history of psychosis often experience the dissolution of all reliable structures of their world during a psychotic episode. They can't hold on to anything, and despair about a world that allows no more unambiguous distinctions and decisions. This often painful experience has its roots in the fact that people with a schizophrenic sensitivity have to take the world literally and aren't capable of holding on to that which they once believed. Rather, they have to repeatedly figure out this new world. Since for these sensitive people there is no default setting for the world almost everything has to be calculated and decided over and over again, so they cannot reach a point where they know that this is the ultimate right decision. Their systems can't avoid overheating because the one and only correct decision in a world of so many possibilities just doesn't exist, no matter how precisely they try to proceed. The world is too complex and too fast for them to be able to act with the precision they need and to manage to cope.

With victims of extreme violence everything is completely different. Due to the constantly encountered and genuinely life-threatening violence they have endured, they have been forced to learn arbitrary distinctions that don't come from the usual external world but from the foreign world of the tormentors. Their hard disk is structured in a world without attachments, without security, where the only security is in learning to split themselves off in such a way (namely distinctions with barriers to other distinctions) that it is always only inner parts that react to certain stimuli with reactions that were necessary for survival. In contrast, a person raised in a healthy environment develops a world of inner decisions and distinctions which all relate to each other. A sufficiently integrated ego can accordingly react to the demands of the external world methodically and effectively. But if you are raised with imposition of decisions and inner separations, inner splits occur (since as an integrated being you couldn't survive this violence). And since the tormentors' demands in addition are completely impracticable, another split takes place at the same time toward the external world.

Let's visualize what is happening. At first inherent presuppositions about the world as a place of care, security, and orientation are brutally broken. Then the tormentors impose on the victims just how distinctions and decisions have to be made in order for the victim to survive, and how each inner part has to behave, and what they have to be able to do and learn, in order to survive. Learning is always both learning distinctions and performing different behaviors of varying complexity tuned to those distinctions.

Because the human organism is born with the instinct to try to survive at any price, it's easy to understand how the tormentors can succeed in training human beings into being parts and robots, to substantially shut down their cerebral cortexes and their consciousness. In this way they make them so controllable that they act in a certain manner, automatically, without any emotion, and without any possibility of resistance. As this happens bypassing their conscious awareness, in the deeper structure of their organism, the conscious mind does not notice it. These people don't need to forget because they acquire their knowledge in dissociation, so this knowledge is dissociated from their consciousness right at the start. Very often with such tortured patients we encounter much more than simple threats or orders to remain silent. There are entire inner interaction landscapes in which the inner persons prevent each other from speaking or watching. This makes it impossible for individual inner persons at the beginning of psychotherapy to examine their experiences more deeply, to remember or share memories of what happened, or to be co-conscious. It is surely evident that the hard disk of such a client, the hippocampus, has to have a completely different structure than that of a secure client with attachments and without such an early experience of violence. In the final analysis, this tormented client began her life with a maximal shock to her presuppositions, was exposed to relatively direct violence and danger to her life, did not experience protection, care, or consolation, and could only retreat to the inside because it was not possible to flee to the outside. The world she experienced differed in practically every important aspect from the normal, comprehensible, orienting world of a human being. As the human hippocampus needs a few years to mature, early experiences of violence create maximal damage.

These early experiences of survival and indoctrination are especially stubborn because they don't originate from the purely cognitive area, but have their roots outside the waking consciousness. At first, because it is attached to our senses, much seems to be so consistent that changing it would mean treading a long path. We have to understand and help our clients to understand how our encounters with the world form or deform our senses, in order for the survivor to have any chance in cautious therapy of taking the first steps into a humane world.

If you want to explore the inner world of the patient, it is helpful to get your hands thoroughly dirty in the perpetrator's intellectual world. For me as a therapist this means grappling with human sadism and envisioning how the tormentors tick. In this way it can be possible, together with the victim, to enter the still closed, dissociated worlds full of shame and disgust, and to reach out your hand to those imprisoned in them.

As therapists at times we have to be able to endure living in a world that also calls a very violent and dehumanizing parallel world its own. We have to be aware that in our society there is an extreme amount of violence, and we have to decide for ourselves whether we are willing to confront this violence without trivializing or denying it.

It is hard to do this and it is hard to endure. Most people wish that extreme violence against children and helpless people was an invention of novelists, an exception, something we can oppose vehemently and indignantly. It is perfectly legal (if not justifiable) to arrange your world in such a way so as to close your eyes and ears to this violence and to consider your side of the world to be the only one. As long as we do this, however, we have no possibility of doing anything to change these conditions.

We have to visualize the personality and goals of the perpetrators who use torture to design the inner structure of multiple systems for other people. Ultimately it is what they want and consider desirable that determines how the "hard disks" of the victims are formed. It is the vision of the perpetrators that determines which conditions of torture the victims have to face, what outcome they want to create, which ways are best suited to breaking resistance, and what steps will lead to unconditional, automatic subjugation. It is the task of the therapist to understand this path of inhuman creation and dehumanization and to observe it without any voyeurism, in order to derive a way back from that world into a human world.

The knowledge about the inner system of the patient is just as indispensable. With whom am I dealing, and how are her thinking and actions structured? It is clear that an inner judge will need to be addressed differently than a small, terrified child, that an inner part loyal to the tormentor understands words differently than a motherly, caring inner part. And the therapist needs a compassionate understanding for the inner parts that had to do terrible things and see themselves deeply ensnared in guilt. Only if we are able to understand that they came into this situation desperately and blamelessly, and if we can also communicate this in our actions and our words, can these fundamentally different inner worlds of the therapist and client finally meet in a beneficial fashion.

CHAPTER FIVE

Inside views from a sadistic world

From the inside view of the person involved and from the therapist's point of view, I want to show here the nature of the hidden world of sadistic perpetrators. I shall try to communicate how their pitilessness (absence of empathy) was already learned in early childhood, and what happens between perpetrator and victim. As we more often encounter perpetrators who, behind the façade, reveal a neo-Nazi mindset in their staging and contemptuous treatment of the victims, this is also described in the example. The reader is invited to enter a world that would otherwise remain locked away. I believe it is indispensable for therapists to gain a perception of this shadow world.

"I have forgotten the past. If you haven't forgotten me, that's your problem," says Klaus Barbie in Max Ophüls' documentary, Hotel Terminus: The Life and Times of Klaus Barbie.

With this one specific example I would like to illustrate how we can imagine these circles that use other people, and the way their world is portrayed to those people inside the group and to those outside. In order to become a perpetrator, first of all you have to be born into the right family, or buy your way into this world through possessing a child.

In these families we almost regularly meet a perpetrator generation starting with the grandparents, that is, with those who were adults during the Second World War. Often enough, it is here in the figures of the grandparents that we meet sadistic perpetrators with far-reaching networks who again, especially for their male offspring, have chosen appropriate partners. Much here reminds us of the Nazi era, of operations like the *Lebensborn* (an SS organization to encourage the birth of Aryan children on the basis of Nazi racial ideology and eugenics). Children are blatantly produced for the marketplace and exploited according to their "usefulness". Children are merchandise, property. The contempt for other people by the supposedly superior master race is applied here in the division of the world into masters and slaves. We are up here—the others down there. And whoever is up here dictates what happens. Those down there are merchandise without any rights.

Dr. Zehn hails from a family that moves in such circles. Coming from a wealthy industrialist family and born during the Nazi era, after completing his studies, choosing a suitable marriage partner, and receiving a doctorate, he achieves a stellar career. Out in the public eye the economics expert is soon in great demand. He advises worldwide conglomerates and is in contact with the upper classes, whether in fields of economy, politics, or sports. His so-called friends are exclusively business associates. Dr. Zehn has no affectionate or loving relationships in the outside world.

Officially he has no time for his many children, since he is heavily burdened with his numerous professional commitments. Within the family he leads a stern regimen. From his wife and children, especially the girls, he demands unconditionally submissive behavior. He possesses a choleric temper and acts out at home in every direction. His wife alternately demands that the children show some understanding for this behavior since he works so hard for the family, or talks to the children in great detail about how she suffers from his actions. When the children ask her to leave him, Mrs. Zehn can't comply.

If one of the girls hurts herself, then Dr. Zehn reacts with uncontrollable fury and doesn't talk to this child for days. Mrs. Zehn refers to this condition of silently expressed anger as "He is worried."

In public, his wife and children are a kind of decoration, ornaments that emphasize Dr. Zehn's importance. He can't stand situations in which he isn't the center of attention. If this doesn't occur automatically, then he makes sure that it does. At first people in his surroundings find him very charming; later, however, they notice that he keeps repeating the same stories. Dr. Zehn is charming when he is the most important man on the scene. There is only one topic that is important to him: "I". Due to his diverse professional activities and international contacts, Dr. Zehn has a believable "stage" for his activities. He is also distinctly successful financially.

In his family he talks about the supposedly sadistic abuse he suffered from his mother, who still tormented him as a grown man, or about the bitter experiences he went through in childcare facilities. The moral of all these stories is always what a good life his family now has, compared to how much he suffered as a child. No one is surprised by the fact, although it seems preposterous, that Dr. Zehn nonetheless still maintains close ties to this supposedly very cruel mother, both in his professional and his personal life. No one questions the fact that his daughter spends a great deal of time with this abusive person over and over again. Or that his wife stopped working in order to take care of the children, even though while the children were younger the family had many nannies and domestic helpers.

Mrs. Zehn has many female friends, who especially distinguish themselves by the fact that they aren't kind to Mrs. Zehn or to the children. Nonetheless these friends and also their husbands have many tasks forced upon them, like having to do something for the Zehn children or having to do specific jobs for Dr. Zehn or Mrs. Zehn. This seems odd, since officially no one thinks much of them or their competence. In words it's expressed as "they owe him". Out in the public eye this is because he did not pursue them in court regarding certain economic damage they have done to him, since they are friends of his wife. Within the family at least Mrs. Zehn has good reason to feel guilty. In the final analysis, it's her friends for whom the Zehns act so selflessly.

This is how you can picture life in the public eye. Dr. Zehn is very successful in his professional life, a typical story from the German "economic miracle" of the 1950s and 1960s. At home he is difficult, which, however, can supposedly be explained by the many burdens he bears. He has a very submissive wife and children for whose welfare he apparently works very energetically.

The biography of Dr. Zehn's wife is perhaps a typical example of a "grandparent generation", where children are unprotected from violence on the mother's side and pedophile tendencies are shown on the father's side. Officially it is a family that is very successful financially and is ready to do everything for the children. Although Dr. Zehn regards the maternal grandfather of his children as a vain exaggerator and their maternal grandmother as a permanently depressed woman, for a period of time the Zehn family moves in with these grandparents. Here Dr. Zehn will also express verbally how much he is being exploited.

When Dr. Zehn helps anyone within the extended family, this help has to have a monetary value for him. Conversely however, he expects all kinds of support for himself and for his family without his having to pay a thing. Masters and slaves—that is his world, and he is no slave.

We can see already in the first descriptions that Dr. Zehn has possibly had traumatic experiences in his world (even if we have to regard the validity of a narcissist's stories of being a victim with some caution). If his stories are correct, then he has dealt with them to the extent that in order to never be a victim again, he concluded that he would have to be a perpetrator.

We could similarly attempt to explain his hatred of and contempt for women. Within the sadistic circles in which he earned his extra illicit income, he has no problems acting out this hatred. He may have been humiliated as a child, but now as an adult he can obtain diverse compensation within the framework of organized violence.

A further aspect of his socialization is his education to become a perpetrator. In such families the sons are the kings of the hill. They encounter criticism only very rarely and they get the message (in the public eye and within the family) that the world belongs to them. This socialization includes the right to make use of other human beings, to do whatever you feel like. So it's not surprising if a boy from such a family backed with the corresponding "education" ultimately also gets furious if someone else in his surroundings gets recognition for his accomplishments—recognition that this privileged boy in fact demands for himself. He should be recognized and admired, not only for his accomplishments but for his desire to achieve, even if he has not actually done so. If this admiration isn't forthcoming, then the accomplishments of others are ruthlessly portrayed as his own, often with such vehemence and conviction that the outside observer is incapable of imagining that the person involved doesn't believe what he is saying himself.

However, in order to practice sadistic violence of a magnitude that has yet to be described, we have to add to the explanation of Dr. Zehn that within his circles he has gone through training in the parallel world of organized violence. It is certainly no coincidence when the rules for behavior which, for example, one finds in LaVey's *Satanic Bible* (2007) say: "Do what you want, that is your only commandment" [translated for this edition], are also the basis for his actions.

For Dr. Zehn, as for any narcissistic person with pronounced antisocial traits, the things that give him kicks and a feeling of power, as well as those from which he can make money, have to increase over time. And this is excluding for a moment his satisfaction from living and operating in a world that is invisible and unimaginable for the majority. He becomes habituated, as with a drug, so that maintaining his enjoyment means that his abuses have to get worse. In plain English this means more pain for the victims, increasingly cruel procedures, and an expansion of possible control over the victims. At the same time every increased action trivializes what happened previously. There can be more; there can be even more. And naturally the doctor's capacity for human relationships decreases even more as does his ability to regret actions or his ability to empathize with the victims. For all intents and purposes, at the end of this development as far as socialization is concerned, there is a completely brutalized human being, who however often portrays himself in public as being especially moral, especially capable of cherishing Christian faith intensively.

The self-portrayal consistently follows the same pattern. He accomplished something because he was so exceptionally gifted. This again makes use of the concept of "masters" and "slaves". More time in the shadow world as well as success in the external world reinforce this view. What reason would Dr. Zehn have to change anything? He can do anything he wants to, no matter how cruel, and no one can do anything to him.

He who is so unsurpassed can't be denied anything by the world. This can go as far as humiliating in the outside world the victims he has abused in his shadow world, because of their inability to operate as powerfully as he does. Or he approaches them as if he is bonded to them in friendly affection. This portrayal has its cracks, but for others is not transparent.

When Dr. Zehn is furious because accidents limit the serviceability of his human merchandise, and he accordingly consistently reacts furiously to his daughter's injuries, Mrs. Zehn stands by him and reinterprets his reactions as an "expression of caring" and his "problems with expressing feelings". This doesn't make him likeable in his surroundings, but people are willing to ascribe his behavior to his being overworked, since he is so successful. And people are willing to agree in general with the theory that men just have difficulties with feelings anyway.

When Dr. Zehn refuses to contribute to the costs of his daughter's education because she moved in with her boyfriend, even though he paid for the other children's education, then he justifies this to the outside world by saying he doesn't want to encourage such loose sexual morals. In fact, again it is all about usability—where there is protection, abuse finds its limits. Where there is a genuine relationship, events in the parallel world aren't as easy to accomplish. A relationship means that there is someone who cares where his partner is, who won't let things happen through his own inaction. When, however, Dr. Zehn emphatically encourages his son to live with his girlfriend while they go to college, this behavior again serves the double standard: "What a man is allowed to do, a woman still has no right to."

Dr. Zehn creates conditions so that after his daughter's relationship breaks up, a circumstance to which he and his wife strongly contribute in the parallel world, he guarantees that his daughter will either have to sue the family to be treated financially as well as her siblings or will have to move back home. His daughter will not know why she actually ended the relationship, but she feels she was forced to, and she is ashamed of that.

Dr. Zehn gets support from the outside world for humiliating his daughter in this way. At her age, and going to college, if she were still living at home, it would be time to move out. That the prerequisites for moving out don't exist remains a secret. Neither the relatives nor the friends learn anything. And the victim has learned to keep her mouth shut.

Here we see another cornerstone of the sadistic world. Dr. Zehn is a highly regarded member of normal society; he has influential friends, some of whom are also at home in his shadow world. Who would now believe the much less influential victim, whose personality and living conditions has been described to the outside world so frequently as "difficult"? If this isn't enough, the family has enough specific contacts in the medical world and by putting on a performance for child psychiatrists, it can ensure that a suitable image is created.

Since the memories of the shadow world, which is so close to the normal world, have to be dissociated, all that remains for the victim are symptoms that she can't explain adequately. If the child were already able to remember in the normal world and were able to put these memories into words, then she would buy herself a free ticket for a long stay in a psychiatric institution.

It is so easy to allege that the victim only had the desire to search for explanations for her shortcomings outside herself and that was why she therefore blamed the parents in such an unacceptable fashion. If you add the barely imaginable dimensions of the acts, then it is only too understandable that the beliefs of even well disposed experts would be stretched to their limits. We don't want such things to happen in our world and so we can deny the reality of everything like that most easily if these things truly only exist in the imagination of crazy women.

Today thanks to the "false memory" movement it is possible to attest that these "poor nutcases" aren't lying deliberately, but that their memories have to be pseudo-memories that psychotherapists talked them into believing, or the products of excessive imagination, or adaptation to a reality dictated by the therapists.

Only a few of us have been disturbed so far by the fact that in the case of traumatic memories only those memories of the victims of sadistic violence have been so massively questioned, and questioned by such a commercially powerful organization like the False Memory Syndrome Foundation. If this were the case with respect to all traumatic memories, then there should be many more such so-called pseudo memories, including those of completely different kinds of trauma. Actually though, this discrediting of memories only pertains to the victims of sexual violence and, above all, organized violence. The fact is that this movement is so successful in selling its product "discrediting of victims and therapists" that a Dr. Zehn can be certain that if anything should "boil over", he will have enough friends and allies within the legal system and among consultants.

This however doesn't change the fact that he still must also punish the victim tenaciously, over and over again, if even a part of her memory should come out into the open or even to some extent some of her own plans should be realized, by writing, drawing, or some other means. If he finds such things, then he goes to work mercilessly. For example, his adult daughter found drawings made when she was a four- or five-year-old girl. Horrified, the split-off and punished inner part of the child had noted and illustrated in childish language that for writing some words she was subjected to anal and oral rape, and for climbing up the swing she was grounded for a week. This house arrest wasn't at home but rather in a special institution, a training center of the group. One can only guess what Dr. Zehn would have done, had he got his hands on this so unambiguous document. Dr. Zehn is merciless, and he knows no mercy or sympathy for his victims. Everything they suffer increases his lust.

Also within his shadow world he knows many and varied "reasons" for punishment. After the victim has been brutally raped and despite the massive injuries on various parts of her body, the victim must then endure Dr. Zehn's sudden lust for more of those "funny games". But when, despite all efforts, his erection just doesn't happen, he tortures the victim again, this time with varying tools of the trade that help him get back into the mood. Obviously he thinks it is the victim's fault for not succeeding in giving Dr. Zehn another erection after his first satisfaction.

Dr. Zehn has many friends. On the one hand they are useful to him in training his children a little further (to the extent that he doesn't attend to it), and on the other hand, in this way he has access to already trained victims. Sometimes he also uses these victims while abusing his own children. This can mean that in the house of his friend Dr. Bescheiden, both Dr. Zehn and Dr. Bescheiden attack a child victim together. Dr. Bescheiden has a fully equipped torture paradise. When this child isn't even able to scream any more but rather just endures everything in a mute agony, then she has to hear all kinds of cynical remarks like "With you it's the best. You just can't get enough of it."

Even though the girl is lying on the floor prostrate and exhausted from torture, the torture is continued. This can mean that Dr. Zehn uses his own daughter to inflict certain injuries on the victim (or to be injured herself), which then increases his pleasure. If at the end of such torture special guests are expected, then you may wonder how that child can even survive. As the girl lies on the floor, rigid with pain, the men make fun of the "good investment" and the fact that it was almost like "doing it with a corpse".

When Dr. Zehn sells his own children into foreign countries for a profit, then for outsiders it looks as if these children are especially privileged. They get to take a trip with a family that others can only dream of. Dr. Zehn films the encounters and sells these films for a profit, a further source of revenue for him. At various business meetings and in harmless-looking advertisements Dr. Zehn lets his friends know about planned events, and using various code words he tells them which special skills they can expect from the victims. If a customer has special desires, he can count on victims being available for such special desires.

The market for sadistic pornography is huge—and likewise the supply in all its aspects. And no one is upset by this fact.

And naturally Dr. Zehn doesn't leave it at selling his own children. He acquires "merchandise", as he calls the children, trains them, and excels at making money in both worlds.

Finally, it is also a fact that his many friends have suitable residences inside and outside the country that they put at his disposal and which are not open to the public; places in which every conceivable protection for the children is destroyed. In these places no one gets to see anything unless he belongs to these circles. And all parties involved have good reasons to keep their mouths shut. If a child should misbehave in school, then the teachers will turn to the respectable parents. If the child should try to get help from other institutions like child protection services by making them aware of her distress, then the social workers would be enormously reluctant to notify Dr. Zehn that his house is to be inspected. If such an inspection does occur, the social workers will doubtless discover that everything is in perfect order.

Should a victim nonetheless dare to go far enough out on a limb that she indeed receives some help and support, and could maybe even begin therapy or find people who would believe what she tells them, then Dr. Zehn still has the option of mobilizing special persecution with the help of his minions, who will then intimidate, threaten, rape, or if nothing else works, conduct new programming or a readjustment on the victim.

Then subservience will be drilled into her again. It hardly ever happens that the victims, instead of retreating in complete shame and fear, have the courage to press charges because of a rape that occurred within such a punishment action. Even if they do, they usually don't really expect anyone to believe them. In addition, because of the multiple splits of their personalities, they aren't able to report coherently about what happened, and they may even be unsure whether what happened to them was justified. Then the results of the proceedings are foreseeable. An additional barrier to the proceedings is the fact that such victims aren't able to name the perpetrators they know.

And the perpetrators can expect to be supported in court by the "experts". This is especially true after a cohort of analytic therapists and experts accepted Kernberg's (2009) classification system. This created the concept of "borderline personality organization", in which without differentiation all personality disorders, dissociative disorders and trauma disorders are pigeon-holed, up to and including dissociative identity disturbances. This had consequences in the public eye. Today almost no court has the courage to contradict the analytic expert who equates antisocial with dissociative, or who follows Kernberg to the point of claiming that traumatizing experiences are not really significant or important, leading right back to Freud and his fantasies about children wanting incest. From there it is just a small step to the testimony of a therapist: "Borderline patients—they all lie."

Another aspect of this world of living sadism is a precise knowledge of methods of torture. On the one hand, many descriptions remind you of the Middle Ages, of witch-hunting and other atrocities. On the other hand these tormentors have also utilized the findings of Josef Mengele's "experiments" in the concentration camps and the modern methods of white torture, for example psychological torture with extreme sensory deprivation and isolation.

And this explains the many descriptions we get in which the victims beseech and beg to be allowed to die and that it is a special variant of enjoying power to deny the victims their release into death. This method is a part of Dr. Zehn's repertoire—bringing the victims to the limit, to a near-death experience, and then bringing them back again and again. Over and over again. Being buried alive, being tortured beyond the limit of life itself. If it occurs that it almost isn't possible to resuscitate the victim, Dr. Zehn will just comment, "That was a close call" and not change his behavior in the slightest.

A further variation, that originally came from methods of white torture and that we find in multiple versions is: "If you don't function (to my satisfaction), then others will have to suffer (or die)." With this method many dictators have forced every conceivable behavior and every conceivable confession from their victims by torturing their children in front of their eyes: "This is all your fault." This technique is also used here. Naturally the alleged protection for another person is not really feasible. Therein lies the special attraction for Dr. Zehn. While his victim consents to everything and everyone, is willing to do everything, absolutely everything to herself if it will only result in someone else being protected, even seemingly offering herself voluntarily, Dr. Zehn already knows that he won't spare anyone.

Naturally we all wish that we lived in a world in which Dr. Zehn didn't exist at all, where he was an invention of the media or perhaps the exception that proves the rule. I believe however that he is not an exception. The problem with the Dr. Zehns of the world is that these people are the ones who profit from the kind of world that we have. This world works for them. In both areas, the internal stage and the public eye, they are the ruling lords; on both sides they achieve maximal profits. You don't even have to draw on any conspiracy theories to understand the reality of this violence. The Dr. Zehns of this world don't need a new world order. They already live as they please and with gusto.

And this explains how President Clinton could apologize for his government's experiments on human beings (about which even publicly accessible documents exist) and there is no outcry throughout the world, that a civilized country within the framework of national security could find it appropriate to completely disassemble and break human beings. For all intents and purposes you could add cynically that this violence and its justification is no different from that in the Nazi concentration camps. Even the ideas have changed only insignificantly. It has never occurred to Dr. Zehn that women or even children might be creatures who have autonomous rights.

When Dr. Zehn therefore ties up his not quite two-year-old daughter and abuses her with electric shocks and punishes every attempt of hers to escape by fainting, he then slices her crotch, because from his point of view it is only logical for him to make room so that he can penetrate her more easily. Watching his friends from the neighborhood rape her later increases his pleasure. To force the injuries and sufferings of this child into the field of vision of another victim further increases his pleasure. To whisper into another child's ear how much he is looking forward to doing the same things to her while his own small daughter screams for her life—that is Dr. Zehn's world.

I have consciously only made allusions to Dr. Zehn's modus operandi. My book is not meant to be a user's manual for copycats and perpetrators so that they learn how to frighten or torture their victims. There is also no need to describe all the abominations in order to illustrate that excruciating and merciless world. But it is necessary to indicate what people in this parallel world are capable of and that they are often respected citizens and "valuable members" of human society. Their official statements containing words like church, humanitarianism, Christian values, social community, and love of one's neighbor sound as cynical as having a blind person in charge of a committee to choose colors.

This is in turn part of the enjoyment of power for such perpetrators. Adorning themselves with all the attributes of humanity, letting themselves be praised for their words, being honored for piety and commitment, and knowing that their victims will read these words and have no one that they can confide in about what is really hidden behind these façades. This provides additional pain for the victims—and an additional thrill for the tormentors: "I see what you don't see." A society of the initiated.

A client formulated it in this way. "I would have liked to ask him why. Why wasn't it enough for you to dissect me, to sell me, to tear me to pieces, to do all those things to me? How could you look me in the eye and claim that you loved me? Why couldn't you even spare my little sister, why was it so important to harm us, over and over, more and more? Wasn't it enough for you, when I was three years old—one rape after another—why still all the disgusting things, why no limits, why still over and over again? Wasn't it enough for you to see my dead eyes, my despair? Hadn't I made enough suicide attempts that you could see how powerful you are? You left me nothing of my life and nothing of my body. You took everything from me—my dignity, my self-respect, my trust, and my future. I never understood the 'why'. What kind of feeling must it have been for you to look into my tortured eyes, to know how complete a hold you had over me? I was your planned child— what kinds of plans …?"

The Dr. Zehns of this world have many victims; the demand for new merchandise is huge. They profit from selling their own children; they train other children, program and hawk these "commodities" to their customers worldwide. They themselves aren't just salespeople, but also perpetrators with especially sadistic tendencies.

This is a small and very moderate excerpt of what we encounter in our work with clients. The tormentors leave in their victims an emotional desert, as the following poem shows.

Life on the inside

My soul, a dried out lake
The grass withered
The fish dead
And no more surface to reflect the sky

My eyes, a deforested woodland
Without life
All roots dead
Nothing will grow back

My faith, a glass broken
Into little pieces,
The liquid evaporated,
No one will take care of it.

My hands, a dead spider
Without prey, simply starved to death

They won't caress anyone any more.

CHAPTER SIX

Inside views from a survivor

This chapter invites you into the mindscape and the experiences of a client who endured extreme violence. At the time when she describes herself Nadja isn't aware of the contents of her dissociated worlds. She experiences herself as separated from the world, as cut off. She suffers, but she can't recognize what the root of her suffering is. Nadja's description is therefore from the viewpoint of a system that sees itself from the outside and attempts to describe what is going on inside. Nadja describes what she is able to perceive consciously from the perspective of an outsider.

When Nadja wrote *Living in a Dream World*, she was not aware of the existence of a single one of her inner parts. Nadja's book is about her life and her experiences. I will reproduce a small part of her story in order to make her perspective clear; to illustrate the inner experience of extreme violence for traumatized human beings.

She has a life story of extreme sadistic and organized violence. In scholarly terminology we would label her DDNOS at the time she began writing. Although she certainly has a dissociative disorder (at this point it isn't certain that she has dissociative identity disorder), she would only be conspicuous in the public eye because of her problems in developing relationships with others.

She experiences herself as dead. Everything connected with feelings is split off from her. Since Nadja isn't aware of this, she considers herself unfeeling. She has no access to the world of her inner experiences. She can't even begin to count how many times she has tried to commit suicide.

Her real story began at the age of six weeks, when she had already experienced extreme violence. She was deliberately and methodically prepared and trained for her role and went through what can only be described as thought control. Later she would be available worldwide for sadistic rituals, films, pornographic productions, and for "live acts". She would program others, torture would be practiced on her, and she would not know anything about all this at the level of the conscious world. She has huge holes in experienced time; she loses time that, as with a blind spot, she is not able to see. What she does notice is that her life seems to flash by her like a film. She seems to know the protagonists but they don't mean anything to her. We could therefore establish that the violence she experienced has cut her off from her own life and the livability of her own life. She sees her life flash by, but she doesn't participate in it.

Living in a Dream World—the Story of an Encounter

Chapter One

Open a passport and you'll find under "distinguishing features" the following personal details: Sex: female. Height: 5' 5". Eye color: green. Unchangeable characteristics: none. This of course doesn't tell you anything. These are only the things that you dismiss as superficialities during a normal observation. But in order to get any impression of the person that this is all about, they will suffice for now.

She was born in Germany, two siblings, an average student whose main interests were music, drawing, literature, and, of course, psychology. Fairly popular among her fellow students, relatively agreeable, though at times—above all when confronted with so-called authority figures—aggressive. Markedly freedom-loving. Attempted steady friendships sometimes break down because of this need for freedom, sometimes because of being incapable of intimacy. Many relationships begin out of pure curiosity "to discover the other person", or from an attempt at self-validation, or to be admired or loved, or to be stronger. Some relationships end abruptly just after they've started. She loves the unobtainable; once she gets it, she loses interest immediately. That gave her the reputation of being a whore, just like the fact that she often expresses her need for affection to certain people but what is important is that she receives the affection; who it comes from is less important.

It is possible that these repeated patterns of behavior lead her to mull things over or to rethink things. She formulates it this way: "I sold myself for the first time when I was 12, that is, it was a kind of exchange. I wanted recognition from certain special people and there was one person, and he got recognition, probably because he was so good-looking, I suppose. And then because he never would have been interested in me, I offered him my body, and well, then people did pay attention to me, saying 'That is the girlfriend of …' and all that. And they didn't know the price I paid, otherwise maybe everything would have happened differently …"

She says all that without any long pauses, as if she had stored it all in her memory, ready to be recited and is now merely accessing it. When I'm a little startled, she laughs and says "Naturally it didn't last forever, I think it was after a year or so that he said to me: You know, I can sleep with you and do everything with you, but I can't be seen with you." She says all that without any sorrow or self-pity, tells the story almost as if she weren't talking about herself. The only thing I notice while she is speaking is that at the beginning she looks right at me and after a while her gaze dwindles until finally it isn't fixed on me at all and she is talking into empty space, so to speak. Finally, as a kind of justification, she says: "I'm just a cerebral person", smiling while observing me out of the corner of her eye. Only a long time later would I understand what irritated me so much. It was this confidence with which she looked at me and tried to convince me of something that she really wanted to believe herself—even though she certainly knew at this moment that she was lying, lying because she wanted to stay alive.

Naturally she wanted to learn a lot from this and, in her own way, she did learn things. She learned where you have to search for the things with which you can buy people. It's funny, she said, that with your body you can get so much, even though a human being has so much more potential. She said that pensively and a little disappointedly, and I think today that she must have known that she was degrading herself with this way of life, because this complete separation between satisfying the body and satisfying the mind doesn't really exist in the way she claimed to possess it.

Perhaps she wanted to possess another human being, using her body as bait—that is, not really possess, she just wanted more from someone than to just sleep with him, and I think that she had to search for the reasons why she ultimately became so hard on herself and others. She was of the opinion that her feelings for others had been substantially reduced somewhere along the line, that she occasionally did fall in love, but then analyzed this feeling for so long and questioned it, until there was nothing left. In this way she proved to herself once again that feelings in reality just didn't exist.

I wouldn't call her schizophrenic in the psychiatric sense. But she had a split soul in the sense that she truly did have wishes, dreams, and hopes, but she didn't act on them. She told herself over and over again the fairy tale about the Walking Head, a creature consisting only of a head and legs, that didn't have anything like feelings or close relationships. This is approximately how the first evening went when I spoke to her. We had met in a little bar and got talking. She was waiting for someone who never did come. "He said he would stop by if he felt like it and it really doesn't matter ... I enjoy just sitting here." The whole time I couldn't get rid of the impression that she constantly felt herself observed, that she planned every one of her movements, and above all, that she actually wasn't all that fond of bars. She sat in the corner, at the only empty table, all alone. She had built up a little protective barrier of ashtrays, cigarettes, cigarette lighters, vases, so that I certainly would have chosen any other table, if one had been empty. While we talked she took down the barrier a little so that in the middle there was a gap through which she spoke to me. She spoke very calmly, without any noticeable excitement, but based on the number of cigarettes that she needed to keep up the conversation, I saw in her, more than anything else, a similarity to a volcano shortly before the eruption.

I wanted to ask her name, but she avoided the question as if she hadn't understood it. I stopped asking because her anonymity seemed to be very important to her while she spoke. Later she remarked that a name was inevitably linked to a perception and that she didn't want me to have a perception of her. There were enough people for whom a perception of her already existed. "It can't be that bad," I said without thinking. "You sound just like my mother," she said, and contempt rang out in her voice. Then I tried to apologize. "Not necessary," she answered, and she sounded a little tired, and then she left. "Will we see each other again?" I asked. "Maybe," she answered, which made further words superfluous. I drank the rest of my beer and left also.

Chapter Two

I saw her again a few weeks later, and that seemed to make her happy. It was summer and mid-afternoon. I lay in the grass next to a little artificial lake. "Have you got some time?" she asked, and I laughed, "Sure". We walked a short distance to a grassy area where there were magnificent trees. "If you lean on one of these trees, then you have a fantastic view of the lake." And then she sat down and leaned up against one of the trees. She sat there for a long time and didn't say anything. Finally I asked her if she was ready to tell me what would have happened after the episode she had told me about last time, and she nodded and began to talk.

I will try to call up from my memory the words with which she described these things. I have often asked myself whether these stories felt so much like stories from a third person because they seemed to be foreign to her actual character. I never asked her this question, and tried to interrupt her as seldom as possible. I was afraid to destroy the frankness with which she spoke. I believe she didn't sugarcoat anything in her stories, but with every word she seemed to search for a justification for herself and for all that had happened.

"I have begun a number of different relationships that were all alike in one respect: I wanted affirmation of myself as a woman. I didn't love any of these people for themselves, not one. I seem to have known as time went by how you declare your love, and the vocabulary for that was available everywhere, in the movies, on TV, in song lyrics. I don't want you to think that I was unfair. At the beginning I really wanted to love, I mean, it wasn't that I intended to deceive, but the role simply surprised me that I played from time to time, though not on a stage. I observed myself and performed automatically, without intention."

I was fairly bewildered, and she must have noticed that, because then she gave me an example: "Look, once I had a boyfriend who was actually only my boyfriend because he wanted to have me as a girlfriend. That means I adapted to his needs, made his dreams into my desires, and then somehow he felt that and left me for my best girlfriend. I got drunk, not because I had loved him that much— I felt my honor was injured, because I would have rather been with his best friend, who didn't love me at all. I know that sounds strange, but I've felt that often, that I always think I love someone that I'm not together with. Then I had a boyfriend who absolutely wanted to marry me. I dreamed about such things through rose-tinted glasses when I was thirteen, but never when I was older. In order to break up with him, I slept with his best friend, and told that friend that I loved him, truly believing it at the time. Yeah, I did want to hurt my boyfriend, because he allowed himself all these dreams that I denied myself. It wasn't until later that I discovered that it was all a farce—or analyzed together, I was just a Walking Head, a creature with only a head and legs ..."

At this point I did interrupt her: "Was there ever anyone that you loved, at the very least for a short time, when you didn't have to overanalyze things because you were so happy?" "Yes, of course, there was one single time when I really loved someone." And then she was silent for a long time. "I believe it was during this vacation at the ocean that my doctor prescribed for me so I could regain my health. I met someone there, and there really was an hour when we sat there and didn't even exchange one word because we were so happy ... But it continued the way it always does. You can't hang on to happiness. We tried to make it happen again. And then all that remained were broken pieces. For a long time we still slept together, probably out of habit and because neither of us had anyone else, and I noticed that I can sleep with someone, and can have an orgasm, without having any feelings for him."

"Didn't you ever have the feeling of an inner emptiness?" She thought for a long time and it seemed that a movie was playing in front of her mind's eye, which she would stop as soon as she found the right spot. "There was one time, at least I cried and he asked why I slept with him if I cried afterwards—and that was the end. I mean, then I actually started to think about everything and to analyze my feelings, until they dissolved into thin air."

"Do you still see each other?" "Yes, he is my best friend," and then she stared out over the lake as if she hoped to drown in it. I believe at this moment she despised herself for this inability to feel more than she did for anything else.

"And after that?" "Many meaningless relationships. Men that I wanted to help, that I wanted to change, whose surroundings sometimes gave me the chance to be the queen, sometimes gave me the chance to flip out—the whole spectrum of fashions, notions, opinions. It was like trying on masks that didn't fit. I mean, I tried to conform until it just wasn't possible any more or I tried to provoke by doing the opposite. With this I want to say that I was standing on the outside, could observe what was expected and observed my reactions. If I wanted anything at all, it was to sleep with someone. Maybe I often convinced myself that I loved him or I imagined that he was someone else that I loved. Maybe that's why in intimate situations I just saw dark rooms where only shadows and contours were visible, but never faces. Illusion in reality, maybe. I think sometimes I am ashamed because I just give my body and tell myself all the fairy tales about love just for my own satisfaction—I can't judge my motivation very well myself."

"Do you actually like yourself?" I asked her after that. "Hmm, it's odd that you would ask me that, but precisely because you don't know me, I'll try to be honest. I can neither claim to hate myself nor to love myself. I mean, it always sounds terribly conceited to say that you like yourself and it's fishing for compliments to say that you don't like yourself. I believe that I sometimes get along with myself quite well, or I get along well with the person I think I am—with the Walking Head, the creature consisting only of a head and legs," she said to remove the earnestness from our conversation.

"Is your head always number one then?" I asked her, irritated. "You know, it's like this, I don't have that many feelings, and certainly no strong feelings, and that's just how it is, mon cher," she said, shrugging her shoulders as if she couldn't care less. "You're flirting after all," I said, not so much to ask a question as to assure myself. "Yes, but not because it is chic," and then she wiped away a seemingly unnoticed tear that remained in the corner of her eye.

"Do you think you are capable of declaring your love to anyone, honestly?" "No, I would always have the feeling of having heard it a hundred times before already; it would sound like a bad novel, and I believe that declaring your love is a paradox. I think, if you were really in love, then the feeling itself would have to make any explanations superfluous."

That, therefore, was what she dreamed of, to be overcome by a feeling, to let herself fall—to live. A feeling that, in the purest sense of the word, would drive her out of her mind. But at the same time she built these walls, these façades. She had been cut to the quick once in her complete vulnerability, the entire nakedness of her soul, and after that she had built a kind of cage, a cage that more and more became a labyrinth that she couldn't find her way out of.

And suddenly, in the middle of these reflections, she said something. It sounded less like a deliberation and more like a wish in which all her hopes would be expressed: "You would need to have the naiveté of a child to be able to say something like: I love you best", and then after reflecting for a second: "But we are raised too much to be adults."

And suddenly, surprisingly, she stood up, ashamed of her spontaneity, and said in a somewhat forced manner: "On with new endeavors," before I could say goodbye. She was gone—and presumably that's also what she wanted.

Chapter Three

When I saw her the next time she had someone with her; I wanted to walk up to her but one glance was enough to keep me away. They took a table close to me and I had the impression that she expected me to observe her. So I stayed sitting there, listening and watching. Even if I didn't understand every word, I could comprehend most of what was said, above all her gestures and facial expressions.

"I'm glad that you came," she said. "Otherwise I would have had to spend this evening all alone. The others are already booked up for this evening," she laughed, as if none of this meant anything. Everything was just a game that she had to succeed at, but for which the result had no important consequences.

He said something about a movie that they had apparently seen together, and in contrast to her, he seemed to regard the movie as a movie, as fiction, whereas she perceived the movie in relationship to her reality. She didn't let him notice, and I only noticed through her choice of words how hard she felt hit by the events in the movie. "I think it was a huge shock when he left her, above all because the other woman wasn't anything special in her eyes." And, after a while she added, musing, "Probably it's always easier to forgive something extraordinary, even if it is a lie, I mean, sometimes it's probably kinder to lie."

He nodded and indicated through a movement of his hand that he was sure he understood. And while she, seemingly calm, made completely uninvolved comments, which apparently showed no personal reference, the tips of her feet drew circles in the ground. She pressed the cigarette that she usually smoked down to the filter into the ashtray very emphatically, as if she could destroy all the dreams and hopes she had ever had with this gesture.

I felt a little like a voyeur, sitting there and fixing my gaze on her over and over again, but it was something like a fascinating theatre play, observing how she created a distance from the man with seeming forthrightness and devotion, through which she deceived him about herself. However, I'm not sure whether she didn't deceive herself even more than she deceived him.

Though she put up these barriers, and though she withdrew, she was actually unable to be part of something that, had she been able to be ruthlessly candid, she considered very desirable.

Her barriers provided an unassailable position from which she was able to chat with some of her friends, needing no protection, no help, no support, and above all no affection; whereas on the other hand there were men with whom she sought physical satisfaction—and probably found it. Therefore she couldn't be attacked because she didn't provide any striking surface; but striking a match also produces warmth, and she sought warmth, even if it was all so complicated that others could barely see through it. She could say the most inconsequential things but for her they were declarations of love. Her sexual advances were so strange and apparently spontaneous that no one could imagine that behind the strong, cold, aloof exterior was a person like any other, seeking someone who would be able to understand her—someone who would not treat her affection with contempt. But she pretended to be independent and since she played her role convincingly, people believed her unquestioningly.

I believe it would have been important for her to find someone who looked behind her mask and understood her inability to achieve closeness behind all her flights to escape. But I couldn't think of anyone who could have seen through this rationally constructed labyrinth quickly enough, and, above all, no one who would have wanted to love her without understanding who she really was.

A few days later she asked the question that was the most typical for her: "Could you imagine falling in love with me?" And without giving me time to find an answer, she said in a tone like a TV psychiatrist doing an analysis: "You couldn't. You would find me cold with no visible need for affection, no real weakness—and in addition to that I'm not even pretty. I mean, with a beautiful person, then you could at least fall in love with her beauty, couldn't you?" "Would you want to be so beautiful?" "It'd be better than nothing and a believable reason for love!" "Sometimes," I said, "it seems like you make fun of everything that you want, everything that is important to you, and you praise what you think is trifling to high heaven. As if you hoped someone would recognize this and ask you about it and finally give you the chance to flee from the prison of your rationality."

"Do you really think I still believe in the possibility of fleeing? And even if this possibility did exist, I hardly believe that I would take advantage of it." And then, after a while she said very quietly, barely audibly, as if she was just talking to herself: "It is more than a Sleeping Beauty dream, with the hope that Prince Charming will jump behind my façade, in order to live with me there."

"Because no one could take him away from you there?" She said nothing, but seeing how much effort it took for her to suppress her tears, I saw that she had touched something there, way deep down inside. "Yes, yes," she said, "The competition doesn't sleep," and tried in this way to remove that which would hurt her from her reality.

She sat on a stone on the bank of the lake and watched herself in the water and suddenly, apparently spontaneously, she picked up a small pebble and threw it out into the middle of her reflected image. Like an apology she added: "You can throw them so they skip right out to the middle of the lake if they are flat enough," and thereby avoided my glance, as if she were afraid to be caught in a lie.

Continuing the story, Nadja describes how she desperately tries to sense feelings, how she begins a search—a journey to flee the dissociation that has her mercilessly under control. She describes her family, analyzes its members, and remains unknown to herself. At the end she allows her protagonist to experience joy and a relationship, but only once and only briefly. At the end the Nadja in her story receives a hopeless cancer diagnosis. With respect to the brief experience of happiness, however, she lets her say, "If I had a pebble now, I could get it to skip all the way to the middle of the lake."

In her wonderful book *Miss America By Day* Marilyn van Derbur (2003) describes the pain and desperation of dissociation breaking open. "If I had only known that there was even one woman in the world who had survived that, it would have given me so much hope." When she finally meets such a woman, it is one more person who has overcome the abuse and is going public with her story of healing.

Nadja doesn't know anyone who has survived what she survived. Nadja doesn't even know what it is that occasionally causes her unbearable pain, or what leads to her feeling so hopelessly guilty and bad. She would like to leave this life, but somehow she also would like to taste a little of what life has to offer; and she wants, which is typical, the story to have a happy ending. No one should be burdened by her. Nadja describes her life to a stranger who is portrayed as approachable and who is capable of enduring the story without greater emotional repercussions.

Her story also teaches us the necessity of really listening in order to understand what is behind the story offered, which on the surface appears to say: "I am promiscuous. There is no reason for this in my family history—it's all my fault. I'm incapable of maintaining a relationship."

If we got to know Nadja in therapy, we would have to begin carefully, trying to put together all the pieces of the puzzle as they presented themselves. It would be a path from recognition to finally integrating what was experienced, to the extent that this might be possible. For Nadja this would mean that we would work with her to place the individual symptoms, which she first describes as "That's how I am" and then describes as painful symptoms of conditions she has experienced, and the statements she ascribes to herself, into a new framework. It would mean asking the question: To what extent does it make sense to begin careful work on the various symptoms? It wouldn't be valid to do what the representatives of the false memory movement describe as "recovered memory therapy". No serious therapist would recommend to Nadja that she see her story one way or another. No one would recommend an arbitrary interpretation of what happened.

It would mean accompanying her with the goal of first diminishing the most burdensome symptoms and, as much as possible, maintaining her ability to function in everyday life. It would be a path through all the pain that would emerge from the gradual dissolution of dissociation. This pain would come with vehemence, physically and psychically. And it would be unstoppable—the only choice would be whether to guide it through with the help of a therapist or to just let it come. If Nadja chose the latter, her everyday life would be overwhelmed by the past.

CHAPTER SEVEN

Death of an assassin

This chapter and the two preceding ones are not all parts of the story of the same survivor. Rather, each chapter provides a different perspective, to help the reader imagine how this world of violence is structured and how differently it is seen by someone with dissociated knowledge as opposed to by someone with very detailed conscious knowledge of the crimes. The theme of the whole book is to invite the reader to look at these matters from various perspectives, giving examples.

Chapter Five provides a perspective to help the reader imagine the world of organized crime in which a victim grows up. Chapter Six shows the perspective of a survivor without any knowledge of the hidden and dissociated world.

In this chapter the perspective is different. This woman knows what happened to her and confronts her dying father in her own chosen way. It is like an inner dialogue while facing him. Please keep in mind that this chapter might be triggering if you are a survivor yourself; and please, do not feel as a survivor or assume as a therapist that you have to confront the abuser. It is this woman's way; other people choose other ways.

Lily White: death of an assassin

They called me. You lie in a coma. Intensive care unit. You will never again wake up alive. Asystolia. Naked fear—your heart could not cope with it. Fear of being called to account for your deeds. I want to bring you before the court, to confront you with all the evidence—but which legal court would have the courage to dare to convict you?

I dosed the fear of disclosure to you, like a poison. It has trickled into every one of your pores. There is not one message I have given you in which I failed to let you know how clearly I now know who you really are. I count on the fact that you have no courage at all—you are a gutless assassin.

I will come to see you. A daughter, visiting her dying father. My intentions are not peaceful. I don't want to facilitate your dying. I want to be sure you die. I want to accuse you—in public.

Here, behind the folding screens of the intensive care unit, with a severely ill person in every bed, is the place where you will die. Here they exercise piety. They offer me the chance to spend time with you alone. They will replace the breathing tube when I have told you what I have to say. As I see it, it is up to me to decide when the instruments finally extinguish the last tiny portion of your life force. As I sit on your bed alone, you react to my voice, and I observe your monitors. They are my witnesses that you won't miss a word. I won't hold your hand—but I will be close enough to be able to. You will be longing for humanity on your last journey. You will not get it.

The goddess of justice is blind, to make her considerations unbiased. Behind the folding screens, no one knows you. On this side, my court is in session; my jury members sit ready:

I accuse you. You are a sadist, a salesman of children, a serial rapist, a murderer. Remember the Heather Caine? Your victims did not die that easily; it is much too easy for you, even in dying. The Heather Caine is a special ship, and so many things were possible because of its enormous size. Particularly below decks. Remember?

I was not even two years old when you decided to present me there, as a sales pitch for one of your programs. Successfully. Internationally. For me it meant being tortured with electricity up to the limit of my survival. It meant being raped by you and your customers, allowing you all to rape me in your bloodlust frenzy. It meant having to injure others. Following a plan, step by step. Nothing happened by accident. Dr. Melven was not part of your panel of consultants by accident. He was well paid. These people are not paid by poor institutions. So much intelligence, so much know-how. And, naturally, spiritual care was not missing. Dr. Goodmice issued a blessing for your projects. Craving power—every one of you.

But back to the details of the accusation. You prepared for every contingency. The so-called mothers kept a record about the babies, as if, like really good mothers, they documented their continuous nurturing. Eating, drinking, special events. With me you lost interest. She had to start the book before the baby arrived—but she only made sketchy notes, months later. She only noted what was of interest for programming. Why did she take on the burden of caring for me? It's not important. I was very isolated and if I made contact with someone, we moved. I was chosen to spend a lot of time with you. I was the darling of Dr. Melven. At home no one loved me and we very rarely visited relatives that did not belong to the group. Distance, isolation, training camp, violence. I was trained only to be of use for you. Mind control. You pushed a button, my consciousness vanished, and another inner part of me for which you lusted came up. The Russian torturer, the Spanish whore, the Queen without any mercy that trains children, or whoever else was in your mind. I was allowed to travel with you all over the world. Your programming was always the same. Torturing, harrowing, killing. Monitoring and assessing. Testing and discarding.

Going back to the Heather Caine. It was a training camp we often went to, to test, to train and to sell children. A ship is a very convenient place. It does not need to ride at anchor, so we were flexible. So flexible that we could include Mishata in our plans. Or, to be precise, you could. You bragged so loudly about only investing a small amount in the kids you bought and trained but you sold them for a lot of money at Mishata. Mishata, "harder than hell", originally intended for the dismantling of mineral resources, now extensively depopulated. Lots of buildings—no disturbance by anyone. You did not get your hands dirty. It was an endless series of medication testing, testing of biological weapons, immunizing against the same things. Your human guinea pigs were two or three years old when they were brought to that place the first time. Besides the normal programming with electroshocks, beatings and rapes, the main task was testing the effects of medications, cold and heat, and near-death experiences. In your words, the idea was to induce artificially allergic reactions, to immunize against certain substances, or to develop medication. I think secret services and the pharmaceutical industries could have been interested in all of these questions. For you it was just an add-on.

Each child's stay there, alone, without any caregiver to trust or to rely on, was only interrupted when they were taken back to the Heather Caine. Change of training—same torments, for those who survived. I don't overlook the fact that you started training them six weeks after their birth. You learned your lessons from biology. Six weeks, that's the period during which a newborn mammal like a kitten has to stay with its mother to be able to survive. You had to accept that much attachment to lay a foundation for your splitting a person by shattering and torment. Many tests, many experiments—you did not try to split someone "any which way". You wanted to know each child's exact genetic capacities. Meticulousness is one of your core characteristics. Research, tests, examinations. Nothing left to chance, not the smallest corner of the soul. You made your decision when you had an idea of your product: premium ware, B ware, or mass consumption ware. The better and more worthy the ware, the more elaborate the training. Your trainings were targeted measures of torture, combined with technical know-how. Everything that allowed you to see into the inside, measuring brainwaves and the composition of blood, hormones and neurotransmitters, using biofeedback and hypnosis.

In the meantime you did not miss out on all the fun. The trained children were pointedly instructed in particular styles of prostitution; for example, to appear to be a little child experiencing rape for the first time. The customer was king—and if the king required something … mass rapes, endless so-called feasts, upside-down church rituals, black masses, cult celebrations—always covered by the fig leaf of "specialness" and always putting the blame on the children, on the victims. How often did you present films of my deeds to me, to show me that I should never even think about getting out of here? My suicide attempts I can´t count. I can´t count my revivifications. I can´t count how many children had to be killed. How many children did I leave in the cult?

Next question. Endless killing. Torturing of children and animals—disgust, fear, panic, being taken to the point of death— I have died so often that I understand your present situation; I have been trained for it. I and so many others had to eat so many things that no mouth ever has to taste in normal life. Would you be willing to have all these things in your mouth? You laughed yourself to death, when with extreme cruelty you ripped everything between my legs with your penis and every imaginable object. Not only between my legs. A hundred times, a thousand times. You made a countless number of films—so many victims, so many crimes. Who would be qualified to judge you? You got so incalculably rich at our expense, and never thought about giving something back.

You laughed yourself silly when my relationship broke in a thousand pieces with your help and the support of another perpetrator. You found it amusing when I was desperately longing for your acceptance and I was willing to go to the best-known experts in the field to call for help. Yes, Professor Grapetown. The luminary for such "cases". And someone who helped with your projects. What chances did your victims have? You had an army of specialists— physicians, pediatricians, hypnotherapists, various kinds of psychotherapists, technicians specializing in targeted use of violence and drugs. We were always under observation. You tested it all, the effects of heat and cold, burial, hanging, impaling, slaughter and … and … and …. I can´t imagine any technique that is not included in your handbooks of mind control. I can´t imagine any technique of torture and mind control which you did not pass on to others.

You considered yourself so superior. You saw the disaster coming much too late. Two years before your death you realized for the first time that I know other victims and I know that they are victims. For the first time the idea came into your head that I recognized one of the perpetrators. You used threats—expensive fun. To threaten me, to try to intimidate me, even though it cost millions for you. This answered my questions. It also let me know that I do not have to fear you or your allies any more. What could you do to me that I had not already experienced over and over again? You have no weapons left. We have no equity in arms—I have defeated you. Remember, I talked publicly about the reality of this kind of violence? You told your close friends that I was sensationalistic, and I was just trying to get attention. You began to understand that there was so much more that I could disclose. You cried out in panic, "She is breaching official secrets!" Who had the right to pledge me to secrecy in the professional field? You confused two things—professional confidentiality and the criminals' code of silence. You did not bargain for my disclosures. You did not see the first stirrings. My hints, my suggestions, my equivocations—manifold. When the noose was slowly tightening on you, you had no way out and no one to help. Dead-end street. Can you imagine how much I enjoyed the idea that all your "friends" would know that you completely failed with me? That you could do nothing, so they wanted to see you dead now, you were a potential danger? Your first asystolia was followed by a second one. This time a deadly one within days. This is my accusation: You are guilty, guilty without any way out. The jury members have condemned you to death. I will call for the male nurse. He will deprive you of breath bit by bit.

I observe you. Your rebellion, your stuttering heart, your fight for defense, your begging for assistance. Your eyes, lost in nowhere, and my coldness, leaving you lost and alone. I observe your monitors. Your breath is slowing. I pronounce the sentence for your last journey: You are not to win *this* fight. You want to say something, so the tube is removed. You recognize me and you understand that only death is waiting for you—a path of no return. Your tongue finds no way to speak—in a last rebellion of the body, you are dead.

An earlier poem by this woman shows how difficult it can be to be confronted with your own truth and to learn to live with it.

I am collapsed
I am collapsed
Broken, shattered
Knocked out

Stroke of butterfly wing—what for?
There is no butterfly effect
Anywhere—for nothing
I am standing up for a truth
No one would want to hear

In my inner house
The candles of blackness light
They illuminate the house
Of never ending violence
As I till the field
Of unutterable agony

I wanted
To know everything
To tell everything

I wanted to survive
To bear witness
To provide proof

How shall I live
With such a heavy load on my shoulders?
My confirmation motto said
One carries the load of the others
Where are the others—who carry mine?

They are nowhere
They do not exist
My roots grasp at nothing
No place—nowhere.

CHAPTER EIGHT

About dissociative worlds

This chapter is concerned with the survivor's present-day immediate family. Sympathetic family members need support in dealing with dissociative relatives. They face special difficulties, not only in the area of sexuality but also in the problems of everyday life. I will present options for supporting them in their understanding of dissociation and of the violence their family members experienced.

The situation of family members of dissociative patients

When, as Marilyn van Derbur (2003) describes it, family members are in the picture who would like to support the survivor, then it is necessary to also make sure that these family members don't have to grapple with the details of the horror their relative experienced. Even especially sensitive family members often want extensive information. If the survivor, believing that this would help, allows them a detailed insight into the shadow world, then both survivor and family member can be overwhelmed by this suffering.

For family members it can be simply unbearable when for the first time they become fully aware of what goes on in such sadistic parallel worlds. By entering such a world they can become lost to the survivor as a support in the here and now. Perishing together is still perishing. If the family member is haunted by the same horrific pictures as the survivor, envisioning what pain the tormentor inflicted on the victim, then a significant pressure to do something builds up. The therapist can only emphatically caution against prematurely embarking on a legal path. Family members often feel such an unbearable pressure that the desire to accuse the known perpetrators can become almost overwhelming.

The goal, therefore, is to make sure that the needs of the survivor that emerge from the dissociative experience are verbalized. In this way she can achieve a stable separation between the times of confronting the trauma she experienced and the times of normalcy, of everyday life. The more of everyday life she is able to recapture, the less of everyday life that is swept away, the better she will succeed at controlling the symptoms.

No family member who has not experienced this shadow world of violence can or should try to enter it, even in imagination. However, family members should know that it will take a great deal of time to work through these experiences, time during which the survivor retreats into working on her own or into consulting with her therapist— and that this does not represent a rejection of her family members. Every other form of facing the past of the loved person would be more damaging than useful.

Yet there are a number of helpful things that family members should know. Among them would be developing an understanding of the emergence of flashbacks, especially those at the physical level. This means that it becomes clear that:

- A flashback is not dangerous.
- It doesn't indicate anything to worry about in the here and now (although any occurrences of pain should be investigated because naturally a person with dissociation could also suffer from other, somatic illnesses).
- Such symptoms can emerge during the person's normal everyday routine.
- If the past experiences that the flashback is about can be integrated, then the symptoms will disappear.

It is very important to inform family members about how structural dissociation functions. This also includes information about how believable dissociated memories are, and how it is possible that memories that the patient was not aware of can still emerge. Here much psychoeducation is necessary about the differences between normal and dissociated memory. At first many family members understandably attempt to explain the whole thing with everyday psychological explanations and with their knowledge from their own experiences of remembering and forgetting. As they themselves have no experience with dissociation of this kind, they fall back on what they know or have heard about processes of repression, forgetting, and reconstructive remembering of experiences stored verbally in their memories. Since, however, we are dealing with disintegrated experiences, these models for integrated memories don't fit.

It is helpful if family members attempt to discover what the survivor expects from them. Which actions can they support her with? Which suggestions can help her? Since this varies from individual to individual, sometimes they will have to proceed by trial and error. However, with regard to this, there are a few basic rules that should be observed in every case:

- No touching without asking and receiving permission.
- No surprises, like for example approaching her from behind and hugging her.
- Respect for the fact that "no means no", and no arguments about limits, as long as this concerns themes like having sex, talking about the past, or being touched.
- No complaining about missing sexuality.
- No investigation about the inner parts if the survivor experiences such questions as intrusive and makes this clear. Do not try to be the person's therapist and ask about inner parts, their names, or their experiences.
- No badgering about promises that have been made regarding future success of the treatment (especially with respect to sexuality). Sometimes a partner will hint: "I'm willing to wait for now, but only if it is certain that I will later get enough sex." This can never work because it functions like a constant threat.
- No criticism about the duration of therapy, especially not along the lines of "It seems like it should be over with by now."
- Don't force your family member to justify her trauma-related behavior, or take it personally. Don't say things like "Is it really necessary that you still hide your diary from me? You should already have learned that I won't hurt you, so why do you still show anxiety? That's not fair. Can you explain why you hurt me that way?"

Justification and reproach were everyday experiences in the sadistic world, and always feeling guilty was a central component: "Because you … that's why this will now happen."

- Put sympathy and your own sensitivities in the correct context, with clear explanations: "I am exhausted from work and if it seems I look unsympathetic, that has nothing to do with you."
- No heroics. It's okay for family members to be worn out, and you don't have to hide it, but you have to make the framework clear regarding where it really belongs. Although it hurts to know that a beloved person has suffered this, it's not the fault of the survivor who now has to deal with this pain. The survivor shouldn't have to hide her suffering or deal with everything by herself. At the same time this is also true of family members. Depending on the dimensions of the trauma, it can be helpful if the family member is included in therapy or if he himself goes into therapy. According to my experience, it is helpful if counseling occurs over and over again at regular intervals. This ensures that encounters do not only occur during conflicts.
- Finally, one last important point. People who have gone through a distinct experience of dissociation and whose memories begin to reveal themselves are often their own greatest doubters. They have to do much work in order to examine critically whether an image is based on an actual experience. It is hard work and it costs a lot of energy. Often it cannot be done in a single exposure and has to be repeated. Only when a memory has become sufficiently clear, can it be dealt with. Therefore at all costs refrain from asking the survivor: "Are you sure that you aren't just imagining things?" You may mean well, intending to support her in not torturing herself with demons that aren't a part of her own life story. However, the question of whether you can believe a dissociated memory should only be asked of the therapist. Do not use the fact that there are indeed processes that aren't understood, even by the person herself, as a reason to express doubt about her memories.

What is dissociation? A possible explanation for family members

Dissociated and re-emerging memories are massive events that can tear apart a person's life. They not only strike those affected but also the entire surroundings of those affected. The survivor and the family members all wonder whether or not to believe the memory that is emerging, or whether the survivor's memory deceives her.

Actually a dissociated memory is seldom deceptive, because it is was split off right when the event occurred. Since material that can't be dealt with or integrated can be split off in this manner, this unprocessed, stored raw material can re-emerge. When it emerges, it is fragmented information that has been stored as a series of images and bodily sensations and emotions, and it can re-emerge in precisely this way. Bessel van der Kolk (1996) says: "The body keeps score." Because, therefore, the split-off parts don't show anything other than information that the person's organism has noticed, these memories contain no reasoning or evaluation by the conscious mind. The material experienced was stored, and emerges, just as the victim perceived and saw it at the time of the initial event. Possible distortions of the situation are included precisely as they were seen or experienced in the original situation. For example, if the tormentors used a trick to suggest to the victim that she was in a special situation such as being in a spaceship, then this trick will also be included in the memory she experiences. If the victim were making up the story, or responding to a therapist's suggestion, she would not report this, because she knows it can't be true and therefore doubts her own mental health. Precisely because these kinds of "unbelievable" things come up, they tend to prove the truth of the situation rather than disprove it, as they display the trickery of the tormentors.

What is also important is that here information emerges as fragments rather than entire stories. Stories you can narrate aren't dissociated stories. Experiences can only turn into complete stories if they have been dealt with consciously. Here fragments emerge that can result in massive consequences in everyday life. When memories of abuse emerge, they will cause the same pain, with the same intensity, as the original situation did, or arouse the same mortal fear as if the situation were now and not then.

Here memory consists of images and bodily sensations, unlike the reconstructive memory of everyday consciousness, which includes a verbal narrative. For such a narrative to occur this memory would have to reach consciousness as an entire story—but that is precisely what doesn't happen, in order to make survival possible. I would like to explain it with a very simplified model of the brain (Figure 15 overleaf).

Seen from an evolutionary standpoint, the oldest part of the brain is the so-called reptilian brain, the brainstem. It contains the automatic

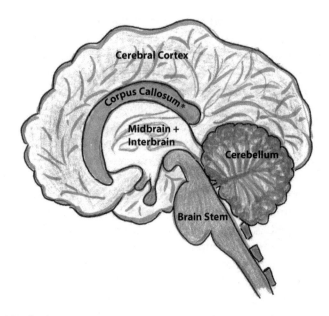

Figure 15. Brain.

reactions that keep you alive, for example breathing and heartbeat—but also the inborn, automatic alarm programs caused by perceived threats. Later the midbrain evolved. It contains the basis for our ability to sense feelings and is therefore the foundation for judging incoming sensations. The amygdala, located in the midbrain, ensures that every incoming bit of information is first evaluated according to its importance. This is where the brain decides whether something is even important enough to be considered further. If it isn't considered to be important enough, then it won't be relayed any further. If it is at least minimally important but not overwhelming, then it will be brought up for further processing. If this succeeds, then a narrative develops. Then that which we call short-term or long-term memory arises, depending on how often the procedure is repeated. The brain is efficient: only that which is consciously used will be retained consciously. Experiences that are important for survival and for triggering alarm status will be dissociated.

In the cerebral cortex, finally, the conscious foundations of thinking and language, and memories that are consciously accessible, are stored. Nothing that is automatic, that we don't need to consciously think about, is stored there. Here are also stored the things that we have forgotten at the moment, that is, things we can't access immediately.

If, as described above, a stimulus is of sufficient importance but not overwhelmingly threatening, then it will be processed further and will finally arrive as a complete narrative in our recall, in our memory. When we remember, we know what happened, how we thought about it, and how we felt. However, we don't feel this with the same intensity as we did when the events actually happened. Here time heals the wounds, and we generally have words to describe the memory. (Earlier experiences, those before the age of five or six, are generally stored in a sensorimotor fashion, and are only partially accessible to language.)

For normal day-to-day living under normal conditions this is a good thing. It means that our experiences of basic security and of relationships are tangibly existent—we don't have to generate them all over again. We definitely know that we have secure relationships. We can rely on the world and on ourselves to be consoled when we are sad, to be held when we need protection. We know that we live in a society and that those around us will help us to survive in a good way. We get to know the most important rules of life and we develop life skills that help us to understand the world around us and act effectively in it.

The surroundings that force us into dissociation are different. They are hostile to life, overwhelming, life-threatening. Dissociation means that as soon as a stimulus arrives, the victim's organism classifies it automatically as too overwhelming to be made accessible to be processed and stored in consciousness. At the same time the victim can't afford to ignore this stimulus. The victim has to react. This leads to the stimulus constantly being split into various pieces; the brain fails to integrate the pieces of the narrative into a complete story and the little pieces remain stored as information to assist in survival. Splitting the stimulus has an evolutionary explanation. If we take notice of a small section of a life-endangering threat (or more precisely of many different attributes of such a situation: how it smells, how it sounds, how it feels, how it looks, and so on) and can recognize these parts without having to think about them, then each attribute provides important survival information. This information is more or less pushed down in the brain, linked to the alarm reactions of the brainstem instead of to conscious memory. The alarm structures will activate every time one of these stimuli emerges, without the victim having to do anything. The organism will react. The body will take notice: This is overwhelming, life-endangering, threatening.

If similar overwhelming experiences are repeated over and over again, then the brain creates inner levels of authority that are automatic procedures for reacting, in order to handle this expected and constantly repeating event. Processing this event would be contra-indicated, because in contrast to the unconscious reaction process that is steered by feelings, our conscious thinking, evaluating, and acting structures take at least ten times as long. If, therefore, a threat continues and we have to react quickly in order to survive, then automatic reaction is the only way to go.

It is well known that in order to survive every species passes on genetically that which is necessary to survive. Acquiring these skills doesn't occur consciously. No creature has to remember that it now has to breathe with its lungs instead of with gills. This important change is passed on genetically. Our brains function in such a way that survival information stored there comes directly from the environment. It doesn't contain any individual evaluation or distortion—otherwise it wouldn't be useful for survival.

Consciousness can't afford to take notice of this for two reasons. First, consciousness would be completely overwhelmed, because no one possesses a repertoire for dealing with life-endangering, extreme situations in his consciousness; that would lead to an inability to function. Second, as described, processing such information would take too long and equally impede survival.

Consciously there are many things that we can't bear; unconsciously we still have resources. This shows also what great significance the survival of the species has had in the history of development. And it shows perhaps at this point a little of the optimism of creation. It implies that there are things that we can't fix here and now. But prioritizing survival gives us time and opportunity to possibly solve them later.

This transfer of survival information occurs in animals and human beings in a similar fashion. Scientists first documented the genetic transfer of survival information when studying monarch butterflies. With human beings we see that children of highly dissociative mothers show a greater willingness and a greater capacity for dissociation, and mind control projects such as Project Monarch (Wheeler &

Springmeier, 2000) deliberately used such children. If a mother is dissociative, her children may dissociate more easily and more quickly if their environment demands it from them.

For brain development and for the development of inner levels of authority you need both. There has to be a basic genetic configuration (we can all dissociate if things get life-endangering and it is necessary) and also forced adaptation to a threatening environment.

People who grow up in a parallel world of violence which forces a process of adaptation on them have often run through two separate processes of development, with each having no knowledge of the other. On the one hand dissociated inner information units have formed which have or are permitted to have no connection to the normal world. On the other hand in the normal world they have been trained for necessary roles and skills to the extent that, while they often lack cheerfulness and lightheartedness, their "otherness" isn't visible to others—and indeed also not to themselves. Peculiarities like not having many friends, sometimes displaying strange behavior, or being afraid of things they know objectively are not dangerous, are often thought to be personality traits. Such people might be perceived as neurotic, sensitive, fearful, or, above all, if there are many painful body memories without any visible somatic source, then histrionic, hysterical.

You could say that these people are split internally. At the level of the brainstem they function more according to the demands of a world full of violence, whereas in their conscious mind they adapt to the so-called normal world.

In the dissociated world inner information units arise which contain certain traumatic experiences and the necessary reactions to them. These units are at first not capable of consciousness, which is why the first step in therapy has to be realization. Only then will this information overcome the barrier to consciousness. This consciousness then for the first time takes notice of the things that were hidden from it and were foreign to it up until then. With very pronounced inner units we therefore speak of inner persons, to simplify things. Sometimes they have names, which serves inner organization. Sometimes the names are invented by tormentors because then they have access to them and know how to retrieve any particular information unit or behavior. Other names come from the victim's system itself. In this way it's made certain that not all information leaves containment at the same time.

Often in these dissociated worlds only a few inner persons have contact with each other (only when it is conducive to survival). And the individual inner persons, when they emerge, have a simple understanding of who they are and what determines them, a kind of partial identity. Therefore it can occur that one inner person states that it has nothing to do with the survivor. At first none of them are aware that everything is interconnected—these are separated "worlds" in the way in which they are organized internally.

The world of consciousness is organized completely differently. It depends on cohesion and on knowing that, in the final analysis, everything belongs to one identity that can find itself in various situations. In this way I know that I possess unpleasant or mean inner parts (ego states), but also that even if I don't like them, they are still doubtless a part of my self. Such conscious inner parts can be more or less close to me; I may know something about how they came into being or I may not—but they are fundamentally something completely different from these dissociated inner persons.

If the information from the shadow world then emerges, this happens at first through a symptom that you yourself don't understand. For example, you may feel compelled to overeat or to buy things, or have an urge to get mixed up with things that you actually reject, to act out suicidal impulses, or to go to places or meet people you find unpleasant or disgusting. Survivors often report how they actually have tried not to do something—but weren't at all able to stop themselves. They felt as if they were observing themselves without being able to have any influence on their actions.

A further source of information is bodily symptoms. They often point to memories, but since they emerge in the conscious world, we don't decode them as somatoform dissociation. Many victims make doctors' appointments for extreme complaints that don't seem to be connected to any medical findings.

Completely inappropriate fears as well as a complete lack of the ability to calm yourself down even when given facts would also point to dissociation. We have to think of this when well-known techniques for coping with anxiety don't provide any relief, helpful information fails to calm, and no adaptation results.

The problem with dissociated information is that it can't be decoded at first. As long as the external threat still exists, for example if the tormentors are still alive and the survivor still has contact with them, even if you don't currently hear about this danger, then the corresponding inner structures or inner persons often remain split off for the most part.

If something changes in the conditions of the victim's surroundings which she can see and recognize, for example if the tormentors in the vicinity die, or if the survivor moves away so that the contact is broken off, and finally also if the survivor doesn't experience any more violence throughout a long period of time (so that these adaptation structures actually are no longer helpful to any extent), then the dissociative barriers begin to dissolve slowly. It is common that survivors are seen as simply depressed for a long time until the first vivid memories appear.

If conditions are conducive to such information emerging, it is good to make sure that the environment is supportive structurally and therapeutically. This is to ensure that no one is completely flooded by the emerging memories but instead remains able to keep separate the times of concentrating on the trauma and the times of concentrating on everyday life. Survival only makes sense if there is a world other than the one of torment. If there weren't one, then it wouldn't make any sense, as Jean Améry (2008) said, "to survive in order to bear witness" [translated for this edition]. For who is supposed to attend to this testimony if not human beings who come from another and more humane world? The perpetrators don't need information about this shadow world—they already know all about it.

Therefore, if a journey begins during which information reaches consciousness by crossing a "feeling bridge" from the brainstem to the cerebral cortex, then finally a connection between the individual fragments develops. Now the cerebral cortex can visualize what it actually means, what has happened. In contrast it often seems less than real if images without emotional content emerge, without emotional or physical feelings.

Realizing what has happened is painful because naturally also old feelings and physical sensations emerge as baggage. But as they can be organized into a context of meaning, these experiences can have a temporal meaning in consciousness and therefore be defanged. What is truly past history and is integrated has much less emotional vehemence. Then the physical pain that existed for so long often ends. It is as if the survivor's organism is reacting to finally being heard.

The better this integration succeeds, the more participation in a normal life is possible. Naturally the amount of possible integration also depends on how much time had to be spent in this parallel world and how much support is also available in the person's current life. For this support it is also necessary that family members and important people in the survivor's surroundings are willing to accompany the process of remembering and its consequences in a loving and caring manner. The family members need to be aware of how much pain and other symptoms of the survivor they will have to endure as she relives, processes, and integrates these memories.

For the family members it's over, as for them these are reports from the past. For the survivor this still has to become so. Along this path, compassionate family members are a huge help. In the world of sadism this didn't exist. There was no compassion, no caring, no support, no language, and no empathy. Back then the victims fell out of the world. Now they need the creation of a good place on this side of the world—despite or especially because of the experiences they have had.

CHAPTER NINE

Therapy to facilitate nurturing attachments

This chapter demonstrates how working models can help therapists to facilitate clients experiencing and learning from a nurturing relationship with a therapist so that they can establish healthy attachments with others. I will show some ways I believe to be helpful in developing a pathway to solutions. If healthy inner structures with respect to the client's inner essence are to develop, clients need support in order to learn: Who am I? What would I like to do? What is "mine", for me, in the truest sense of the word?

> "That I may understand whatever binds the world's innermost core together." (Goethe, 1997)

Restructuring the client's inner world according to the individual's true essence

For every client, the goal of therapy should be to decrease the traumatic pressure and suffering as much as possible and to change as many as possible of the artificial inner splits, the forced splits for a sadistic market. I share with Ellert Nijenhuis and many other authors the belief that the ultimate goal should be integration. It seems to me that for victims of extreme violence an ambitious but attainable goal should be to achieve enough integration to enable them to have an everyday life that is worth living.

Besides changing and removing the deliberately designed, alien aspects created through violence (not the inner persons themselves— only the aspects that originated with the perpetrators), it is necessary to encourage the client's own genuine self-awareness to develop in a world not primarily influenced by violence. How can she recognize who she is in the essence of her being? How can she encourage that which actually constitutes her innermost core?

In my optimistic perception, starting at birth each human being has an innermost essential core that makes her unique. As I understand it, this core can't be destroyed, and success in therapy occurs when all (or as many as possible) other inner parts are able to relate to this core of being—a kind of foundation of the individual's personhood. With victims of extreme violence this essential core has been disassembled, distorted, and hidden. Helping to free this core and to make relationships from the inner parts to this core possible, means, as I understand it, health, in the sense of integration.

Here much work is necessary in perception, interaction, and practiced actions, in experiments in behavior and role-playing, much work to "test and find out". The therapist needs to be a compassionate and responsive person who herself is a role model in many areas of life lived so little by the survivor. The therapist needs to have the skill to provide for the client more than one kind of opportunity to experience positive and healthy interactions. I believe it to be indispensable that in therapy at this point we provide such clients with plenty of opportunities to find out about this side of the world and themselves, to test, to role-play and to get feedback but also to make their own choices. Do not expect that the decrease of the consequences of violence alone and the removal of that which is alien in them is sufficient to create a place for them on this side of the world. A significant part of this work could be defined under the subject heading of "relationship work", but also of "caring psychoeducation". What is normal on this side, and what isn't? And how can the survivor of such violence get along in a world in which the other people generally neither share such a fate nor comprehend it—where some won't even be capable of believing that this shadow world exists?

Psychologist Thomas Bock (2000) expressed this in a sentence that for me is very important and true: "It is normal to be different" [translated for this edition]. Also, I would like to add, to get along in the world with respect for your own difference. At this point I encourage clients to find their own language for what happened to them. They need a language in order to at least communicate partial fundamentals of what happened to them to others who regard them benevolently. Organized violence and sadism are concepts that also exist in the "normal" world. Satanists, so often mentioned in this connection, with an especially huge media response, are nothing more than a masquerade—a variation of sadistic violence.

People need the opportunity to arrive in this side of the world with their own peculiarities, and to express them self-confidently and without shame, as well as to demand what they need. To be who you are is only possible in a world in which differences are considered normal and acceptable.

Cerebral cortex, midbrain, brainstem: how can therapy make use of these distinctions?

Here is once again a general description of the three main areas of the brain and their significance for understanding extreme and organized violence.

The brain stem: the location of our automatic functions

The brain stem controls survival. Here there is no room for reflection, but rather just automatic options for actions. This is where our alarm reactions to threats to our survival are localized.

If programs or conditioning are connected to the brainstem, their course of action is automatic. That doesn't mean that you can see the programs or the conditioning functioning in this way. You have to imagine it as a backpack that was packed under repeated training during life-endangering conditions, near-death experiences, and extreme pain. This backpack is now filled with all these interconnected courses of action, to which verbal pronouncements, patterns of behavior, physical reactions, etc. also belong. It may additionally contain imposed aspects of identity and emotions induced by the perpetrators.

When we therefore want to work in this area, we must first find access, in order to be noticed. We have to make it possible for the inner parts hidden here to begin to experience the outside world, which means we need to be aware which sensory channel is the most effective input for each inner person. Then, in a second step, we try to make it possible for them to discover their own emotions, or at least to gain access to them, and then finally we hope they make a connection to the cognitive structures of the cerebral cortex. Programming at the brainstem level means subordination, following orders, and even giving orders without the awareness of the everyday consciousness. Sensory channels that could be interesting for our work include smell, touching and being touched, hearing (tone of voice), and sight (noticing objects in the room or through the windows). Touch is a very dangerous area for survivors as it is almost always interpreted as violent or sexual, but toys and blankets and pets can be used for safe touch. When we approach a baby, we are interested in communicating to it that we are not dangerous, and this is primarily done through nonverbal communication: voice and body language.

The midbrain

The fundamental parts of the limbic system are localized in the midbrain and contain the basis of our emotions. The hippocampus, with its first spatial-temporal classification of experiences, is also a structure in the midbrain. If inner parts are primarily located at the midbrain and organize their inner world according to it, then for them the topics of relationship and feelings have priority. For example, we have to expect a bond with the perpetrator. There may be inner parts who like the perpetrator and who are valued and respected by him. There may also be inner parts who have an extreme need for a relationship and who might be tempted during therapy to let anything happen and leave every decision in the hands of the therapist—"I accept anything you do, please do not send me away." Bonds to the tormentor due to conditioned fear (or other conditioned feelings) may exist. These inner parts can be reached most easily through relationship, and the task of the therapist is to make relationship and the offer of relationship visible and tangible.

Another important goal is the survivor's regaining access to her own emotions. The task of the therapist here is to make feelings come alive and to repeatedly offer criteria for differentiation between the alien and enforced feelings and the client's own feelings and desires with regard to relationships. Developing a capacity for inner consolation can't be emphasized enough as a task for therapy. There is also the question of which problems can be solved internally through inner cooperation, and which problems need an external model or witness. And the client needs to recognize which desires for relationship are actually feasible for the adult person at the present time, since child parts frequently long for the unbroken nurturing that the child did not receive. The mid-brain is also involved with integrating the different aspects of experience and making it conscious. Therapy can provide a contained space within which the boundless mourning for irretrievable losses can be expressed. The therapist can help the client to learn to deal with feelings attached to specific events at a defined time (with a beginning and an ending) and in a defined setting, instead of being overwhelmed by tsunami waves of each particular emotion.

The cerebral cortex

Inner parts located at the cerebral cortex level may have less access to emotional topics but can be reached at a cognitive level. Here, for example, psychoeducation works; here cognitive restructuring is possible; if the patient finds herself with many such inner parts, we can argue with them logically. The relationship to the perpetrator appears at first to be genuine loyalty, because of the clear advantages or the noble values of the cult or perpetrator group. You can expect pseudo-rational explanations for belonging to such a group. Meanwhile, some parts localized in the cerebral cortex don't know anything about belonging to a group. They have knowledge and understanding about everyday life but might follow rules that were created on the "other side". Inner parts that are localized in the cerebral cortex generally shape everyday life, but the therapist must figure out which side of the world is the source of their understanding of everyday life. What are they capable of, what do they know, and which rules are valid for them?

And you must not believe that having explained the conditions and rules to certain parts about normal life versus life in the perpetrator group, the psychoeducation has now been taken care of for the whole system. It helps if you as a therapist regard the whole system as a family and are constantly aware that in individual sessions not all the members will be present. And you can't use the same mode of explanation for each individual "member of the family". For example, you have to ask yourself whether you are dealing with an inner person that has many cognitive skills and is able to perceive the "normal" world around her as it really is, and understand explanations the therapist gives as they are given, or whether what she can hear, see, or think contains huge distortions of reality. This distortion is typical of some mind-controlled clients, and you need to learn how to deal with it. If your client, for instance, hears the opposite of what you say, you can try to find out whether she is able to listen to your words on a tape or can see them the right (real) way if you write them down instead of speaking them. Sometimes I have had to deal with inner persons who genuinely believed that their ideas about me, and what I was doing, were a result of what they had experienced with me and what I had said, when their perceptions were far from reality. They actually believed that their statement of "I heard you saying ..." was true to what I said, though it wasn't. We therapists need to ask ourselves over and over again which intervention strategy can reach any particular inner part or inner person. Which senses can they use; which senses are locked away from them? Do they have access to feelings, or can we help them to develop feelings?

As we get to know each inner person, we don't always know right away what capacities she has. Some utterances or behaviors might mislead us into thinking that an inner person is closer to understanding our world than she is in reality. Sometimes certain skills fool us into believing that the social skills and flexibility of the inner person must be extensive, when they are actually quite limited. It's easy to overlook the fact that an inner person might be involved in therapy without recognizing that she is part of a larger system. Or we might overlook the fact that much apparent cognitive flexibility is only the capacity to acquire large amounts of knowledge rather than genuine mental flexibility.

Part of therapeutic work is developing hypotheses about inner persons, maps, connections, possibilities, skills, and resources, testing these hypotheses in practice, and then modifying them over and over again. Inner persons also tend to grow, to mature with time, and to change in their inner structure. Flexibility is essential for psychotherapy.

Seven structures of dissociation—how do these distinctions help in therapeutic practice?

In the first chapters I described how, following a working model, we would deal with a total of seven different dissociation structures. However, we must not lose sight of the fact that in every individual case, for every individual client, and for every inner part, individual characteristics play a role.

In connection with the varying splits we have to ask which possibilities we can expect with which structure and, consequently, which principles we have to take into consideration during an intervention.

I would like structures to be understood as structural characteristics for inner parts, not in the sense of the sickness of the respective client. Inner parts are different and also differently structured. As a reminder, here once again are the individual structures:

1. Simple PTSD
2. PTSD that becomes chronic
3. DESNOS
4. DDNOS/DID with inner parts conditioned by experience
5. DDNOS/DID with inner parts conditioned by outsiders
6. DID with programmed inner parts
7. DID with programmed and inversely programmed inner parts.

To plan a therapy you would look at which of the seven different structures your client has, with respect to the sections of the brain you would most likely have to address. That would mean taking the location of the inner persons or parts into consideration in deciding upon an intervention, and then imagining which resources would be necessary to address this level.

1. Simple PTSD

With the first structure of the model, we are dealing with a simple PTSD (post-traumatic stress disorder) without relevant comorbidity or previous traumatic experiences. In this case it is likely that we as therapists might have about a ninety-five percent shared world view with our clients and that the PTSD and the experience of their symptoms represents an exception.

For therapy this means that there aren't any major difficulties in getting involved in the world of the client; we have a relatively easy task in agreeing on a mutual consensual reality. It is quite simple for us to negotiate basic rules for living together in the world. And if the client additionally comes from our cultural group, then we share a great deal with each other. For therapy we need a mutual, consensual reality between the two human beings so that we can really effectively "connect".

At this level of simple PTSD the individuality of the client is also still the most important element in her understanding of the world but, to the extent that it is important for therapy, the client's world view can be negotiated and bargained with. Therapists can easily and effectively do what the neurobiologist Humberto Maturana (1992) calls "structural coupling". We share the same consensual reality, and the fact that we do not map the world (the "multiverse" in his words) in our inner worlds in exactly the same way does not matter. In general, the client's conclusions about the world around her are sufficient for her to make sense of the world and intervene in it successfully. The client can interpret social connections adequately enough and can behave according to social rules. We can assume an extensive mutual basis for understanding much of what goes on in the world. The client's need for dissociation is only for a small part of her experience; most of her experience in life is conscious.

This implies that psychoeducation and teaching about self-soothing will work, that social resources are accessible, and that the client still remembers skills and resources she had previously. The level of hope here would be significantly easier to raise.

When simple PTSD is the only disorder that has to be treated with therapy, it is very possible to establish a working bond. A mutual understanding with respect to atmosphere of treatment and methods of intervention can be reached easily through straightforward dialogue.

The work is relatively simple in that we are dealing with a human being whose main inner parts or ego states are consciously aware, and who has a relatively integrated ego. That is, she has a part that gets along relatively well on this side of the world, so that in working on relationships you only have to deal with one person who can also recall your mutual work to a great extent. A relationship develops, and indeed a reliable one.

In this situation, most of your interventions can take place by means of language, through conscious processes of thinking and managing behavior. Although you have to take the therapeutic relationship into account, it is not so much in the forefront as it is in therapy with a more complex dissociative structure. Clients with simple PTSD want competent consultants who are well-acquainted with their disorders, who can explain to them how they need to understand the exceptional situation of their trauma, how to respond to it, and finally how to integrate it.

Since the experience of feeling powerless represents an exception for these people, we generally are concerned with clients who are thoroughly consciously aware of their own expertise and resources and who have had many experiences during which they were able to have influence over and control things in their lives. It is fairly easy for them to achieve this control again. The dissociated parts of experience are therefore not so many and the clients are not as extremely traumatized as others.

We are dealing here with clients who are relatively secure about their place in the world until an event changes everything. They possess a basic trust, a security about relationships, and knowledge about how the presence of other people can be a consolation. In their mourning and despair they long for people with whom they can talk, to whom they can entrust themselves. They are able to seek and find a foothold in the community.

With this group of clients cognitive work is possible to the highest extent from the very beginning. The clients are capable of reflection and introspection. Apart from the PTSD they are able to control their actions consciously and to regulate their impulses. They merely have one poorly integrated experience, but still have an integrated self.

With this group of clients you can confidently fall back on well-known and publicly recommended courses of action. You don't have to fear that these somehow have been distorted by perpetrators and could now cause damage. The entire repertoire of trauma therapy can be implemented in a relatively speedy fashion. After a short stabilizing phase, confrontation with the damaging experience is also possible.

An important criterion for the selection of your intervention is then: How much normalcy, how much "everyday life" is pitted against how much experience of helplessness and trauma? It is helpful to specify how much positive life experience the client has as a resource, and how much knowledge of the "normal" side of the world can be assumed.

The further to the right we come in Figure 16 on the next page, the fewer have been the client's normal experiences of relationships and interactions, the more powerful has been the parallel world, and the more the inner structures and knowledge of the world derived from the abuse will dominate the person.

What is shown as steps in Figure 16 in order to provide a better over-view can in reality naturally also be subdivided within the seven steps into yet more steps. However, models need to be presented fairly sim-ply, which is why I chose this display format.

Now you could think it doesn't make much sense to give thought to how to treat simple PTSD when there are other more serious and

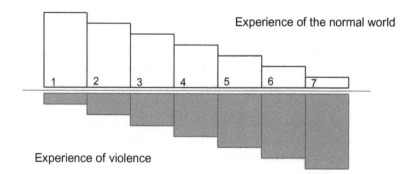

Figure 16. Experience of violence and experience of the world.

longer-lasting traumas. But that would not be right. According to my model, extremely dissociative people have inner persons on all levels of functioning. And intervention with these inner persons can be adjusted to what each of them is capable of accomplishing.

There are inner persons who can engage in a reflective attitude; there are those who have not experienced any traumatizing; and there are those whose tasks lie in coming to terms with everyday life, who are obliged to function in the world on this side. Naturally, because the person is split up into many, they don't have the mental efficiency in their actions of integrated persons, because no part has the same mental energy as a whole person (van der Hart, Nijenhuis, & Steele, 2006). But it is very important to take the differences between the inner people into consideration for access and intervention planning. Otherwise you might, for example, indulge in constant psychoeducation and in epic explanations without recognizing that you are dealing with an inner part that lacks the capacity to answer adequately. Inappropriate interventions strain the relationship between therapist and client as well as the client herself.

2. PTSD that becomes chronic

Let's continue with the model and observe PTSD that becomes chronic. Here we have to consider additional accumulating stress factors. They can originate from varying sources, which have varying consequences for therapy.

We have to ask ourselves what is responsible for PTSD becoming chronic. These factors could come from the person herself, or from the environment, or could also be secondary consequences of the traumatic experiences that caused the PTSD. If the factors come from the person herself, did she already have a personality disorder? Was she already sick and thereby especially weakened by the occurrence of the traumatic experience? Did the experience lead to a complete destabilization of her functioning, or to feelings of shame because up until now she has always been able to take care of everything by herself and therefore she delayed starting therapy for a long time? You need to identify the stumbling blocks to therapy and to creating a therapeutic relationship. And naturally, you as a therapist now have to place your treatment decisions into a specific hierarchy based on which source of suffering is the greatest right now.

Further typical problems that have an impact on the therapeutic environment could be bad experiences with previous therapists, or with institutions for victim compensation, or with compensation from damaging events determined by appraisers.

Finally, and this should also not be underestimated, one-time traumatic events can also produce lasting effects, for example a permanent handicap, lasting pain, or disfigurement. And some events, such as the murder of a child, are so heinous that they can never be atoned for. This can have a substantial impact on the person's participation in the world.

Basically, with chronic trauma, the inner map of the person is changed.

It is necessary for the therapist to question many tacit assumptions. The connection between client and therapist will become more difficult and the creation of a mutual consensual reality for treatment can already be damaged by distrust or hopelessness. Chronic trauma asks the question again regarding which "reality" is decisive, that of the traumatic event or that of normalcy. How this question is answered will depend to a great extent on how many effects remain from the traumatic event.

As with PTSD, inner persons may find themselves in such a situation. If an inner person up until now had no experience of trauma, the world she lives in could have collapsed, for example after a rape in the here and now.

3. DESNOS

With DESNOS (disorders of extreme stress not otherwise specified) a line has been crossed. In most of these cases, the client has experienced violence that sprang from human beings. Of course there are exceptions such as living in an earthquake zone, or growing up in starvation, but in those situations you have to ask what proportion of the devastating effects result from the actions of people. No matter what the source of the trauma, with DESNOS there is still a considerable portion of the normal world, and many aspects of life, that are devoid of trauma. This results in the dissociated parts of the person's life experience being fewer than in the more complex disorders. Sometimes victims are aware of the source of trauma. When they are, body memories and flashback emergence of feelings characterize the picture.

DESNOS as complex traumatization means that the traumatizing events have repeated themselves and have arisen either cumulatively (as in the case of serious neglect) or sequentially (repeated individual substantial traumatization, such as with sexual violence, imprisonment in a concentration camp, or torture). Depending on the stage of life in which the damage to the client and her previous trust in the world began, we may meet inner people in therapy who possibly have no reason to trust other human beings or to expect anything even rudimentally positive from them.

With DESNOS we have arrived in the section of man-made disasters and—if the damage began early enough—also in the area of dysfunctional relationships. In practical terms, this means that these clients come from life experiences in which they could not achieve a stable assessment of their world. Like borderline clients (who may or may not have a complex trauma disorder), it is difficult for them to judge interactions correctly, and they make hasty judgments, because of the great inner tension that has characterized their situation continuously for a longer period of time. You can interpret this as a method of quickly getting back to safety. The sooner it is clear to them what is going on, the faster they can react adequately. This results from the fact that the consciously perceived world when they were children (even if some defining pieces were missing) was unstable. Sometimes one thing was valid, other times the opposite. Sometimes certain feelings were acceptable, other times not.

It is probably helpful to spend much time in therapy trying to construct a meaningful relationship, beginning with the conduct of the therapist. Since these clients have essentially experienced two worlds and been unable to gain any clarity, it is now important that what you, the therapist, see as a valid interpretation of the world is communicated unambiguously. This process includes explanations about how they could have developed such an unstable view of the world, along with reassurance that the difficulties that arise from this are completely normal. For these clients it is important, along with psychoeducation, to assist them in regulating their feelings and restructuring their cognitive processes. It is all too easy for these clients to respond in the moment as if there were only one single evaluation possible for a given set of facts, and they can react with fury if this evaluation isn't accepted.

In my opinion, a further important point in understanding DESNOS clients lies in the fact that they still experience themselves as one individual and therefore in therapy you encounter one person or inner person who, normal memory loss notwithstanding, can remember situations including the history of the relationship with the therapist. Of course, the client will remember things differently, depending on which ego state she is in or which inner person is speaking.

If you apply this pattern of dealing with relationships and experiences to those inner persons for whom it fits, this would mean that they also can retain memories of past experiences with the therapist and can see these as a continuous experience of a relationship. A basic capacity for relationships is there, as well as the ability to learn, to understand, and to change.

There is also the possibility for training or for "homework", therapeutic tasks to be accomplished at home. A relatively functional inner person may be able to take responsibility for having all inner parts write in a book, and can make interior arrangements with other inner persons or parts. Such an inner person can potentially get all the others from the differing levels on board. However, it is important to be aware that inner persons normally are not capable of looking into more deeply dissociated parts of the inner world, even though they can see what is on their level and what is more conscious.

It should be apparent that there is a lot of room for misunderstanding. Often the intention of the actions of another individual or his supposed thoughts about the person in therapy will be misconstrued. A client or an inner person with this problem will benefit from a verbalized, benevolent relationship (which can include telling her the reasons for this benevolence). She also benefits from therapy being a place where she receives help to bring her intentions—also with respect to relationships—into greater agreement with her actions and habits of thinking.

Here it is also clear that she needs an active therapist who won't create endlessly long pauses filled with silence and will combine words with visible actions. Listening and talking is no longer enough.

4. DDNOS with inner parts conditioned through experiences

In accordance with Figure 16 (p. 124), I would presume with a case of distinctive DDNOS (dissociative disorder not otherwise specified) that the person's experience in the traumatizing world and the world of the normal experience of the world are about equal. One peculiarity is that many DDNOS clients at first know nothing about the configuration of their inner world and truly assume they have only lived a life within the normal world. They explain their symptoms by their own craziness or by an undiagnosed illness.

The brain does fill gaps of consciousness in the client's perceived biography. For instance, if you have spent time in school, your brain knows what school means, and gaps may be filled with "I was in school" or other similar assumptions. In my description here it is the way everyday knowledge and memory works. We do not remember every single day of being in school, and we use general assumptions when we think about the past. Alison Miller (2014) has encountered a programme to fill in gaps in which a client has attended a ritual with some ordinary experience ("I was walking along the railway track"). This is another way in which gaps in knowledge are filled. Corresponding to actual knowledge from the truly experienced world, an inner person is taught by perpetrators to copy the client's conscious experience until all the gaps are filled and are no longer noticeable for the client.

The inner parts in naturally arising DDNOS should be distinguished from inner parts that have been conditioned by perpetrators. In this case an inner part comes into being because a specific overwhelming experience is produced often enough to force the existence of such an inner unit that reacts to it.

In the interests of correctness, I want to mention that you may also see DID (dissociative identity disorder) as a clinical picture under these conditions. However, this reaction as a result of repeated trauma comes from the inner core of the client. The emergence of an inner part is a sensible answer from the client's organism to this specific type of event.

If such split-off inner parts or inner persons ultimately emerge in the therapeutic setting, then, besides the task of creating rapport in your relationship with both the client and the inner person, there is also the task of helping the client find a relationship to this split-off inner part as well as making the case for an understanding among all the inner parts. Emerging inner parts often feel responsible for the events that created them, or the main person blames them. It is necessary to throw light on this error. Words are often not sufficient to convey the message that the client's parts are not responsible; the words have to be supplemented with nonverbal activity, with actions. Your body language and tone of voice convey what you really feel. At this point the therapist fails if he is not able to adapt his own repertoire to the needs of his client.

You may need to explain to inner persons that killing or evicting a particular inner person is not a solution, because this would not get rid of the unpleasant feelings of pain or grief that inner person evokes. Instead, they need to recognize that each internal entity performs a function in the inner community—and did not cause the pain that it bears. In *Psychotherapie mit entmutigten Klienten* [*Psychotherapy with Discouraged Clients*] (2001) I describe such a course of action with a client whose baby inner part still bore huge amounts of pain that the other parts didn't have to bear.

Basically then, we have two system levels that balance each other out. The system level that can be classified as belonging to the normal world differentiates itself in roles and ego states that can be consciously engaged in and exchanged. The system level of the parallel world consists of many apparently conditioned inner parts. If the tormentor made sure over and over again that it was indispensable for the victim to react to the tormentor's violence with lust, then an inner part developed who was precisely capable of doing this.

The inner parts function according to "when—then". When they recognize a certain pattern, the everyday person will be switched off and the necessary reaction proceeds. For everyday functioning it is also necessary that the parallel world is not consciously perceived, even when it causes loss of time.

What is important is the fact that the emergent inner parts are derived directly and functionally from the overpowering experience they had. It made immediate sense. The experience of violence and the response to the violence, specific to the client's organism, are the only decisive factors.

The therapeutic setting has to be suitable for understanding and learning how inner parts have become that which they are, and which alternatives they can choose or are allowed to use today. Psychoeducation, working on perception and feelings, and learning to evaluate perceptions are important. And don't forget: The road map to solutions, especially for small inner parts hidden from conscious memory, is only possible via physical experience and emotions. These inner parts have a sensorimotor memory and also a corresponding self-representation. They have to have the hands-on experience that the danger is over with.

5. DDNOS/DD with inner parts conditioned from the outside

With DDNOS as with DID we encounter what I would like to call inner parts conditioned from the outside. These split-off parts are no longer only due to the variables of violence and of the client's organism. These inner parts have passed through a deliberate training program with the goal of forcing them to participate in certain actions completely contrary to their own interests, wishes, and beliefs at the flick of a switch. Since each of these inner parts itself—and sometimes the front person—is directly aware of the actions and their consequences and perceives these actions as "I am doing this, therefore this has to be a part of me", it actually has no alternative other than to experience itself as perverse and equipped with incomprehensible motivations that nonetheless exist.

The fact that we are dealing with conditioning but no programming is still a determining factor. It is possible for the therapist and the client and/or inner parts to begin to search for how the inner parts came into being. A good guideline for me is the recognition that perpetrators usually create something specific for their own purposes, so each inner part has some specific quality or behavior different from the qualities or behaviors of the other inner parts. And naturally the client isn't consciously aware of this repertoire.

Therapists shouldn't be overly surprised if affected inner parts at first offer a peculiar explanation, such as "I was bad and had to be punished". It is necessary to extend the context, to get a proper explanation. That is, to look back in time to the start of the training program, and to observe again more precisely how the tormentors justified their actions to the victim.

For this topic the book by Werner Haas, *Das Hellinger-Virus* [*The Hellinger Virus*] (2009), is really helpful. In particular, abusers' unspeakable statements with regard to sexual violence and the perpetrator-victim relationship are examined very well. Another book specifically concerned with this topic is *Tat-Sachen: Narrative von Sexualstraftätern* [*Facts: Narratives from Sex Offenders*] (Buchholz, Lamott, & Mörtl, 2008).

And, as a marginal note, it is advantageous for the therapist to consider the sources of inspiration that the perpetrators may have used for creating conditioned inner parts. Knowledge of works of world literature is helpful, as well as the Bible, myths, legends, and similar sources, as perpetrators use all these.

When certain inner parts emerge, the names the perpetrators gave them can hint at their functions. In certain circumstances, you can even deduce that there have to be still more inner parts, in order to complete the picture.

Put simply, we're talking about deliberate complete distortions of the original reality. Recognizing this is only possible if what actually happened is clear enough that you can comprehend the distortion or the false reality that was created. Then corrections will also be easier to carry out.

Nonetheless you should still at all costs make sure ahead of time that the dissolution of such conditioning is not prevented by a "barb mechanism". A barb mechanism is a built-in negative consequence of any change that might be made. So, for example, if you want to help a client to stop acting on her conditioning to drink alcohol, you should be aware of what will happen if she does not drink. If there is a barb mechanism it could bring up something like a suicide attempt. If there is one, it must first be counteracted, since if this isn't done, the client will pay an unacceptably high price. It is important to discuss possible interventions with the client in advance, working with the respective inner persons, and asking systematically "What would happen if ...?" Then you can find out right away whether, for example, a healing idea that includes "water" would act as a trigger, or whether specific rooms, colors, symbols, animals, and so on would present any dangers. Therapy is a custom-made suit—not something from a catalogue. What can each inner part do at which level, and which of our intervention ideas are really useful for it?

6. DDNOS/DID with programmed inner parts

We now enter a risky area for psychotherapists. We are no longer dealing with individual inner persons but rather with inner persons that the perpetrator has fixed in place in relationship to the other inner persons and whose behavior has been primarily determined from the outside. A fundamental understanding about this is that the programmed inner parts at first aren't sensitized to their programming. They perceive themselves as doers without any context of how they came to be this way, and they assume that they are implementing their own intentions through their actions.

In contrast to inverse programming, here we have programs running which function in the same way as the emergency programs of the client's organism. If defense is indicated, then it now proceeds in the way the perpetrators designed it to, including the interaction between all parts involved. This is also true for the interaction with the outside world. The therapist is well advised to keep in mind the fact that in this situation he is dealing with an internal family rather than just with a client who, well integrated, talks about the varying intentions and opinions within her.

One well-known "program" draws on varying aspects of sexual availability. In the first chapters of this book I gave examples of how within a sequence of violent sexuality a transformation must take place from a frightened and sensitive-to-pain inner person to an insensitive-to-pain inner person and finally to an inner person nearly lusting for pain. The distinctive feature is that these interactions are perceived by the other inner parts and that the inner persons mutually judge themselves as acting independently of each other.

For the client this means that at first she hardly perceives these inner persons as parts of herself, as being in her body (a phobia described by van der Hart, Nijenhuis, & Steele, 2006), and even where she does perceive these parts as being within her, she generally regards them as something external which was added to her. Meanwhile on the other side, those inner persons might see the front person as separate from them and not living in the same body. In this situation opinions arise among the inner parts about each other. Quite often these opinions have a negative slant: "I can endure things that she isn't able to." Or, "He is evil and you'd better stay away from him." Some of these negative opinions arise from deliberate training of the inner people to believe that some parts of the person are demons or other evil entities.

The therapist therefore has to educate the client's system about the fact that all parts belong to a single system, and every inner person's contribution to survival is equally necessary and important. This also applies to every individual inner part: it needs its own psychoeducation, attention, and explanations. Each inner part has its own pattern with respect to physicality, physical contact, touch, language, and silence, as well as its own perceived age and its own framework of understanding. How exactly this therapeutic work can be done is something we discover when we access the memory of the original traumatic event of this inner part and how its training proceeded. We can then use this knowledge for helping the network of inner persons.

7. DDNOS/DID with inversely programmed inner parts

Inverse programming completely separates a human being from all of humanity. This programming means ultimately that all the victim's desires and capacities to think and feel are preprogrammed at this level, including her interactions with others and with other inner parts of her system. It means also that every positive impulse she has in relation to the outside world is accompanied by escalating destructive activity. So, accomplishments that were once possible don't get easier each time, instead they become more unmanageable. Every remnant of a relationship or humanity mutates to the experience of being betrayed and forsaken. Every step requires enormous exertion—and yet failure is often preprogrammed. The client feels robbed of any and every hope, as the poem *Innenleben II* [*Inner Life II*, translated for this edition] expresses:

> There's nothing left
> Nothing of the dreams
> Nothing of the hope
>
> Only nothing has remained
> Into nothing slowly but steadily
> Suspicion infiltrates
> Fear flows in
>
> Only the never has remained
> As a final refuge
> Charred shooting stars
> In an already long closed sky
>
> There's nothing left
> That could still die a death

The further to the right we proceed with the steps in Figure 16 (p. 124), the more difficult it is to develop relationships with the inner persons; each meeting with a particular inner person is more like the first encounter with that part. At first nothing grows—and no learning is possible. And it is of pre-eminent importance not to equate this with the client's "not wanting help" or "boycotting the treatment".

For therapists it is initially a completely confusing stage of therapy. If in previous years your client was apparently able to integrate her inner persons on system levels one and two relatively well and she finally achieved a relationship of trust with you, you can no longer rely on that automatically continuing.

Opinions, actions, and interactions are simply and bluntly set, and we encounter many of the perpetrator's sentences that make any kind of thought and reflection impossible. These sentences are far removed from what we might, for example, find as opinions of the dark inner parts at system level two ("That's the law ...", "It is written ..."). These are in fact sentences that come from the structure of the perpetrator's logic and the poisoning of the normal world. They twist and pervert any knowledge gained at other times regarding relationships and actions as well as regarding the commitment of the therapist. These sentences seem specific and personal due to their contents, but they use the same structure over and over again, without any reflection. Every attempt to get these inner parts to reflect on their automatic views and actions fails at first. The underlying structure says: "First they lured us into this world, now we are forsaken."

The capability to reflect and make distinctions is necessary to make it possible for such an inner part to comprehend that its perception is the result of a program, and its reality has been determined and perverted by this program. If we attempt to explain to such an inner part that its perception denies the reality of the present situation, and that perception can vary depending on the situation, it will say briefly and succinctly, "You're quibbling" or "You're talking nonsense—you make distinctions that are completely unimportant." Unimpressed by our intervention, it will adamantly present its only true view of reality. Anyone who doesn't agree is a liar. Because of the way this interaction proceeds, the therapist may have the impression that this inner part really thinks and reflects, and that its statements must be the result of a comprehensive process of reflection. We experience such inner parts as evil, manipulative, and distorting reality, and the seed planted by the perpetrator sprouts.

Then the evil of the program comes between the therapist and the client. The inner person experiences the therapist as evil, as a failure, as someone who suddenly stops trusting the client. The clueless therapist, unaware of any fault on his part, assumes that an introjection of the evil tormentor is acting in the client, or even that the client herself has an evil core. There may be another problem too: Inner parts who pretend to be other inner parts or the host personality.

Admittedly, many therapeutic efforts fail because of dark inner persons. Various supervision sessions in this area have made it clear to me how difficult it is for therapists who have caringly tried to help a client. They suffer because this client possesses inner parts that appear dark, evil, and hostile to therapy, that have done terrible things, or that possess horrible convictions inside.

Many clients have difficulty tolerating their own inner parts that are so enduringly different from them. You don't only have to think of injury and death, but of inner parts that apparently enjoy prostituting or even torturing or killing themselves or others, or who speak positively about the tormentors. This is what those parts are trained to say and to believe about themselves.

Since at first these inner parts oppose the world and the values of the therapist, the therapist's experience is much like that of the client's front person, who has to endure inner parts whose views, actions, and so on are so foreign to her own self.

If as a therapist you are getting into conflict with inner parts and their values, it is helpful to clarify this for yourself. If you are conscious of this, it can prevent you from urging the inner parts to become "better people"; instead you can approach them respectfully and determine how they became the way they are. At least at level one and level two it's possible for the inner parts to describe how they became the way they are. This simply means explaining which experiences shaped their behavior. The more clear the inner parts are on level one, the more easily they are able to come to other explanations through reflection.

But the therapist who truly does make progress must not assume that he has now won the battle. On this basis it is important to truly know which inner persons you are encountering in the victim's system and at which level they are. Repetitions of positions that have been expounded upon many times and that sound recorded are a sure hint that your intervention is not being effective.

Broadly, I can say that inner persons who are at the level I call borderline, that is on the system level one including dissociation structures of one, two, and three, are accessible for cognitive interventions and often benefit from it. Just as with personality disorders, it is possible to get the inner parts to scrutinize reality. Cognitive restructuring, though often with many detours, is feasible. It is possible to encourage new and different views of the world through thought processes. Thinking, learning, and change are possible. Insight can be achieved and behavior changes can be planned. Explanations can be understood.

At system level two, where I would arrange dissociation levels four and five, an effective intervention is more likely to be possible through the senses than through cognitive arguments. Only after you have plowed a path through senses and emotions can you try to move the inner parts into the direction of cognitive thinking. First feelings and sensitivity have to become possible, otherwise meaningful thinking is not.

At system level three we find dissociation levels six and seven. Here much is lacking. There is no relationship to each other among the inner parts, no automatic cooperation. Perception is extremely restricted and predefined. There is little or no freedom in evaluating things, nothing is calculated by the parts themselves; everything is set by the tormentors. The inner parts have no feelings of their own, no habitual ways of thinking other than those installed by the perpetrators, no conceptions, wishes, or hopes. The further we get toward the right in Figure 16 (p. 124), the more we are confronted by inner parts that behave like machines. We are beyond humanity. Much seems robotic; much is automatic and kneejerk. Identities are modified by the perpetrators rather than developed through experience.

This means the therapist must first come up with a way to be genuinely perceived by the client. The therapist must plow a path through a multitude of disappointments and reproaches. He must try over and over again to invalidate the negative presuppositions that the client has about him. The therapist must come up with many creative ideas so that the inner parts that have lost touch with their senses can learn once again how to use these senses. And the therapist needs patience, patience, and even more patience.

System level three, involving inverse programming, is the level of automation, of almost complete external control, from which the distance back to the victim's own consciousness is the farthest imaginable. The inner persons at this level hold the tormentor's thoughts to be their own consciousness. They can't put things into context, they don't comprehend a "before" or an "after". The inner persons respond to hints from the outer world that they are wrong in their judgment with hurt feelings and accusations of betrayal, as if the circumstances they know as normal are just a "given" in the present situation. They sometimes believe they uphold noble ideals in their actions and are serving honorable purposes like sacrificing the child to a worthy deity (while in reality they are killing for a "snuff pornography" video), and they can't recognize the fact that their behavior doesn't really serve such ideals, that they are being used. They don't attempt to understand the world at all but live in a world in which they believe that they already know and perceive everything.

Their references to the perpetrators or their actions, and to the person's experiences, differ considerably from what inner persons on the other levels might say. Whereas on the other two system levels you can get detailed evidence—for example naming the father clearly as a tormentor and describing a rape that he performed or a place where he sent the victim—on this level the messages sound different: "Person X is also one of them." "That other client is a traitor." All our attempts to get more precise information, even when we state that we can only protect the client and ourselves if she gives us more exact information, fail. Every attempt at obtaining more concrete information is rejected irately. If we allude to the fact that earlier information from her was quite different, her immediate comment is that the therapist has apparently lost interest in the victim, or that the inner part has made a very costly effort and now she is no longer of value to the therapist. The victim may claim that previously the therapist was different towards the client; something has changed.

It is truly apparent that the inner part believes that it has given decisive information. The part believes that it has all possible information at its disposal and therefore has made sense of it and come to a logical conclusion from its point of view. It has a giant blind spot—but the inner part doesn't recognize the fact that it is a victim of a preconceived evaluation from its programmed brain and that it doesn't possess genuine insight.

If we get far enough to achieve contact with such an inner part, then we must remain aware that such contact may make this inner part's way of perceiving, seeing, and knowing become more powerful in determining the views of the other inner parts that are on other levels of the system. This is likely to change the perception of the inner parts that at first were favorably disposed toward the therapist. The client suddenly sees her therapist very differently. Some of her understanding becomes distorted, and she loses comprehension of what is going on. If the therapist takes away a pair of scissors or a knife that the client was trying to use to hurt herself, she does not believe the therapist's explanation. If the therapist doesn't answer the phone when she calls, she is convinced that this is a message to say "You are not important to me" and then she feels herself increasingly lost and separated from the therapist. She may begin to believe the therapist is fraudulent. She may begin to imagine the therapist's voice has changed, or the therapist's eyes have changed color.

Whereas on system level one a client knows that someone has threatened her and has said she shouldn't see the therapist, and at level two she develops extreme anxiety when she goes to the therapist, fearing something might happen to him, on level three the inner parts are convinced they never wanted to leave the old world and had no interest in therapy. At least for the inner parts that experienced inverse programming, this is valid. These inner parts have no access to our world, which is exactly opposite to the world from which they come—and they simply don't perceive this, our world. When what happens contradicts their past experience, their models for explanation are already predetermined.

The result of this work is therefore at first that what seemed to be well integrated suddenly blows up in your face. Not because you performed an unsuccessful therapy, but on the contrary because therapy was successful. In a certain sense at this point you just start all over again. Probably you will only be willing to do this for clients who have grown on you, and hopefully you will be ready to do more than you can charge for, and you want to commit yourself personally to the challenge.

This programming to create inhumanity and betrayal undermines all trust and has enormously destructive repercussions on relationships— both internal and external ones. Therapy has to learn how to oppose this inverse programming.

Inverse programming has generated many ways to attack benevolent people who mean well. For example, therapists receive unambiguous sexual offers that pervert their kindness and their efforts toward the welfare of the client and make them appear sexual. If a therapist resists, explaining that no such sexual feelings, as in a love affair, exist in the therapist toward the client, then the client will tell the therapist that she can manage fine on her own, taking the therapist's statement as proof that she is not considered to be lovable. Then when the therapist tries to assure the client that she is lovable and important to the therapist, but he doesn't combine such devotion and love with the need for a partner relationship, the client may reproach him for leading her on and encouraging her romantic interest willingly, just to deny everything now.

Then a massive disruption can result that withstands all attempted explanations. Because through the closeness that the levels, the inner persons, and the waking consciousness of the client have to each other at this moment, now the original client is convinced that the therapist is at fault, what is true is what she sees at present, and without a precise transcript of events those gaps in understanding and sometimes even in time which were not perceived can't be filled with knowledge of what really happened.

In contrast to the same situation at levels two or one, no discussion is possible. These inner persons do not have behavior options of their own and simply repeat the same things over and over again. They have been created to prove to the client that there is no life worth living outside of the shadow world. The perceptions of these inner persons have a huge blind spot so that they also can't see that they don't see. The therapist's task is to help these inner parts to move toward the possibility of gaining consciousness. From the position where they were designed to live as robots, without feelings and without their own thoughts and motivations, they have to develop feelings, to learn to have their own thoughts, and so on. (This is referring to the brain, from the brainstem to the midbrain to the cerebral cortex.) The therapist has the task of making sure that the possibility of their finding out how the world really is can even come into existence at all.

A simplified picture would be that on system level two the surroundings are perceived through the client's senses but there is the baggage of pre-assembled meanings and intentions. For example, knowing that the therapist works hard to help another client can't be interpreted any other way than as betrayal and definitive proof that the therapist no longer cares about this client or even has a double standard.

It is already set in stone what things mean and it's not easy to correct these false impressions with a little psychoeducation. The therapist needs a lot of patience and empathic understanding of the hardship of the client in this situation, above all. It isn't about a well-ordered objective talk involving differing opinions but rather where the client experiences the therapist as betraying her and reacts emotionally with massive accusations—and therefore represents a challenge at the very least, even for a good-natured therapist. When we lower our guard and become involved, we are especially easy to batter. But there is no other way to truly reach these deeper levels.

At level three at first you can't accomplish anything with cognitive arguments or with emotional care alone. Although the client is unaware of it herself, a kind of scanner runs constantly, which mercilessly destroys important contexts. Every attempt to make it clear that you didn't say something like that, that you didn't intend to give it that meaning—none of that works any more.

At the level of inverse programming in this way an inner reality is created that is believed to be the outer, real world. As a result, people who are positive influences and have the client's best interests at heart are quickly perceived as betrayers.

To shake up this fundamental and inaccessible world view requires more than just patience. What is needed above all is loving care and imagination in order to come up with ways to make it possible for the client to recognize her own blind spot. You have to take into consideration that at this level mistakes are connected with great shame and possibly suicide programs. It's about making insight possible, as well as dealing with the unavoidable shame, when insight is achieved, about the unjustified insults and blame placed on the therapist.

What was said of the other levels is the same here: This level arose out of a life-endangering situation, in which all the important possibilities of orientation conducive to accomplishing goals in everyday life were destroyed. Instead of these healthy possibilities we are confronted with the fact that present-day external reality is being inserted into the internal reality only as a tiny fragment. In the client's internal reality everything is set in stone—nothing is validated or tested to discover the truth. Everything is assumed to be known—always.

We therapists frequently despair: "Can't you see ...? Don't you know what you used to know?" For the client all this seems to be useless argument. If finally the third level has reached and influenced a client with whom we share much interactive history, then the therapist and what he has to offer appear completely changed to the client. She herself believes that she is dealing with a reality just like the one she was used to in the past, that she knows what it all means and that what she perceives is the truth. She saw it and heard it after all, and she is completely unable to see that what she perceived came much more from her internal world and not the external one. The inner persons of the third inversely programmed level can't see present-day reality. It's their blind spot, because their programming has such distorting effects here. They can't see how their perception of the world came into being and that it was changed from a source within them. In one sense, all people are unable to perceive the process by which the world arises in their heads.

Therefore we can't construct a consensual reality with our client, because a very large part of the client doesn't connect with us. And indeed that means a major change in the reality of the relationship. The meaning of what we see in the relationship is really extremely different from what the client sees. We have to ask ourselves: What can we still connect to? Which pillars are still standing? And only then when there is an answer, when something remains, can we try to proceed with the last segment of the journey.

For the therapist this means learning to deal with hurt and mortification, knowing that our previous work only provides a small amount of support as there is scarcely any trust left. It's not only as if there never was any good, but rather as if the bad and the misunderstood now take center stage.

From my own experience I can only give the advice not to react to attacks immediately or directly. The attacks can be very fierce, and I myself have cried many tears when I was subjected to them directly. Or I got into a genuine rage over so much injustice inflicted on me. It's necessary not to strike back in the same fashion but also not to act as if it left you cold and unaffected.

Much empathetic supervision or counseling is necessary for the therapist in order to make room for these feelings. They need space. And they are also an important clue in the sense of countertransference, in order to understand which feelings have been released in the client. For she is experiencing two things at once: She is suddenly confronted with especially brutal memories, and she believes that an important person is no longer available to help. Since she can no longer trust an important attachment figure (who may be the only person who knows the story), this is pure horror for her.

One inner person said to me once at the beginning of such a journey into hell: "It doesn't go any further. If you continue to work here, everything will blow up and you will need every skill you have as a therapist and more."

Here it can't continue the way you were used to. Direct psychoeducation is as ineffective as addressing the patient directly and emotionally. Misunderstandings, threats to break off therapy, and frustration on both sides are the results unless the therapy plan is changed. What is necessary is as much control over the interactions as possible. Therapists who work with cameras or recording devices are at an advantage here, because these make transparency of the interactions possible. You have to consider how much of the relationship is still feasible when the inner people of the third level come out. What can still show that you are serious about your efforts?

At the level of inverse programming your goal is to contribute to the client's desire to discover the world outside and become curious about it. You have to be willing to let yourself in for an adventure, to question once again your firmly established knowledge and feelings. For this to work there has to be trust in blocking certain of your client's channels of knowledge for a restricted time, in order to make new experiences with the senses possible. To give an example, one client had been trained to be unable to smell what she was cooking, but to know how things smelled because of their color. She would tell me that she was cooking green, or red, or yellow dishes for her son. When she was asked how something tasted or smelled, she was unable to answer because she could not smell what she was eating at all. She believed that she and her clothing stank like feces. I asked her to test the smell of a scarf she was wearing and one I was wearing, with open eyes. To her mine smelled wonderful, but hers smelled like feces. I asked her to close her eyes and tell me how each of the scarves smelled. I put the perfume I personally use on her scarf and repeated the test, all while her eyes were closed. To demonstrate to her that I was not faking the situation, I later showed her on video what we had been doing and her reactions. Before trying something like this, you need to first make sure that your client is able to do the testing without extreme consequences resulting from active programming. So a lot of communication should be done in preparation for this kind of work.

At this point the complete untrustworthiness of these programs implemented by the perpetrators shows itself. The client has experienced traumatic events at all levels, yet has with a great deal of effort and despite many fears let herself be involved in a trustworthy working alliance with a therapist. Yet a second time at the conscious level she has to confront herself with what is happening here and now. Despite all her pain she has been successful on the first two levels. Now she can't continue to build on that, as the price for reaching this goal is the destruction of the relationship and an almost complete loss of foothold. Here she feels she has to start all over again, right from the beginning, which means in her mind she can no longer trust the idea: "I will do my work with my therapist and we will find a way out." The therapist is no longer a person she can trust. And this isn't the first time in her life. She knows people who have promised, "I'll get you out", and then turned out to be the worst offenders.

So it is no wonder that at first the client reacts negatively to all attempts to get her to see things in a new light, and to prove that the therapist is conspiring against her and blaming her for his mistakes. "Why don't you believe me any more? I have never lied to you!" For example, the client wants to give you information to protect others. But she can't recognize that a clue like "At the XY event there are two people who are dangerous" isn't as helpful as a clue that describes a certain person engaging in a particular action at a specific location.

Still, and therapists should never forget this; those disclosures that seem so vague to us come at significant cost to the patient. Only she, and some of her inner people, know and will feel how massive the backlash will be because she talks at all and because she talks about such things. It can result, for example, in massive self-mutilation or in retaliation by the perpetrator group that thinks it owns her. It sometimes helps to ask the client directly about the price of disclosure and why she wants you to have this information. If there is still a personal motivation here, such as to protect or warn the therapist, then there is still a small piece of relationship to be found.

We must never forget that the intention of the tormentor is hidden behind all the actions at level three, even though the client is unaware that it is being carried out.

Despite everything it is worth examining all information carefully over and over again, in order not to be forced to act or to blame too quickly. Otherwise at the end of an essentially successful therapy we will be standing in front of a small pile of remains.

The most important thing, besides a very individualized selection of therapy and an elaborate plan of treatment that constantly adjusts for various necessities, is great care and extreme diligence. These clients come from parts of hell that we can't begin to imagine. Therapy must avoid any appearance of similarities to this hell. The therapy must be transparent, and the therapist's character must be transparent, including a willingness to let the client do as much as she can without abandoning her, but with a willingness also to become involved beyond the norm when appropriate. Much patience is necessary, but the effort is worth it for every single human being who entrusts herself to us.

There are at this point many things we can attempt. To me the most important thing is to be authentic yourself as a human being, and to continue to answer the accusations with friendliness in your attitude, without denying that some of those accusations hurt you, and without accepting lies as if they are true simply because the client believes them. Yes, it hurts, and yes, the client is important to you. The form of these gestures of goodwill can't take place imaginatively enough. Words are not adequate here. Words have been used wrongly too often; the client needs contact, actual human contact.

It's about contributing to making it possible for a human being to experience her world again with all her senses (or at all). A human being should be able to rely on her perceptive organism for orientation and should be able to structure her inner order in accordance with the surrounding reality beyond the parallel hidden world of abuse and torture.

In addition to all these aspects described there are naturally many technical details that are helpful in order to dissolve programs. These technical things only become important when the quality of the relationship has already been developed. It is worth knowing how the programs were created, since you can deduce from that what would also be necessary to dissolve them. From my point of view, for example, it appears to be good at this point to clarify whether you are dealing with a complex ritual or with a sequence of individual shorter sequences, and so on.

In my practice I find a thorough knowledge of program architecture helpful in order to understand how complex many entanglements look, and which programs are bound to which inner persons in which ways. In order to find that out, the therapist must first acquire expert knowledge about how these programs come into existence, and with which barbs (or booby traps) they are furnished. Finally, the therapist needs to take into consideration the varying types of inner persons involved when creating a complex plan of treatment.

As with other aspects of treatment, you may also be ambivalent about whether to be concerned with program architecture. I have tried to present my working model in its various aspects without implying that it is the only way to treat our clients. I don't believe that it would be advisable to prescribe specific interventions as gold standard and pamper vanity in such a complex area of therapy as treatment of dissociative disorders. What I hope for is that my deliberations will prove beneficial to other colleagues, that they will experience them as starting points or additional skills to aid their work, and where necessary they will provide a critique of my methods.

If you would like to help people to find a way to their own selves after such an abundance of abuse in which they were deceived, distorted, and confused, after so much agony and inexpressible torture, you may find it useful to keep these various perspectives in mind:

- The world of the perpetrators from the viewpoint of the perpetrator and from the viewpoint of the client
- The world of the therapist from the viewpoint of the perpetrator and from the viewpoint of the client
- The viewpoint of the therapist with regard to the world of the perpetrators
- The viewpoint of the therapist with regard to the inner world of the client
- The viewpoint of the inner world of the client with regard to the therapist
- The social reality of the perpetrators (their reputation in the external world)
- The social reality of the client (her position in the external world)
- The social reality of the psychotherapist.

There are a few things that are especially important for successful work with victims of extreme violence:

- Love for the human being and your own ability to form relationships
- Patience and time
- Carefulness and caution
- Imagination and creativity
- Profound professional expertise and clear plans for treatment
- The capacity for self-criticism and the willingness to learn from mistakes
- The capacity to hope under adverse conditions
- Humor, work on your own resilience, and mental hygiene
- And the courage to repeatedly embark on a journey, over and over again.

CHAPTER TEN

Truth, lies, deception, and fabrication

This chapter is about doubt. When confronted with stories of extremely monstrous and inhuman abuses which have until now been hidden, not only the false memory movement but also our clients themselves, as well as the courts and society in general, ask whether these things can actually be the truth. It is indeed possible that narcissistic and histrionic clients may well "adopt horror" in order to access longed-for care and attention. How can we distinguish one from the other? This topic is a chapter of its own because within the framework of therapy it is such a frequent theme with clients.

Various authors have said that dissociative clients, because of their great internal hardship and difficult feelings, invent stories of ritual abuse or other outlandish situations in order to make these feelings more understandable and tangible. How can we tell whether this is happening in any given case?

Hannes Fricke (2004) tells of an inmate who was bullied and neglected in an institution his whole life. Many emerging fragments of memory showed a huge amount of violence and events that could have been found in a concentration camp. As a grown man and author the boy has now told his life history as if the individual stories were from an experience in a concentration camp. In reality the author was verifiably never an inmate in a concentration camp. The events he was describing had been a mixture of the real experience in his own life and the experiences and circumstances in the concentration camps. He was surely aware of the fact that his story never happened in the way he was telling it. Some parts might have sounded very convincing because he had genuinely traumatizing experiences.

Many who can't believe that such a mechanism as dissociation really exists use such stories as proof that it is all just fabrication. This man's example demonstrates that it is possible to confabulate "facts" by putting fragmented memories into a familiar context (after the Second World War, reports about concentration camps weren't exactly scarce). In addition to details he actually remembered of "what" really happened to him, he added the "where," which was completely imagined.

This does not provide evidence for or against dissociation. But it does clearly show that dissociated fragments of experience are pre-served undistorted; the mistakes come via conscious attempts to clas-sify and order them. This is why it is so important during therapy never to suggest interpretations or to propose information. Even if in a cli-ent's memory it appears obvious that it's Father coming into the room, either his identity will appear as dissociated material sooner or later, or it won't.

When we classify memories or try to put them in order or make sense of them, it can happen that we succumb to deception. What happens to completely dissociated inner persons is entirely different. In their disso-ciated preservation of experiences they don't succumb to or create any deceptions. What is reported in dissociated conditions is precisely what was saved in their memories, as it was experienced by them. Under these conditions their credibility must be a given, as bizarre as it may appear. At worst, the facts could be furnished with deceptions inten-tionally introduced into the situation by the perpetrators (like a magic trick where you don't see how it was done, for example the illusion of pulling a rabbit out of a hat). The senses save the experience in a one-to-one correspondence with what happened. Generally the patient is also unaware of these facts in her conscious mind.

But here painstaking caution is again in order. When a client has an apparent memory emerging, what kind of material is it? Does she appear to be experiencing it directly, or is she merely describing it? Knowledge of something described, as for example in the case of Heidi

Kastner (*Väter als Täter am eigenen Kind* [*Fathers as Perpetrators*], 2011), doesn't come from dissociated experience, but rather from the imagination, in this case intensified by hypnotic suggestion. Knowledge that is merely suggested rather than lived remains bland, without any color or feelings, and lacks all the repercussions it would have in everyday life. This is not the same as dissociated material. We have to distinguish between normal hypnosis, which just makes use of the subconscious, and truly dissociated material, which emerges into consciousness, if at all, as bits and pieces, flawed, with a huge question mark. Normal hypnosis makes use of inner resources in the subconscious without having access blocked by censorship. In this way repressed or shameful or forgotten memories break loose and are accessible to consciousness. But memories that can emerge in that way have not been dissociated but repressed or forgotten. These memories are integrated and have previously been known consciously. Such memories were never dissociated, just not made a focus of attention.

To put it objectively, when another person such as a therapist suggests a supposedly dissociated experience that is hypothesized to explain a client's symptomatology, which tells the patient what happened without her first questioning the completely foreign knowledge that is being put into her consciousness—that is a deception, whether or not the suggestion is made to a hypnotized client.

An example of described "knowledge" is shown by the following case. A therapist suggests to a severely bulimic client while she is under hypnosis that the only possible explanation for the up-until-then unexplained bulimia she suffers from must be oral sexual abuse by her father. Under hypnotic conditions a picture comes into being in which the patient can be seen as she is penetrated orally by her father. She recognizes her father; she recognizes herself. It is just a small step to get her to envision this picture. If she can accept this picture without any doubts, then from a therapeutic standpoint you should consider reviewing her diagnosis in the areas of histrionic and/or narcissistic personality disorders. But emphatically not in the area of borderline—for generally these clients misjudge not reality, but rather the intentions behind the actions, and a borderline client would for example suspect that the care she receives was steered by evil motives or that her abuse actually had to be understood in the context of aid.

Let me be perfectly clear. As with every symptom or syndrome, the diagnoses of dissociative identity disorder or other trauma disorders are not immune to abuse. Here it is useful to ask regarding the diagnosis: *Cui bono* (who does it benefit)?

For example look at the sensational murder trial of Yvan Schneider (which the press called the "cement murder" because along with three accomplices he murdered someone and put the body parts in cement which they threw in a river). The main defendant, who was later diagnosed with antisocial personality disorder, decided (along with his lawyer) to pretend in court that he was mentally ill. He posed as a psychotic. Scuffling and stooped, in shackles, glaring at the family of the victim with hatred, he made a show in court. He tried to create the impression throughout the trial that he was a delusional schizophrenic. His behavior in jail at that time made it clear that he was not schizophrenic at all. It wasn't until two years later that he admitted officially that he was not suffering from such a mental illness. It is therefore nothing new in the context of court cases for such illnesses with advantages for the defendant (because they imply diminished capacity) to be simulated.

A famous example in which for these reasons a split personality was claimed is a well-known case of murder in the United States. The alleged murderer showed himself to two expert witnesses as a person who, like Dr. Jekyll and Mr. Hyde, switched from a good to an exclusively bad person, who was responsible for the murder. It was only the third expert witness who twigged what was going on. He suggested to the defendant that he was surprised that he was only divided into two personalities, as normally such disorders would result in at least a third personality. The prisoner then immediately produced a third personality, which in this particular case made clear that it was all a lie, and the murderer admitted he had made it up. He was diagnosed as having a personality disorder. But we can keep in mind that in other cases it might be true that a third part would exist, as splits often produce three parts: victim, survivor, and ignorant front person.

In this context of telling a story for your own advantage we also see lying in a dispute about child custody where one partner claims the other abused the child. If such a claim only emerges when it is to the advantage of one partner, it is wise to be cautious.

We also find out-and-out lies, even with understandable motives, coming from persons with narcissistic-histrionic disorders with a long history of neglect and being overlooked. After inpatient treatment they almost always wish for the same attention as those patients in the clinic with a dissociative diagnosis. The stories of the narcissistic patients make an impression through the fact that their supposed inner persons are mainly involved with trying to impress the therapist with incredible skills, special appearances, and remarkable character traits. Their stories are an accumulation of how they imagine things occur, especially in the area of Satanism. This is different from horrible stories victims tell us about real experiences with Satanists. I do not want to say that a story is not true just because there is so much violence. It is the way it is presented, just as stories that seem not to affect the life of the client at all. Generally they are about devils as supposed occult symbols, and bloodlust. Here it is also useful for the therapist to assess the client's motivation. A truly dissociative patient struggles with everyday life; she doesn't need this kind of attention and she will make sure not to (and not be able to) produce believable well-organized narratives about extreme violence.

There is no question that someone who adopts such disorders needs therapeutic help. But it doesn't help anyone for the therapist to get mixed up in this defective construction. Careful consideration of the client's motivation is necessary, recognizing that it may be an expression of great inner hardship, and that the client probably lacks the words for the genuine hardship or can't perceive it well. Getting mixed up in this story, however, means overlooking the patient's hardship yet again.

A client, herself a nurse, represented herself in this way as having multiple personalities. Unfortunately she did not understand the disorder very well. She presented herself as having forty talented inside people whom she knew by name, and as consciously knowing everything that had happened to her, while she did not present with any of the typical problems of dissociative clients. She had the impression (not incorrectly) that with such a disorder crises are frequent and therefore seeking help would be legitimate. It however wasn't part of her staged production to realize how difficult it is for patients who truly suffer from this disorder to ask for help. She therefore demanded extra time, sent dozens of faxes about appalling abuse and from the beginning presented an epic list of inner persons. This moved us so little that we finally exposed the whole thing. At first the client gave in and decided to set off on working on her great inner emptiness, the narcissistic disorder and her suffering from constantly being overlooked by her family (one sister had been very ill in need of constant care since birth). But she couldn't endure being this normal for long and presented us as a further cause for her crisis a suicide attempt by her sister that left her in a wheelchair. From the start of the interview she showed little distress about this supposed suicide attempt or its results, which made us realize that it was really about her rather than her sister. Only one day later we heard from another source that this sister, supposedly so seriously injured because of the reported suicide attempt, was seen walking on both legs while making bulk purchases. She had never made any suicide attempt and she was definitely not in a wheelchair. At this point we ended the treatment of the client, whom we at this point in time didn't regard as capable of engaging productively in therapy. This turned out to be accurate. Only a short time later she showed up once more, this time at one of our colleagues' offices, with the story of her multiple personalities. There is of course no question that anyone who behaves in this manner has great inner suffering—but it is not dissociative and this person very probably does not suffer from the claimed ailment.

A further form of expressing yourself is shown by the example of another client, Ms. Schmitz. She has a documented family history of being a victim of violence and neglect. Her father is an alcoholic; her mother abandoned the family. The client comes to me because her previous therapist says she can't deal with such dreadful things. Ms. Schmitz, the mother of two children, tells me, while sobbing uncontrollably, how she lost her best friend to cancer, and describes an extremely tearful final encounter at the airport. The story sounds definitely believable the way the client tells it (this is just a short summary), accompanied also by the respective emotions of being heartbroken. She says that she is upset because these feelings continue although enough time has passed.

We begin with working through the traumatic core she presents. Something very surprising occurs. The client wants to stop working through this—but without being especially overcome by feelings. She says the story "somehow does not work". A short time later I get a phone call saying, "If I tell you what I have done, you won't ever want to see me again. You will break off treatment." Finally the client describes how it was just impossible for her to talk about her genuine suffering and that was why she invented this story.

Ultimately it becomes clear that her genuine and her invented stories are similar in the immensity of the trauma. The genuine story is that when the client was nine years old she came home from school and found her mother leaving the house with a suitcase and no goodbye. "I'm leaving you with the old man—I'm going." Her mother never returned and the daughter had to stay with her alcoholic father. This genuine occurrence was later confirmed by a third party. This was a different kind of motive—not an out-and-out lie but rather a substitute for the actual source of suffering.

To summarize, we can see that whether a ritual act, an act of extreme violence, or sadistic torture took place can't be determined merely by the contents of the story. An important clue is the way in which the story is presented. Both of the above examples show clients who are aware that they aren't telling the truth. However, their motivations are quite different.

There is a common assumption that people who were subjected to ritual violence in particular are making up their stories, putting unbearable feelings into a context that explains them. We need to recognize that the emergence of fragments of dissociated experiences (as such, not narrative memories) or entire scenes *never* creates more peace of mind for a truly dissociative person—on the contrary it creates more agitation.

The consciousness has never seen these contents, and they may possibly involve people known to the client whom she has trusted up till this point. For all practical purposes she stands before the ruins of her life history; she has to restructure her relationships if the new information is true. She may have to break off contacts. She has to and will despair, and that will last for many years and will recur over and over again, as in this quote from a client: "There are those who know about event XY and that my father was involved—but I'm not one of them."

You notice the stories are put together with difficulty and hesitation, with many of the pieces missing, and that they are accompanied by great distress. What is absolutely essential to recognize in my opinion is that clients start therapy because many of the symptoms resulting from the abuse and from having multiple identities (that is, the inner splits) are no longer bearable. I know many clients who, after many years in therapy, still express doubts about whether the emerging fragments of experiences and scenes could be made up. In order to make them up the brain would have to make use of available knowledge. The areas of experience that I often encounter with my clients have absolutely not been set down in writing before. They contain specific details, often knowledge and actions that specifically identify a perpetrator, and they function within a programmed logic. For the clients themselves it is often absolutely frustrating. For example, five clients, independently of each other and without knowing each other, describe in different words a specific tool of a particular sadistic tormentor. And they all ask questions like "But that has to be crazy. Is there such a thing? Does anyone do that?" They give this description even though some of them immediately experience massive flashback pain.

Often, when working as an expert witness, the question comes up whether we can trust the material, when it appears that the patient is dissociating during questioning. Previously forensics answered these questions with "No". That is too bad, for under such circumstances survivors provide especially authentic material.

For this I would like to give a conclusive example. Ten years ago a woman told the therapist treating her about the violence she experienced as a child from her sadistic father. Now she has pressed charges against her father. The background, as with many similar court cases, was the fear that her father could abuse other children. For the woman herself, pressing charges didn't result in any advantage. If during the assessment by the expert witnesses very painful experiences were addressed, then the client viewed these experiences from a perspective as if she were sitting behind a glass partition. You could say that she dissociated during observation—due to the massive feelings that emerged. However this circumstance didn't change the accuracy of her descriptions.

Assuredly during the assessment she didn't have an undistorted perception of the assessment situation, and she therefore needed time in order to gather her thoughts and to report. But the derealization regarding the traumatic situation derived above all from the assessment situation rather than from the contents of the traumatic experiences. Those contents were saved in fragments and that was why such an effect was even possible.

Naturally a certain depersonalization is also involved. When a human being slips into a split experience, he then experiences things that aren't integrated. But pulled back into the assessment situation, he can talk about this dissociated experiencing. Naturally not as a simple narrative, because that's not how the information is saved in his brain.

Dissociation is the impossibility of assembling sensory impressions that belong together as a complete narrative and preserving this information in your memory. But precisely the lack of a connection and the preservation of impressions for future emergency situations ensure that the information is stored without being changed. You can't think about dissociated experiences and you don't think about them—therefore they are only accessible to changes when they reach your consciousness.

And because it gets questioned over and over again, let me repeat this statement one more time: Where there is trauma, there is dissociation—where there is dissociation, there is trauma. However, this is only valid when we truly understand trauma as being an objectively overwhelming situation for the human organism, when he has to take material he hasn't dealt with and store it as fragments far from consciousness.

For experiences that are truly horrible but for which it is necessary for survival to perceive the situation objectively, it can be helpful to split off and put away things like pain or fear but not the event itself. This also is dissociation.

In Amstetten, a city in Austria, a father kept his daughter imprisoned in the cellar of his house, without any daylight, for many years, and when she was rescued she had with her seven children (the results of her father's rapes). This trauma was definitely severe enough to create complete dissociation in a child. This young woman could not afford to dissociate the events completely (at least not long term) even if she was able, because otherwise the care and support of the children and their safety would have been in question. So she could split off only physical sensations such as pain, and some of her emotions but not all, as she had to be a caring mother to her children.

In a similar way this is also valid for survivors of concentration camps. They can often communicate events with verbal descriptions and drawings (the B of the BASK model). Later, feelings and physical memories are constant companions.

And this should also be mentioned here: Trauma and dissociation are concepts that are currently used as catchall categories, as were "schizophrenia" or the "borderline" syndrome previously. They are a kind of reservoir for all that can neither be understood nor justified. That can lead to our receiving requests for appointments from clients who state immediately that they desperately need trauma therapy because their previous therapy didn't help. And in everyday vocabulary a somewhat stressful experience gets described as: "That really traumatized me." This is not helpful. It leads to a good and useful concept being diluted, and makes the identification and treatment of genuine trauma disorders more difficult.

It does not happen by chance that some therapists have already spread the dogma that no traumatization requires stabilization, that exposure to the traumatic memories is possible from the very beginning, and that all trauma disorders can be treated within the framework of regulated allocations of a set number of sessions, and anything that takes longer is simply impossible to treat.

If I were a perpetrator, I would be laughing myself silly. If I worked for a health insurance company, I would rejoice in my extra profits. As a therapist for massively traumatized human beings, this makes me very bitter. Who gives people with a successful resumé and good living conditions the right to penalize those who are defenseless and without rights yet again? They have a difficult enough time already obtaining victim compensation. Often they "fall between the cracks". They can hardly make use of the courts because people can't evaluate their disorders adequately and generally leave that to the psychiatric assessors who are not trained for work with dissociative clients. If they are certified as having a dissociative traumatic disorder and if they are possibly dissociated in the assessment situation, then because of this their testimony in court will be considered invalid. After all they have suffered, to then take away their psychotherapy means doing these people an injustice yet one more time.

In our everyday concept of memory we assume that we remember things that much better the more impressive and dramatic they are. Often though, we lack the awareness that we have had to split off information that was too overwhelming in order to survive. Dissociation is a bigger thing than missing pictures and stories, that is, it is not just amnesia. I don't know any dissociative clients who at first didn't seem to suffer from completely different problems: a variety of physical disorders, compulsive behaviors, and so on. Proponents of the false memory theory claim that such people can't endure these symptoms and then, with the help of psychotherapists, piece together false memories. But the majority of my dissociative clients have downright begged me to give them a diagnosis of schizophrenia: they have tried meticulously to convince me that they are in fact crazy, or have asked me to say that they just made this stuff up because it couldn't be true. The situation is therefore exactly the opposite of what the false memory proponents describe. They would rather be diagnosed as schizophrenic than to have a disorder as a result of traumatic experiences, because the term "trauma" already says what it's truly about. You have this disorder because something happened—something you would prefer not to know about.

At this point I want to add that I neither reconstruct memories with clients nor do I participate in any therapy aimed at disclosing previously unknown events. I am not trained in hypnosis and will not take this training. And every day I make the effort once again to avoid attributing interpretations or meanings under any circumstances, but rather to be the objective chronicler and companion that my clients have earned. I could quote Picasso here and say "I don't seek; I find." But I don't invent. My "demand" for gruesome things was satisfied long ago, and I rejoice in every human being who was not subjected to gruesome violence and who was allowed to enjoy a childhood as a child. I believe in the goodness in my fellow human beings, up until the point where I am forced to acknowledge the opposite.

And I will allow myself one further comment. I have repeatedly heard of colleagues who publically make fun of people who talk about their inner persons or inner parts. Neither the commitment of those therapists who get involved with such fragmented systems nor the phenomenon itself deserves ridicule. I hope that I have made it clear by now that those therapists who truly involve themselves with highly dissociative clients have to talk to the inner persons because no other person and especially no rational adult front person is available at first, at least not constantly. Therapists who don't do this either have no such clients or are fooling themselves. Neither situation would seem to be something to be proud of. People whose fate never demanded of them that they survive extreme traumatization don't have the right to ridicule those who had no choice—or those who try to support them.

Here again we see the conceptual weakness of many critics. If you mistake dissociation for imagination, then you treat therapists who work with inner persons as if they were talking to the "Kitty" in Anne Frank's diary. We, however, talk to the split-off parts of a human being that contain split-off experiences that can help us understand what went on. These experiences can't be compared to invention in the outside world that was created by imagination for completely different reasons. And only in confrontation with the split-off knowledge are we able to discern the reality that we hope to integrate later.

This work is different from work with parts of people who might have had hard but not overwhelming experiences. In such cases, in dealing with problems and conflicts we can talk about "parts" when dealing with preferred patterns of reaction or behaviors in therapy. We can talk about the client's psyche as if there is a manager, or a vulnerable child, or an anxious part. This conceptualization just helps us to deal with ambiguity or to externalize different motivations and behavior. We invent those parts as a useful tool for therapy. But with dissociative disordered people these parts actually already exist as real entities, and are so enduring that on the one hand they can be seen when they emerge on a PET scan, and on the other hand they have specific impacts in everyday life, for example in varying reactions to medication, loss of time, and varying degrees of vision exhibited by different inner persons.

It's hard for many people to believe this, but there is a long way to go before the concept and reality of dissociation can be continuously recognized in the professional world of experts.

CHAPTER ELEVEN

Dissociation, imagination, and fantasy

ere the reader is invited to join me in neurobiological and epistemological speculation. What is the essence of dissociation? Which areas of the brain are affected and how much conscious activity of the human being can be expected at any one time? How conscious do you have to be in order to develop imagination, to be creative? My thoughts here are working models that should provide practical assistance, not ultimate truths about any topic.

I believe it is essential to use the term dissociation as a concept defined within strict limits. According to my understanding, dissociation means only and exclusively that contents that must not reach the consciousness level in order to ensure the survival of the organism also don't reach the consciousness level as a narrative. Many contents don't even reach the consciousness level as fragments. This explains how inner persons, even when they are created completely without active assistance from a perpetrator, aren't accessible to the main consciousness of the client, who is not even aware of them. The existence of these internal entities only makes itself known through consequences, such as time loss or body sensations—changes in the outside world. ("Why isn't my book where I left it?" "Why am I dressed in pink—I'm an adult and I hate pink.")

159

Note, however, that there may exist inner persons who "float" above the traumatic events and can give a perfect narrative, without believing that those events happened to them (Alison Miller, 2014). The front person (the main everyday consciousness) is unaware that this narrative exists. Some perpetrator groups deliberately create and train such parts as reporters, with the job of reporting any disloyalty to the abusers. Other such observer parts are self-created and can observe secrets of which the trained parts are unaware, such as hidden microphones. Perpetrators are aware of the existence of such "floaters" and try to capture and imprison them.

When authors claim that such internal entities arise from the imagination, from using make-believe, and that dissociation is a result of imagination, I have to disagree. Imagination is a conscious act. If a person is able to consciously develop healing beliefs that oppose certain problematic conditions, it does not mean that he is capable of creating fragmented memories. Our imagination can develop narratives, little healing stories that can condition us to think in new ways. Through imagination we can also breathe life into objects: holding onto a little seashell can calm us down effectively because we have learned to associate it with an imaginary inner safe place. Conscious repetition is necessary to make imagination work reliable.

Without a doubt imagination can be a healing process and can be spontaneous rather than planned. Dissociation, on the other hand, is an inherent survival mechanism. In my work as a therapist I have not discovered an inner person in any system who contained more than that which was necessary for survival—including the concepts of its identity, its behavior, its appearance, and its self-esteem. For example, only those inner persons for whom it would be important have a concept of the body. Others, for example, who don't feel any pain, also see themselves as having no body. For those inner persons other characteristics are more important.

As the research of Nijenhuis and colleagues (Reinders et al., 2012) also shows very clearly, there is a difference between imagination and dissociation. When an actor imagines and plays the role of a person with multiple personalities, completely different areas of his brain react to his invoking this imaginary reality than those areas that are activated when a dissociative patient switches or an inner person reacts to an external constellation of stimuli. Even the brain of an excellent actor who involves all his senses in his craft and truly feels what he plays reacts in different areas than the brain of a person reacting to external stimuli.

A further point shows the difference. A person who has imagined an inner helper, for example like Anne Frank, who called her diary Kitty, will never forget that she herself is the inventor of this reality. Similarly, we all willingly take on roles in everyday life, while being always aware that they are roles. For example we have learned to adapt to our professional roles successfully and to show appropriate behavior at work.

It is important to pay attention to this distinction. If it were the case that roles are part of the continuum of dissociation, less dissociated than ego states and even less dissociated than inner persons, then this would mean that the inner persons of dissociative people would be a creative invention of the clients themselves. But then how do we explain the fact that different inner persons have different skills that only they can use? We can devote ourselves to imagination, to fantasy, we can consciously surrender to it, we can drop ourselves into it—we can do such exercises when they happen to be necessary, and we can also decide not to do these exercises. But we can't just decide to speak a language we have no knowledge of and no memory of learning. However, one of my clients has an inner person who speaks fluent French. The client herself can't access this talent consciously at all. Other dissociative people have inner persons with special artistic talents that are not shared by their conscious front persons at all. Perhaps some inner persons also have imagination they can use, but they are nevertheless not created through imagination.

Imagination and dissociation are simply not the same thing. Imagination is an ability of consciousness, being able to think beyond your present reality. Dissociation is being forced to flee to the inside in order to survive. While the process of imagination allows conscious design and freedom, with dissociation there is absolutely no freedom to design. Some people (including, for example, Colin A. Ross in a personal communication in 2011) have described dissociation as a little girl imagining she is somewhere else while something bad is happening. Psychologist Alison Miller (2014) states that this is inaccurate; rather, dissociation is just never putting together overwhelming, life-threatening experiences in the first place.

Dissociation may appear to us who don't experience it as a creative lifetime achievement, a survival achievement of the organism. From the outside it seems so. It is a survival achievement, but it is not accomplished through creative imagination; it comes from necessity.

Maybe this is a stretch, but if automatic care of infants is made more probable by giving them cute childlike characteristics, perhaps the splitting off of child parts for survival is also a part of creation. If dissociation was just technical and did not involve a creation of inner persons, it would be much more difficult to accept them. Seeing parts as individuals, as children, perhaps makes acceptance of them, and thereby survival in this world, more probable. If the splits weren't formed this way (even if they were only formed to serve survival), how much more difficult would it be to accept these inner parts? We can use our imagination consciously to accept these parts, but not in order to create them. A threat to life is what creates them, or, rather, splits them off.

Imagination, fantasy, and make-believe are therefore just as much accomplishments of consciousness as are forgetting and suppressing shameful and guilt-ridden memories. You can only forget that which you once knew. Often we are aware that we knew something once, and we know that it is our shame or guilt that is blocking this knowledge. In order to suppress something, it has to have been previously accessible for evaluation and for the conscious mind.

There is no question that naturally inner persons, especially those on levels one and two, can possess even further creative abilities. But the mechanism of their splitting off as such is not creative in a real sense, even if they vary in shape and form. Human beings should not think that they know better than the way the natural world is designed. It is organized so that it does vary in shape and form but its shape and form always serve a purpose and are never superfluous. The hummingbird's beak that fits so perfectly into specific flowers, the diverse and intricate courtship dances of birds, and the sheer variety of color and form in nature, all make us think that they are creative accomplishments. Perhaps dividing our selves offers the most possibilities for survival and growth, for evolution. The greater the possibilities and varieties of adaptation, the better the chances of survival.

Whether some creator enjoyed making nature so multicolored and varied, or whether it is just our imagination that lets us experience the world as formed so imaginatively, has to remain open for discussion.

However, one basic principle remains. Nature, including human nature, is concerned with survival of the species. Probably it isn't completely absurd to assume that the things that we experience as being attractive incline us towards a healthy diet, good relationships, safety, procreation and thereby the survival of our species.

CHAPTER TWELVE

Power and powerlessness

This central topic in the public eye and on the internal stage needs to be clarified once again from a social perspective. From the viewpoint of the therapist, changes at many social levels are necessary in order to dismantle the societal structures that make the shadow world of organized violence powerful and that maintain this power. I agree with Salvador Minuchin (personal communication, 1994) that intervention on many varied levels is necessary and that therapists should definitely become involved in social activism for the benefit of their clients.

Traumatization to the degree described is only possible if the tormentors are in positions of power in both worlds, simultaneously ensuring that their victims remain permanently powerless. The more powerful people are on this side of the world, the more influential they are in all-important areas of society. It's about power in a double sense: real power and the power of decision-making and defining reality. For the perpetrator network to function smoothly, it has to be assured that pivotal positions in the wider community are occupied by people who will keep the secrets.

The system of the parallel world is a system of mutual dependency. "I know about you; you know about me." Anyone who becomes conspicuous, for example through alcoholism or through uncontrolled behavior in public, ends up either becoming the "fall guy" or having open season declared on him. He will become the person at whom everyone can point a finger, of whom it is said publicly that everyone knew that something wasn't right about him. The group shows how much power it has, and how much influence in so many places. So you had better not try to say no, to get out, or to tell any outsider about the things that happen in darkness. No one would now dare to be a state witness against a member of this group, whose leaders always appear honorable. A member in such a position, starting to drink or attempting to leave the group because he can no longer stand what happens, can only hope that the evidence against him isn't sufficient for a conviction.

And so, just as we are dealing with a system of mutual favor in the parallel world, this is also the situation on this side of the world. Years ago, for example, it was no secret that anyone who wanted to be successful as a politician in the German state of Baden-Württemberg would fail without the support and acceptance of a certain politician. No one was surprised when politicians who openly opposed him couldn't get anywhere in politics. Candidates openly admitted that they didn't like this person but knew they could only have a career with his help. You could, however, also decide against a political career in favor of your own values. It is a personal decision.

The impressive career of district attorney Vogt from Leipzig shows that there are also people in important positions who have earned our support. He made a name for himself through targeted and successful prosecution in the area of child pornography. At the end of 2009 he resigned from this position. He admitted publicly that he couldn't stand dealing with the fact that he was forced to return computers to the accused without examining them, and that after a year and a half he failed to obtain successful criminal convictions because he had too few qualified and honest people working for him. He didn't want himself to be used as a "fig leaf" to cover up the abuses and so he went public with his complaints.

Did this do any good? It is always better if society believes that law enforcement is able to adequately prosecute criminals and that victims of violence will receive justice. Why should the right to get your property back (the computers) outweigh the right of criminal prosecution in such an area? Why is property more important than the right to your own body, the right to protection from violence? What would it cost to give the accused other computers while theirs were being examined?

Questions, and more questions. One answer given in criminal law is centered on the determination of guilt or innocence of the alleged perpetrator. Justice must be done to the accused and his guilt must be evaluated appropriately, which means that a certain timeframe must not be exceeded. However, as valuable as this legal requirement is, it is questionable whether we are able to fulfill it, with the number of law enforcement staff available, in such a way that it isn't one-sided—to the disadvantage of the victim. Whoever has the power can arrange things—with all the advantages and disadvantages for the alleged perpetrator and the victim.

In politics we like to talk about the "heirs apparent" of a certain politician, and precisely the same phenomenon is valid in the parallel world. A British TV show dealing with the upbringing of daughters of aristocrats in Great Britain made the point that these daughters would later have the option of marrying into the best houses. The show, "Ladies for Gentlemen", demonstrated how these young women learned to grow into a compliant and custom-made role that had to be in accordance with the needs of their future husbands. No one asked whether this was what these women wanted or valued; the only question was what was expected of them.

Meanwhile, the sons (and generally it is the sons) and heirs apparent in abuser groups in the parallel world learn which fundamental structures underlie power, how power is exercised, and over whom it is exercised. They learn to equate their power with being in the right and to feel nothing but contempt for the powerless. They learn which methods and instruments make victims compliant, and they themselves learn, depending on the status in the group into which they are expected to grow, how to program—or how to use existing programs. They all learn to torture and to torment, and they learn that there are no limits for them—at least none as far as the suffering of victims is concerned. In the parallel world they learn early that above all, children and women are the natural victims of violence and they learn to ignore others' pain and fear, or to experience it as increasing their pleasure.

The lack of a sense of guilt in the parallel world is widespread. A colleague told me in confidence about a major customer, himself a professor in the area of social work, who wasn't ashamed to brag about a brutal rape in a disgusting fashion in a bar, where even a nearby drunk moved away from him.

Within perpetrator groups in the parallel world there are definitely preferred professions for male candidates: medicine, psychology, law, politics, religion, economics. There are good reasons for this. Such a group would never exist for any length of time if it didn't have members in important positions. For the development of such programs, you need more than basic intelligence (for using such programs, you of course need less), and you also need a constant fresh supply of victims in order to hold on to such positions in the parallel world. In some cases we have found that a person's standing in the parallel world helps him to obtain and keep important positions in the "normal" world. Medical knowledge has many advantages, among which can be excellent knowledge of hypnosis, which is used extensively in mind control. In addition, many tortures require the assistance of a doctor because of the well-known brutality of the torturer. If necessary doctors can make sure that victims are resuscitated or otherwise taken care of through insider medical treatment. Beyond that there is also the possibility of getting medical equipment and drugs more easily, including narcotics and other pain medication. And it's also handy when, for example, academics who are perpetrators have contacts with students, especially female students, in order to recruit a fresh supply of victims or to make the necessary "readjustments" to those already programmed.

There is no lack of experts who will confirm that a patient has always made ridiculous claims or has tried to commit suicide or suffers from schizophrenia. Psychiatric expertise means that they can also use medication or electroconvulsive therapy to silence the patient.

Such experts are also needed to participate in the commissions who set standards. They can be experts in diagnosis (if there is no such thing as dissociative identity disorder, then there is no such thing as the violence that results in it). They can be experts in therapeutic treatment who can decide, for example, to only allow a method of treatment that benefits certain clinical pictures but not others. They can be experts who contribute to standardizing certain methods, or experts who determine guidelines and procedures and standards for treatment, and the right to psychotherapy. Such experts can have a say as to whether extremely traumatized clients have a right to therapy or whether these clients are defined as untreatable.

In the health professions there are other bottom lines. Who determines the standards by which social workers, psychologists, and childcare workers are educated, and whether they are trained to recognize or not recognize risks? Who is responsible for the entire range of recognized procedures and the lack of available trauma therapy in this field? Or the regulation and restriction of admission to treatment via the health insurance companies, or the return of biological psychiatry? All these things disadvantage people who have already been given a raw deal in life.

The legal realm holds the power to determine believability, which is only demanded of witnesses, not of perpetrators. This is a huge field of major possibilities for intervention by perpetrator groups. If it is determined that a dissociative patient is not believable when giving testimony, then with one stroke of the pen all people with dissociative disorders, that is all victims of extreme violence, are defined as incapable of testifying. This is even more useful than accusing them of lying. Here it is easy to simply determine that the dissociated witness probably believes that she is telling the truth, but since unfortunately she is not able to tell her story consistently, she is disqualified as a witness. Therefore the dissociative human being who talks believably about what he has suffered cannot be a competent witness because he cannot report in a constant, consistent manner. And if he can report clearly, then he isn't believable because after such experiences, it isn't possible to report them in this way.

Of course I also want to state here that naturally not everyone who supports such rules and ideas is a violent perpetrator. But he serves the interests of such tormentors to a vast extent. It is important to remain aware of this. We need to be clear how far the perpetrators' power can extend.

If we look at the area of politics, it's clear that rules can be found for many areas of society. But in the same way, rules can be blocked or demanded by lobbyists. Is anyone surprised that each new government fails at reforming a healthcare system to make it deserve the name, that restructuring a welfare system always burdens the poor the most, and that the redistribution of wealth once again functions to transfer it from the bottom to the top? A welfare recipient can't threaten his government by claiming he will move his main residence out of the country if his needs aren't met! We have a bailout safety net for banks—where is the safety net for victims of extreme violence? Who advocates for them, and who helps them stand up for their rights, other than a few caring citizens?

It is an open secret that there are people in high positions who are willing to pay, no matter what it costs, to take advantage of opportunities to torture human beings sadistically. Not only in my practice are there reports about certain people and their procedures, which are never put into writing but which demonstrate how perpetrators always behave the same way and always display the same preferences and tools of the trade. And here neither the claim that the therapist suggested things to or manipulated the patient, nor the claim that the patient is one of those people who always cried ritualized suffering (or who just made it up) in order to explain her otherwise inexplicable symptoms is valid. As if there were a single explanation for every human being's symptoms!

Politics also defines the legal scope of who gives whom the right to punish and in what way. Politics defines the legal foundation and the amount of leeway that every judge has at his disposal. It defines the requirements for pressing charges, and the focus—whether criminal law centers on the criminal, on the question of guilt or innocence, on the sufferings of the victim, or on protection for society. Political agendas, along with expert witnesses, even define who is allowed to testify, what constitutes evidence, and what is allowed as evidence. In politics it is the lawyers and judges who are the authorities with respect to the rules in the legal arena. This is how the German law for preventive detention after a sentence has been served, and the North American dangerous offender designation, came about.

Lawyers determine how they defend the accused, and how they use the margin of discretion that a judge has at his disposal. They decide how long a trial may last and which witnesses are called. District attorneys decide about whether and when preliminary investigations are opened. Do not forget that it is always advantageous for a perpetrator to have friends in certain circles. If inopportune pieces of evidence emerge, it is useful to find that out so that you can arrange for evidence to be destroyed. If you have the appropriate contacts, you can naturally also try to influence the question of the particular crime for which the accused is being tried. There is a fundamental difference between being tried for supposedly harmless abuse or for crimes against humanity.

Doctors within the framework of psychiatry and jurisprudence have opportunities to decide about freedom or imprisonment for a human being. They can decide to set him free (because he has been healed, or because he has served long enough), or in the case of Mr. Klar, a member of the Red Army Faction (popularly known as the Baader-Meinhof Group) in Germany, to keep him in prison. And here it is legitimate to ask why a shoplifter who resists arrest stays in jail and probably gets a jail sentence as well as probation, whereas a man proven to have sexually abused his daughter, who even fathered a child with her, can continue to force visitation rights so that he can have contact with this child/grandchild.

Politics and the economy are also intertwined. Both are powerful, both need each other, and both inevitably influence each other. Wherever there is power, it can be used for the benefit of all or it can be abused.

The economy, especially the financial economy, defines living conditions not only in Europe but worldwide. This is the only way to explain how the industrialized countries can make so many rules for the poorer countries. The reverse is unthinkable. And naturally this is how it also works in Germany where I live, according to a cynical revision of the Golden Rule: He who has the gold, rules. Many politicians and business leaders set shameless examples with their displays of wealth, legitimizing greed and overtly wielding the power that comes with affluence.

As administrators of public ethics and morality, we have the representatives of religion, the churches, and church dignitaries. We all shudder when we discover that for a long time the Catholic church had slush funds for the purpose of paying hush money to victims of abuse without doing anything to change the deplorable situation. At best, the clergy who committed this abuse were merely transferred after undertaking "treatment" programs. Misconduct among the ranks has been treated leniently, this leniency being rarely extended to parishioners.

Observe with what contempt the use of condoms in Africa for preventing AIDS, or abortion in cases of true hardship, is met, and note the double standard being applied. There is one procedure for the powerful and a different one for the powerless. The church, whether Catholic or Protestant, has great influence and it offers something that is otherwise hard to acquire. If we publicly pledge ourselves to the church, if we make sure we are seen in church, then this is more or less proof of our ethical conduct. But we should not forget that the conduct of many church dignitaries during the Third Reich can hardly be described as "ethical", and that the so-called "ratlines" were a way for Nazis and war criminals to flee Germany at the end of the Second World War under the smokescreen of the church.

It doesn't hurt to have allies in key positions in child protective services, institutions, and other inspection authorities. If a victim seeks protection here and wrongly believes herself to be safe, then she can find herself paying a high and painful price for this error. Not yet mentioned but also of great importance are teachers. They are often in the key positions where behavior becomes noticeable. If they belong to the "club", this simplifies a lot of things. Sometimes it seems as if it doesn't matter whether public or private schools are involved. I have reports of various named perpetrators from both sectors. When it comes to paying financial compensation to victim of violence, it can happen that victims just don't encounter people who are well disposed to them. One victim recognized one of her tormentors working in such a position.

I speak about this so explicitly not with the aim of casting a slur on any particular profession *per se*, but to emphasize that in these positions there is power—and whoever has access to these positions can exercise power. How he does that depends on his own inner attitude and his socialization. It's a question of which values are important and with which people and goals he sees himself connected. No one is compelled to remain faithful to a group's goals, not even if he was socialized into such a group as an adult—no Nazi in a high position had to fear anything more than an end to his promotions if he said "No". Even in those circles it was possible to get out, you could even get out and just keep your mouth shut—and forego your participation in further torture. When you find yourself in the situation of being in a powerful position on both sides of the world, in contrast to the victims you don't have to expect to be disposed of, you just have to forgo some advantages.

That you can even act courageously in these circles without any disadvantage to yourself is shown by the protest of the director of the mental institutions in Wilhelmdorf. When he was ordered to register the names of the mentally ill in the institutions, Heinrich Hermann didn't just let the deadline go by, he sent back the blank forms with the following commentary on 6 August 1940:

> Being told to register the wards of the institution forces me to make the following assessment. I know the purpose of this planned economic compilation. I know about the many death notices which the families of many patients at sanatoriums and mental hospitals

in the state of Württemberg have received in the past months. **My conscience won't let me keep quiet or go along** [author's emphasis]. I know very well that we're supposed to "be subservient to the authorities, who have power over you". Therefore I have also completed the yellow form. But now I can't continue. I simply have the conviction that the authorities are doing a great wrong by killing certain ill people (...) God says: "I require it, and of the hand of man and of the hand of every man's brother, will I require the life of man so that he which sheddeth man's blood, shall have his blood shed by man again: for God made man after his own likeness." (...) With killing (...) we act against God's will. That is why I cannot participate in this. I am sorry, but I must obey God more than man. (Faltin, 2008)

If we look again at the chapter about inner views of a sadistic world (Chapter Five), then we recognize that Dr. Zehn is at home everywhere. His professional career brings him into contact with leaders of the economy, with the jet set, and with politicians at the highest level—and because they know each other in both worlds, he can enjoy all the privileges and advantages of power. He can use doctors to have his daughter diagnosed according to his wishes, and psychologists to lead her to a therapy that he finds suitable. If he wants to have suitable facilities (such as a torture chamber) built for his special purposes, he knows the proper construction tycoons for such work; if he needs a permit for things that cannot be permitted, he knows ways to get this done. For the victim there is no escape.

Whereas perpetrators choose to behave differently (play different roles) depending on whether they meet their friends in public or private places, victims can only survive through splitting themselves off. The tormentors don't have to split anything off because they are at peace with themselves, on both sides of the world. The perpetrators I am talking about in this chapter are integrated, here and there, whereas their victims are split up on both sides of the world and within themselves. Both here and there they have no place for themselves and no consistent identity.

When they see one of their torturers, for example, on TV receiving an important award, when they are "allowed" to travel with him when he receives such recognition, knowing too well what will happen afterwards, they find it hard to bear.

Victims remain powerless on both sides of the world. At the beginning of their history of suffering they are powerless because they are children and unable to escape the sphere of influence of their tormentors. Inside the parallel world these tormentors determine the rules just as they do in the so-called normal world.

In order merely to survive, a child learns not to know anything about the hidden world in everyday life in public, and to make herself at fault for things that can't be explained. What becomes public works in one of two ways. Either no one notices the child's distress, or an empathic teacher or childcare worker recognizes it and turns to the supposedly well-meaning parents, because she can't see beyond their façade of respectability and honor. If someone in authority approaches the parents, they make sure that the child's mistake that led to this never occurs again.

By the time the child is able to talk, her basic level of dissociation is complete. She functions in each of her worlds at the push of a button. She doesn't consciously know about the parallel world, and she experiences the "normal" world only in bits and pieces, but is unaware of the missing time. Absence in the external world is explained (depending on the case and age of the victim) by visits to family, sickness, use of drugs, bad friends, and poor parenting. Skipping school and running away complete the external picture of the child. It is hardly to be expected that any teacher will become particularly fond of this child. The child will either go through school in a streamlined, inconspicuous manner, or will appear rebellious with a behavior problem. She will find herself shriveling into a permanently subservient mode or she will alternate between subservience and defense.

In the external world the survivor demonstrates mood swings that result from having different dissociated personalities who deal with everyday life. It's a short distance from this point to receiving a diagnosis of various mental illnesses. As a result she's a long way from making any kind of friends or maintaining stable relationships. If it isn't clear who you are, if who you are isn't sufficiently stable, everything in life is problematic. This instability makes it difficult to maintain a continuous interest in educational or recreational activities, or have the ability to persevere with them successfully. In addition there may be various physical limitations that some of the inner parts have while others don't. This prevents sensible medical diagnoses. Since the person has no access to the origins of the disorders, she has no way to adequately communicate them. Just like those around her, the person herself thinks she must be crazy.

No one is present who represents a divergent opinion and mindset. No one makes corrections and no one helps. So the victims in the parallel world of torture are speechless and compliant, and in public they aren't capable of making use of any resources. They lack knowledge about what has happened to them. They often lack permission (and the punishment for disobedience is terrible) to seek out clinics or well-meaning doctors, and the thought of seeing one leads to panic-stricken fear that can't be overcome. If it is possible for a victim to overcome these fears, the result is more abuse, with terrible injuries, which does even more to prevent the next visit to a neutral helper. No wonder that therapists are also on the list of people that the client has no right to consult.

If she nevertheless does take such a step, she is subjected to multiple threats that don't fail to have the desired effect. Sometimes the therapist gives up, sometimes the client, and sometimes both. If the client manages to get into a stable therapy, and if the worst complications are somewhat controllable, then she faces a seemingly insurmountable mountain of traumatic experiences, which lead her to despair and to wonder whether it will ever be possible to work through them in a way that allows her to have a little bit of life left.

Often therapy is the first stable, benevolent human contact for her, and that is far too little to make her life satisfying. With all these abuse experiences behind her, the client experiences herself as socially unattractive, too chronically distressed to easily connect with her partner if she has one, and therefore socially isolated.

If she acquires resources, for example finishes high school and goes to college, then she will have to make much more of an effort than others. She can't apply for financial aid because then her relatives would find out where she is and she would again be in danger. She will have to work her way through college. She will get less sleep than others, but will have to work harder than others, and she will ask herself over and over again whether it is worth it.

She won't have many days without pain and flashbacks and won't have many nights that don't trouble her with bad dreams. And at the end of her journey she will say that she already lost so much time as a child which no one can return to her, and that she now has to spend a great deal of time in therapy, just to limit the degree of permanent damage.

She will have to come up with a lot of imagination in order to take further steps in life and to regain lost ground. Along the way she will ask herself over and over again whether it is worth it, and she will repeatedly experience suicide attempts and suicidal thoughts.

If she is lucky and finds an understanding and stable therapy situation, if she is lucky and has friends or even a partner to support her on this path, then she will—because none of these clients lacks intelligence—slowly reach a place where she is a person in her own right. At the end of the journey she will have gained an ability to speak, control over her bodily functions, an ability to satisfy her needs according to her own feelings, and the integration of the most important inner parts.

And at the end, that will allow her to live with a relative measure of freedom and her own decision-making powers—no longer directed by the will of sadistic people. She will still have to work harder than other people in order to experience any quality of life. She will always have to tend to internal cooperation and inner dealings. Over and over again she will have to acquire trust in others, in herself, and in the world of possibilities. Every single day, she will have to work at recognizing that she has a right to her life; the old convictions will still have so much power over her.

When it becomes clear to you that these clients come from a world in which the perpetrators truly dictated everything—thoughts, feelings shown, actions taken at the push of a button, refusal to satisfy basic needs (eating only when and as much as the tormentor allows, drinking when he allows, going to the bathroom when he allows, no speaking, no screaming, or screaming and crying at the push of a button, no relationships, no caring, no protection, no connections with other people) up to and including the decision over life or death—then this apparently small victory, achieved with much time and effort, is actually a huge one.

This victory rectifies something important: the basic human rights of every human being. I have rights! For many that is inseparably bound with an enormously important step: Only when I can recognize that all human beings have basic inalienable rights, and that I am a human being like everyone else, can I perhaps say that I have a right to my own life, with no ifs, ands, or buts, and without any additional accomplishments on my part. Only when I have reached this point have I really understood that those things that were done to me were wrong.

Something else is also apparent at this point: the extreme powerlessness of those affected. The power of the tormentor who controlled her wasn't restricted to one single aspect of life, but instead included everything imaginable: What she learned, where she went, whom she had contact with—nothing was left out.

Figure 17 illustrates the quality of human needs with different situational goals. Two situations can be described based on this drawing.

In situation one, the tormentors dictate all areas of life. There is no room for the victim's own decisions. The tormentors have 100 percent of the power over their own lives in all areas and almost 100 percent power over the life of the victim.[1]

The three rings can be symbolized with hula hoop rings on the floor, one after another. The client starts in the smallest ring and the therapist stand behind the biggest ring, stretching out a hand to help if needed.

The therapist can encourage the client to find out how it feels to stand in each of the different rings and to discover that she is able to move from one ring to another. Often victims of mind control have initial difficulties realizing they can stand somewhere other than in the smallest ring, "survival". They are overwhelmed by fear and anxiety in the other rings. You can describe for each client her own individual issues for each of the three rings and what she wants to change.

Situation two presupposes a maximally successful therapy, in which we would assume that both inner circles of the victim's control over herself are 100 percent accessible and a quality of life of at least forty percent can be achieved. At the same time we have to bear in mind

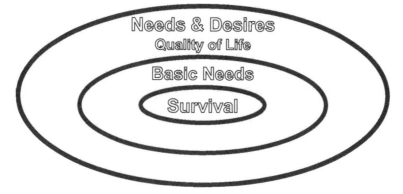

Figure 17. Quality of human needs.

Figure 18. Invitation.

that this goal is restricted by the permanent damage, the losses that can never be compensated. A good quality of life would then include entering a relationship in which she can perceive her own body as something other than an enemy and a source of constant pain, have a sense of identity, and an extensive integration of inner persons that allows her to control her own life and pursue her own professional and personal goals.

If we consider these two situations, then it becomes clear that at the beginning the situation between the perpetrators and victim is maximally imbalanced. If we observe the situation after longer-lasting successful therapy work, there is still a clear imbalance. However, and it is important to understand this, we can do much more than just resign ourselves to something. We can begin by changing a little at a time in order to get the scales to gradually shift more and more in the direction of greater justice with respect to power and powerlessness.

The power–powerlessness situation between tormentor and victim is the same on both sides of the world, because the tormentors possess power and influence on the visible side of the world but also have the means of being significantly instrumental in creating rules and in exclusively dictating the definitions of rules and rights within the parallel world.

This splits the victim in various ways. On the side of the parallel world there are all the inner parts desired by the perpetrator, and within these inner parts yet another split takes place. The more extreme the programming is, the more inner parts are trained to mistrust and keep away from the other parts. Then there is not only distrust directed outward but also distrust among the inner parts themselves—a huge obstacle to integration. Much also separates these clients from the visible world. For the most part they have never experienced the accepted rules for other people there. They aren't familiar with them, or they know that they must not apply these rules to themselves. Here, too, a split goes through the entire person. There are inner parts that can function on the outside, in chosen areas and professions that were designated acceptable by the perpetrators, and there are inner parts that make sure that they abandon this incomprehensible and from their point of view false world again as quickly as possible, whenever they see that another inner part comes into contact with this world. Again, the client experiences herself as not integrated, but instead split apart. What one inner part wants, the others don't, or aren't allowed to—in any case it is difficult to speak of "wanting" where the person has no identity, no goals of her own, and no coordination between her inner parts. Surviving used to mean splitting herself apart, and that is what happened in many different ways.

The power on the side of the perpetrator consists of being maximally powerful in both fields, of making the rules in the external world and in the internal world and having the power to enforce these rules. As a result, equipped with all the rights and no bad conscience at all, the perpetrators experience themselves as "lords" of the world (a minority of perpetrators are women), in the same position in both worlds. They are optimally adjusted to both of their living environments, which they shape themselves; the victims are split to fit into these living environments.

If the "lords" in this world and in the parallel word have only an inflated ego, then the victims don't even retain a tiny ego. It is important to know that there are also inner parts of our clients that experience themselves as being weak, that submit and that can't imagine that anything will ever change, as well as inner parts that feel strong and who have contempt for weakness, who believe themselves to be in solidarity with the perpetrators or with their value systems. Consequently the topic of power and powerlessness becomes an internal psychological topic for therapy. Power and right, who rules over whom, and with what right—who makes the rules today? The power structure in the supposedly democratic world influences the way we see the world and how we are able to act in this world, as well as influencing the way inner structures are created. If you grow up with a concept that gives certain rights to certain groups in society, you will not question that in the inner world. For everyone outside, it is unquestionable that the law is applied fairly and that bad people are put in prison.

And here is what we dare not overlook. We are talking about perpetrators who have *genuine* power in both worlds and for a long time also in the inner worlds of our clients. That has consequences in therapy sessions, but also outside therapy. The tormentors do not simply wait when we treat our clients; instead, as far as it is possible for them, they use their power to deflect potential security risks (Figure 19 on next page). And it is not just those providing the treatments who are endangered but also, if they haven't carefully, step by step, established very sustainable safety nets, our clients' lives are endangered from without as well as from within.

Behind these people who seek their "enjoyment" in this way, there is much power and money, both of which they are willing to deploy. That means that we won't get anywhere with a mentality that would prefer to go out into the field alone as one lone fighter against a well-organized, well-resourced army. On the other hand we need the courage and wisdom not to let ourselves be maneuvered into a completely powerless situation. Do something, yes, but not mindlessly, because there is a danger also for therapists. Whoever leans too far out of the window unsecured can easily fall down. It is easy to ruin someone's reputation and much more difficult to free him from evil insinuations. These perpetrator circles always have the power to ruin a livelihood. It's up to us therapists to behave in such a way that this ability becomes less feasible.

It's about making the strategies of the perpetrators fail and about making it possible for people to live a life of human dignity and with less human suffering than they had before. To this purpose we cannot and must not restrict ourselves exclusively to the realm of therapy, but need to direct all our efforts toward creating public awareness of

Figure 19. Balance of power.

these survivors and the wrong that was done to them and still exists among us. And as therapists we must make use of honest people in powerful positions. We need lawyers and doctors with whom we can cooperate, district attorneys and judges who are interested in this problem, organizations that help victims, the staff of child protection services, politicians, police officers, and more. To put it simply, it's about opposing the network of the indecent with a network of decency and human rights.

CHAPTER THIRTEEN

The language of violence

There is a language of violence within the inner world of our clients, as a result of a language of violence used in the world of violence where they grew up. But there is also a language of violence far beyond this narrow sphere, in the public eye, visible and respected. Language defines reality and language is power. It is the intention of this chapter to try to sensitize people to this fact and to set this perspective in relation to organized violence.

> "Understanding being nothing else than conception caused by speech." (Hobbes)
>
> "If language is not correct, then what is said is not what is meant; if what is said is not what is meant, then what must be done remains undone; if this remains undone, morals and art will deteriorate; if justice goes astray, the people will stand about in helpless confusion. Hence there must be no arbitrariness in what is said. This matters above everything." (Confucius)

In the analysis of the suffering of many of my clients, it has become clear to me, over and over again, what a central role language plays. Language defines reality, describes distinctions. Language can offer orientation or it can confuse. Language can authentically describe actual situations, and it can hide intentions. Language can be forbidden or it can get lost, so that inner persons lose their capacity to speak. Language can make communication and contacts possible. It can define obstacles within and without. An example familiar to us all is the Tower of Babel. It worked until God stopped its construction by confusing the tongues of the builders (making them speak with different languages), and the project failed.

Things function in a similar way in the parallel world. Having different groups of inner persons speak different languages isn't coincidence and isn't just to satisfy a worldwide customer base. It is deliberately designed to make inner communication impossible. For instance, it is common (at least in Europe) that inner parts exist who speak perfect French whereas the client herself doesn't. In such a case, there are only a few inner parts fluent in two or more languages, which then makes translation among the inner parts for the purpose of communication and coordination at the very least more difficult. And of course it takes much more time. There are often very many inner parts who have to make themselves understood somehow or other and, as often reported, don't share the same ideas, moral concepts, and so on, which means that their differences derive from more than the fact that they do not speak the same language. It is advantageous if therapists are fluent in many languages. But here you have to be careful: Some words or phrases are connected directly to programs and make them run or turn them on or off. It's worth examining things cautiously and proceeding on an individual case-by-case basis.

A further language is the language of rituals. Many of the rituals of torture and the staging of such events are derived from rituals of the church, passages from the Bible, Greek mythology, sagas of heroes and gods, fairy tales, movies, and the like. It is helpful to understand the reference. A simple example would be if a therapist encountered an inner part who believed himself to be one of the four horsemen of the Apocalypse, it would be reasonable to assume that there are three more of them. When passages from the Bible are used, I almost have to assume that they stand for important things in the parallel world such as the devil in the form of a snake. Many tormentors are well educated in the humanities (despite their lack of humanity) and are fluent in many foreign languages. In Europe, at least, you should always assume that this is the case.

Now, the last person who knew everything lived a few centuries before our time, and we therapists cannot become specialists in all fields.

But we can learn to make use of other specialists and their knowledge in order to serve our clients. That saves suffering and time.

A further step in the world of violence is poisoning language. It isn't a product of individual imagination when a programmed girl lets us know that her rape was called *love*, and experiencing that was the most wonderful day in her life. In these groups many words are poisoned, and they mean absolutely the opposite of what they mean in normal life. That means for therapy at many points we need paraphrases and new wordings in order to use language that does not have a toxic meaning. Many words have been forbidden, or their use leads to punishment in the internal and external worlds. It is not a coincidence that these are words that therapists often like to use.

Language defines the environment we live in. Language is what we use when we define reality. For many abused clients language is used to lead to a reversal of reality. In the parallel world they are told that they are nobodies, without rights, unworthy of any respect. The injustice and torture done to them is denied, and instead it is labeled as right and simply the proper order of things. In the other world they feel guilty for being unable to manage their lives, and blame themselves for not overcoming their experiences. If they remember violence and neglect, they assume that they have deserved it. The victims are blamed in the parallel world, and blame themselves (and often are blamed by others) in the ordinary world.

The White Ring (*Weißer Ring*, an organization dedicated to helping victims of crimes) used this phenomenon for a series of posters. One showed a five-year-old girl with the caption "This whore seduced her uncle."

For many of our clients this is the reality in which they grew up. They were told, "When you were born, a light flashed which means that you wanted to be with us in the group." Beginning on the day of their birth they were forced to "learn" to do certain unwanted things and then after carrying them out they were told, "You wanted it." Or after failing some tasks they were told, "This is the proof that there is still evil in you" and then they were punished. Everything is logically consistent.

It is not a surprise that perpetrators claim to the child that they (I am deliberately not describing the method here) have the special ability to look into her soul and have seen that the childlike soul is black and depraved. And if the perpetrators didn't look into her soul, there is still original sin as an explanation to show she is evil. And this provides another opportunity for the most terrible torture under the smokescreen of love and the pretense of assistance so that this terrible child can eventually become good.

Then there are a number of so-called prayers that she has to learn, which structure the balance of power over and over again in the same way. She has to use titles that emphasize the power of the torturers. They are borrowed from the visible world: generals, masters, emperors, kings, and so on. The only thing that's important is that these are powerful terms that appear to have legal authority, showing her that she can't get away and that she has to submit. She is told that objects or places associated with the abuse are alive (the teddy will watch and report everything, walls have ears), and they instruct the child that objects, places, and people have a hidden meaning, combined with the group. So looking at the teddy will make you know that you are always watched, and looking at a red rose tells you to keep silent, and so on. This guarantees that once set in language (under conditions of torture and a threat to life) the messages will be cemented over and over again every time these people, things, or places are encountered. The saying that evil is always and everywhere becomes a certainty for the victim, because those who are powerful in the shadow world are just as powerful on the visible side of the world, and the language of power isn't all that different on both sides. If the ceremony of Holy Communion is abused, every correctly performed Christian ceremony will cement the training of the shadow world.

Therefore it's also not surprising that all ordinary life rituals that are expressed in language, such as prayers, create huge problems for our clients. The holy days and the feast days all have a completely different meaning in the shadow world. For example, on the visible side of the world, a birthday has a positive meaning. On this side of the world we celebrate the fact that it is joyful that someone was born: "It's great that you exist." On the shadow side of the world it means: "You were born as my possession, for my enjoyment, and without any rights. You live because I allow you to live, not because you deserve it. And on every birthday you will pay once again."

Victims pay a lot. Many of them are born on cult or group holidays (often due to medical "assistance"). In Germany we had a holiday on 17 June, in remembrance of the national uprising of 17 June 1953. When in 1989 the wall between East and West Germany was destroyed and Germany was united again, the government abolished this official celebration day and instead celebrated the day of German reunification on 3 October. A client's birthday was deliberately dated 17 June, a day that was celebrated with a lot of violence and pain. This gave the perpetrator group another opportunity to punish the victim, though not of course to release her from her sufferings. When this day lost its meaning as an official celebration day, the cult blamed her for this and began torturing her on both this date and 3 October. One might have expected that if such a day loses its meaning it will bring better times, but this never happens on that side of the world.

In chess there is a saying: "White begins—black wins." On this shadow side of the world you would have to change it to: "Black begins—black wins."

Language is also used to turn everything upside down over and over again. If the child is brought into a specific state (that is, a specific inner person is brought out) for the purpose of torture, they might say to this inner person, "You came out because you wanted to be rewarded" (implying that the torture is pleasurable). Or after a child is made to commit a horrible act, she is punished again because "this shows what you are like. And you're lucky we accept you; there's nowhere else that would take you." Children who are horrified by their "crimes" and horrified because they believe they are evil have no option other than to internalize these teachings.

A further reason for children to internalize the abusers' words is that they are assigned the task of repeating them word-for-word with the correct pitch and emphasis. This makes them more credible later when they have to speak the words. Words are also used in staged events. If you are proclaimed guilty within a staged court hearing, and as a result later have to host inner judges (deliberately created inner persons) who repeat this verdict over and over again, you can hardly expect to be able to shake off the guilt and to evaluate the world without the assumption of "I am guilty".

Words can do even more. They convey a mindset. If they are used together with actions, gestures, and facial expressions, they appear to give a consistent (and therefore true) message. A perpetrator threatens to kill a victim during a simple rape if she doesn't say the words that he tells her to say, words that insult and humiliate the victim as she begs to be tortured and abused. How then can she experience it other than "I wanted it," especially when it happens often? If the victim does not pay enough tribute every time to the "reality" conveyed via language, or if her subservience is not one hundred percent successful, she can be punished in any of a number of ways, including extreme pain, near-death experiences and great guilt over the suffering of others for which she is made responsible. She has to "learn" quickly.

The use of language for self-expression is reserved for the powerful. The child, however, must remain silent, must scream when the customers want her to, must smile, must flirt, must engage in conversation when commanded to, and must express total availability, also in language. The child generally doesn't have suitable words for what is happening to her, because no one has given her the language to name the wrongs done to her. Since she has no rights, what is done to her can't be wrong. It's that simple. Hans Christian Andersen used this phrase for much simpler situations: "Whatever father does is always right." Here, it is: "If someone powerful says something, then the truth of it doesn't matter; it is valid because it comes from him."

The child also has no right to express her suffering, to speak, or to communicate—she bears the guilt of her very survival. And if she believes her tormentors, then she was already guilty as soon as she was born, guilty because she is alive, and that justifies every act of violence committed against her. The child is a possession, at the mercy of others and without any rights. If it's convenient, then the child will be declared a powerful authority who forced the poor tormentor into this situation. In my own work and also in the work of linguists, for example, we find the same pattern in the behavior of the perpetrators: Violence is rationalized by blaming it on the actions or the existence of the victim.

The self-proclaimed therapist and former missionary Bert Hellinger began in the early 1990s to travel around promoting an approach called "family constellation work". In Germany he was helped by famous promoters who owned their own publishing house (Carl Auer Verlag), and as a result he and his followers produced a huge quantity of CDs, DVDs, and books to provide his answers to almost every question. He adapted techniques such as David Kantor's family sculpture, based on the ideas of the founder of psychodrama, Jacob Levy Moreno, without crediting the originators (Künzler, Böttcher, Hartmann, & Nussbaum, 2010). He held huge meetings with 500–600 people in the audience, including physicians and psychotherapists, and promised easy resolution through speaking so-called "healing sentences" for even severe somatic illnesses such as cancer. He was acclaimed as a healing guru, and his books are now published in approximately 20 languages.

Hellinger's approach to incest is to see a girl victim as compensating for her mother's withdrawal from the sexual relationship with her husband, so that the girl is a hidden perpetrator. The damage to the family will be resolved if the daughter confesses to both mother and father that she engaged in the incest for her mother's sake. Hellinger also states that rape and incest create a bond, and the victim must give the perpetrator "due respect" before she can bond with anyone else. He has similar controversial and victim-blaming approaches to such things as cancer.

From the very beginning, it was shocking for me, my colleague, and many other therapists dealing with victims of severe violence to see that somebody whose work involved in our eyes blaming victims and humiliating women could be celebrated as a psychotherapy guru. How could well-educated doctors, psychotherapists, and other professional helpers believe this is healing?

Truth sometimes appears simple: It is easier to trust the lies of the perpetrators, than the truth of the tortured victim. It is a matter of who has the power, of whether you have courage, and, last but not least, whether you are willing to risk social and professional ostracism for not going the easy way. Famous therapists and parents cannot be wrong, and only children and clients are unwilling or unwise.

If someone doesn't heal as a result of Hellinger's approach, it means they are not willing to heal. Well, it's really resistant not to heal, if the way to healing is to obey someone who tells you to kneel in front of your abuser and tell him: "Father, I thank you for your love." Citing Hellinger (Hilgers, 2001) in a case of cancer: "Now it is time to kneel in front of the father, to bow—but the client is not able to do so. He prefers to die." To me this means that if you do not pay your parents this compliment anyway, you will have to die (of cancer for example). And if you don't forgive your torturers or pray for them, you are ungrateful. "No one can flee his fate" (Hellinger, quoted in Studentischer Sprecherrat der Universität München, 2005). The victim's fate is to be a victim, and to want to live a normal life is not right.

The false memory movement started with a lot of money and publicity, and so did Hellinger. It seems that for many people it is more attractive to side with the ones in power. Maybe this is what is happening for some of his followers, because being on the side of power you can avoid being a victim yourself. If victims are guilty, you don't want to be a victim.

Maybe we shouldn't even be surprised that it was only after public opinion slowly started turning against him that many of Hellinger's longtime professional companions started to separate themselves from him. Eventually it became impossible to sugarcoat his moving into Hitler's old chancery offices. (It wasn't until 2004 that this became public knowledge.) In 1995 my colleague and I published works rejecting Hellinger, before it was "in" to do so. We stated clearly our own horror at how few in the field were appalled by Hellinger's position. How can someone glorify tormentors and support them with his pronouncements? We felt that no one was watching what he was doing. It is interesting to see, if you follow Andrew Vachss on his website *Merkt Euch Ihre Namen* [Keep their names in mind], that Hellinger's followers now use the prescribed terminology that should enable them to separate themselves from him: "I work differently—or not quite so dogmatically."

It's even more interesting that not only clueless and poorly educated people followed Mr. Hellinger but also doctors, psychologists, and other trained therapists. And naturally I ask myself as a therapist: Was it not possible to recognize the inhumanity of his attitude through the language used in his supposedly healing sentences? Was it really so difficult to discover that a self-chosen healer who claims visionary qualities for himself is being unethical when he thinks it's wrong for the therapist to position herself on the side of the victim, and instead insists that she must dignify the suffering of the perpetrator, that these tormentors are the true victims? Remember the poster with the five-year-old "whore"? We live in a society that is loyal to power, that finds it difficult to bat for victims. If this were different, then the White Ring wouldn't need to stage campaigns like the one against the ostrich with its head in the sand syndrome. ("Stop the ostrich with its head in the sand syndrome" was a poster campaign against turning a blind eye to things.) It takes courage to say "Stop!" and courage to admit publicly that you were mistaken about something.

I'm still eagerly waiting for the human being who can admit: "I committed myself to the wrong thing. I wronged people. I behaved horribly and should have known better. I am guilty."

Linguistic confusion is useful to support perpetrators. I can't count the number of times clients have reported to me that they had to apologize for their wrongdoings and had to take responsibility in trials in the hidden world. The stronger person is right; the loser is guilty. Ignoring the context, as described previously, of course actively supports this. Here I am quoting Hellinger (2001): "Only when the last Jew has spoken the Kaddish [prayer for the dead] for Hitler ... can the world take a turn for the better." [translated for this edition]. To me this gives the message that the Jews have to apologize to Hitler! And that people should just accept their fate, even the fate of being born into certain families.

Hellinger (1995) states that "Parenthood is independent of morality and beyond good and evil [whoever here reads Nietzsche and his superman with special rights into this isn't that far wrong] and therefore parenthood must not be looked at in terms of good and evil. Every judgment of parents is presumed to be right. Parents cannot be judged. They are always right." [translated for this edition]. Then you don't need to be surprised why a client whose parents tried to murder her many times asks herself seriously whether she can just simply forgive. Let it be understood that this is without even a hint of regret or apology from the perpetrators—simply because victims must forgive. "You must not carry a grudge!"

"Parents don't need to honor their children, but the reverse is true." You got it. No wonder that Hellinger also has fitting sentences for the perpetrator down pat: "An unbelievable intensity of love that flowed between father and daughter" and another sentence for the victim to use: "I thank you for your love. I was glad to do it for you." Or he has a woman say to a rapist (to a proxy in a line-up): "I used you, and I'm sorry."

Finally—and I quote Hellinger because then I don't have to quote the perpetrators who abused my victim clients, as their text barely differs—Hellinger suggests that the victim should bow before the tormentor and the therapist should place himself on the side of the perpetrator, who after all is just a victim of entanglements. Sex, it is also clear for Hellinger, takes priority over love. If sexual acts occur, no matter how early in life, a bond arises, and the experience is then just a little premature, not wrong.

And in this respect Hellinger with his oppressor mentality, his sentences and rituals, is a source for therapists to help them understand how the tormentors think. Contempt for weakness, elevation of power, irresponsibility, and smugness—it is all in the spirit of Aleister Crowley's direction to "do what thou wilt" (Crowley, 1977).

Language is therefore involved in many ways with the horror that befalls our clients. Precisely for this reason is it very important for therapists to use language that doesn't send our clients back to the chambers of horror from which they come. This implies also that the language of violence and elaboration of revenge fantasies are not helpful.

Much well-meaning language can be triggering. Much religious language has been turned upside down and used for abuse, thereby losing its positive meaning. Many clients can no longer find any God to whom they can address their hopes. Sometimes they are able to tell us that even if we use words that are not poisoned, in their minds they hear the exact opposite of these words.

This is also a part of their training, an almost Babel-like confusion of language: Good is bad, black is white. For every meaning there is at least a second meaning. What appears to be an invoice can be a legal document, apparently innocent colors and symbols in a card or an email can be demands for actions, and on it goes, almost without end. Whoever has the power of definition and the power to enforce it can force others to see and hear things their way.

And for therapy sessions this means we are never alone with our clients. On the contrary, many others within each client listen and speak, and they have different realities and different linguistic truths. Realizing and taking account of this is a fundamental condition for successful treatment.

CHAPTER FOURTEEN

Differences that make a difference

What relevant modifications can be made for the practice of treatment? Here I summarize and give an overview of the different kinds of adjustments to therapy described in the previous chapters.

Anthropologist Gregory Bateson (2002) stated: "Information is the difference that makes a difference." From the viewpoint of information theory, everything else is random noise.

In this book I have tried to illustrate the areas in which, according to my view, variations can be made that can be useful for therapy. Here I want to list them one more time as a summary.

Seven different structures of dissociation

I elaborated distinctions within the BASK model and illustrated these with a cube to help further understanding. Chapters One to Three are concerned with this working model.

Three different primary areas of the brain

In Chapters Seven and Eight I described the characteristics of the cerebrum, the midbrain, and the brain stem with respect to the inner persons/inner parts, and the implications of these distinctions for therapy.

Three different system levels

In Chapters One to Three and again in Chapter Eight I described the different levels of the inner system. These levels determine the distance to the inner core of the person, the distance to his consciousness and the degree of external control by the abusers he experiences.

The different sensory systems

Inner persons can differ from each other with respect to their capabilities for using their senses. Many chapters address dissociative people's "blind spots" or complete blackouts of functions of perception and their substitution by perpetrators with trained beliefs.

Inner maps

Different inner maps exist from the view of the client's conscious mind (and therefore how many inner persons she can perceive and how she perceives them), from the view of the therapist, and from the view of the individual inner persons. Generally inner persons who are localized further back in the mind (or deeper in the unconscious), can see inner persons at the front levels, but those at the front can hardly ever perceive those further back. Whoever is localized on system level three may possibly see an inner person on system levels one and two, but they don't see anything on level three. Inner maps can also describe the membership of various inner persons to internal groups and make various functions of the inner persons clear.

Functions

Inner persons can differ in the functions that they carry out and the degree of freedom they have in perception and presentation of the function.

Technical aspects

Programs and conditioning differ in the triggers that they install, in the sequences and the progression with which they were implemented, and in the rituals, symbols, languages, tools, etc. they use. Technical aspects demand somewhat technical solutions to reverse what was done.

Differences among inner persons

These are numerous and include:

- important distinctions in the internal and external worlds that contribute to their world view: criteria they can use to know what is important and what is not, what belongs to what, and what is extra
- concept of self, perception that they share the body with multiple selves
- activated survival systems (for relationships, defense, etc.)
- age, gender
- cognitive, emotional and relationship capabilities
- resources, preferences, interests, functions, competences
- degree of restriction of each sensory system
- ideas, value systems
- languages spoken or understood
- loyalty to the tormentor(s)
- degree of freedom to choose their behavior
- relationship to the therapist
- ability to reflect, flexibility
- capacity, and need, for spirituality.

And naturally also the groups in which the people were tortured have differences between them. For example, the child trained by Dr. Zehn's group for international use would contain within her inner parts for dealing with child pornography, brutal sadism, and various cult variants (for example, satanism.) And this daughter would, if programmed for all this, also contain torturers, self-destroyers, etc. within herself. Here it is worth looking at the technical details of programming, the perpetrator group, the structure that might be useful for the group to implant in the client, and so on, as they tell us something about what we might find within the client and what help she might need in order to change it.

General aspects

This listing does not lay claim to completeness but it does what I said at the beginning of the book: It describes a pathway to solutions. From this pathway we can create individual plans for healing. Our clients must then shape them specifically according to their needs. Therapists can be traveling companions and sometimes mountain guides in apparently impassable terrain. It is always the responsibility of the client to define a place suitable for her in the newly conquered reality. We are trying to develop helpful modifications to therapy to create a different reality for our clients. Especially with respect to programming and conditioning, this simple principle is valid: While the paths designed by the abusers point to "always this way" and "always the same" with respect to the client's behavior or beliefs, it is the job of the therapist to develop new detours, ways out, and secondary roads. It's about contrasting the world of forced inhumanity and violence with a world of loving, creative solutions, a world where space is provided to grow. On the basis of a cherished and sustainable therapeutic relationship, the client receives an invitation to develop a new curiosity about the world of humanity.

CHAPTER FIFTEEN

Prospects—so much is missing

Despite all these encounters with victims of extreme violence I am still generally an optimistic person. I am absolutely convinced, and the revolution we had in East Germany backs me up on this, that you can get things moving from the bottom up, that small strokes fell big oaks, and that while perpetrators of extreme violence can be found in decision-making bodies, they aren't the only ones. There is always cause for hope. Just recently a judge in a state court was heard saying that as a result of the false memory debates there was now hysteria about the power of suggestion.

There is a long way to go, simply because society isn't focused on this form of violence. The guidelines of health insurance companies do not provide for treatment of such experiences. Research on trauma has continued to grow after its initial intensive years, but research on violence is still in its infancy.

The possibility of receiving compensation for damages, the opportunity to press charges against the perpetrator, the possibility of protection such as changing your name or preventing release of your personal information, the classification of such crimes as crimes against humanity—these are all unavailable at present for these clients. The question of who is capable of testifying is just as unresolved as the question of evaluation of trustworthiness in witnesses regarding such crimes. Specialized therapies are lacking, as well as therapists, doctors with knowledge about dissociative clinical pictures, specialized clinics for these clients, and shelters, as well as material resources, appropriate medication, and safe rooms to where clients can retreat in emergencies.

Secure places for clients to live, protection for clients who are trying to flee their situations, and so much more—it is all lacking. We can see this situation as cause for despair or as a starting point for defining the tasks in which we as individuals must productively engage ourselves. This gives us space for creativity.

If we can succeed in making the burden smaller, step by step, then the balloon of hope can rise higher and higher in the sky.

Discover the possibilities.

Figure 20. Hot air balloon.

GLOSSARY

Adjustment disorder

A pathological reaction to an event, with which people can normally deal, because of a special sensitivity or pre-existing deficit.

Alarm programs

Emergency programs of the organism, which are automatically called on in the case of emergency, life-threatening stimulus constellations or those experienced as such. At first they increase activity in order to make fight or flight possible. If neither is possible, the freeze response sets in, and the play-dead reflex materializes.

Amygdala

An almond-shaped mass, part of the limbic system, located deep and centrally within the temporal lobes of the brain in complex vertebrates, including humans. It evaluates stimuli upon their arrival with respect to their emotional importance for the organism. Unimportant stimuli are ignored. Life-threatening stimuli activate alarm reactions.

ANP = apparently normal personality

The part of the personality that is in evidence most of the time, strives for normal life, and phobically avoids reminders of traumatic experience. ANPs often manifest a range of negative dissociative symptoms. The very emotional experience inherent to trauma is split off, and the personality that shows itself as the ANP appears whole but is actually incomplete.

Antisocial (or dissocial) personality disorder

A personality disorder in which the person deliberately hurts other people and is completely heartless and detached from the suffering of other people (antisocial).

Attachment system

One of the two systems of motivation for survival that are described as fundamental by attachment researchers. Only when secure attachment relationships exist can a child turn to exploring the world. If the attachment is shattered, the child stops any kind of exploration and tries to re-establish the attachment to obtain safety.

Body memory

Memories at the body level exist in the form of pain or other physical sensations belonging to earlier situations. For the body it feels as if the previous event is happening now (for example when a survivor feels a knife at her throat or the heat of a fire).

Borderline

Borderline personality disorder: in the narrow sense of the word a personality disorder characterized by fierce mood swings. Borderline clients have a huge dread of intimacy. Their relationships function more like an oscillating pendulum. These clients can often appear quite functional but have a defense program that can be activated very easily. Rage for them occurs much too often and too violently. Expressing sadness is often difficult for them. There is discussion about whether "borderline" could possibly also be understood as a complex trauma disorder.

Borders of fear

There is a normal realm of experience in which people show fear appropriate to the situation. Fear can get out of control in both directions. Either an actually non-threatening stimulus can provoke feelings of fear, or a life-threatening situation can exceed the biological limits of fear. Fear can then no longer function as a useful warning mechanism that helps to avoid something, and all that is left is fleeing inwards.

Classical conditioning

Simultaneous presentation of stimuli leads ultimately to their being linked so that the reaction to an originally neutral stimulus (e.g., the sound of a bell) is now the same as it was to an unconditioned stimulus (food). Pavlov always offered a dog food at the same time that a bell rang. Finally the dog started salivating as soon as it heard the bell.

Codes

Symbolic language, or a system of symbols or characters that have certain meanings.

Cognitive restructuring

Restructuring of thought patterns. Changes in the basic assumptions about one's own self, the surrounding world, and other people.

Compensatory trauma pattern

The idea or scheme developed by a human being after a traumatic experience regarding how to avoid re-victimization.

Conditioning by deliberate training

In contrast to conditioning through experiences whereby the organism develops habits of behavior through repetition, like Pavlov's dog, this designation shows that conditioning is not a product of coincidence but instead occurs intentionally, planned and implemented by human beings.

Contain

To keep or preserve internally, sometimes to keep away from consciousness, to preserve in such a way that prevents the existence of a conscious, enduring, recurrent recollection.

Contextualization

The context defines the framework of meaning in which something is found. Without a description of the context, the meaning of "being naked" is neither appropriate nor inappropriate. If we add the information of being in a bathtub or being on a bus, then it is quickly obvious that the condition has to be evaluated differently. Within the framework of organized violence, often the original context of an action gets suppressed and a new context distorts the meaning of the action.

Coping strategies

Strategies for solving problems and minimizing stress.

Cult

A group that provides an ideological or pseudo-religious framework for the abuse of its victims, often in connection with satanic sects and rituals. A cult doesn't necessarily have to be satanic. The principal aspect is the repetition of rituals that reinforce secrecy and members' sense of belonging, usually on particular cult holidays.

DDNOS—dissociative disorder, not otherwise specified

Dissociative disorder in which the individual, separate splits already also have qualities of personality. According to Nijenhuis's classification there is only one ANP (apparently normal personality) but many EPs (emotional personalities).

Deconditioning

Dissolution of conditioning.

Deprogramming

Disabling a programme.

DESNOS—disorder of extreme stress, not otherwise specified

Clinical picture involving primarily functional and physical complaints rather than dissociative characteristics of the personality. There are more likely to be fragments of trauma memories split off from everyday consciousness. DESNOS includes both complex and event-specific trauma disorders.

DIS-client

A client with dissociative identity disorder.

Dissociative barriers

Internal divisions that can separate individual dissociative experiences from each other, above all keeping the dissociatively stored information away from everyday consciousness.

Dissociative identity disorder

According to Nijenhuis's description, a split in identity that possesses at least two, but can also possess more, apparently normal personalities, and also more emotional personalities than would be seen with a client suffering from DDNOS.

Ego states

In this book I use the term for ego conditions of which the person is either aware or which she can discover through introspection, even if she isn't able to maneuver them consciously and doesn't know how they came into existence. They are states that one person can experience consciously as parts of herself.

EP—emotional personality

The emotional, split-off information from a traumatic event. Depending on the configuration and complexity, it can also develop a personality.

Episodic memory

A category of long-term memory that stores our complete experiences of specific events, situations and experiences: your vacation, your sports activities, your arguments, and so on. From this important system memory storage we develop our sense of identity, who we are.

Externalizing

Presentation of an inner process as if it were external. Instead of letting himself be characterized as a thief, for example, a child who has stolen something learns to get a "little thieving devil" under control. Something on the inside becomes symbolized on the outside, and this expands the person's ability to change the behavior or emotions.

False memory

Concept invented by the false memory syndrome foundation, which then named itself after the phrase. Insists on characterizing the process of dissociation as insignificant and extremely rare. It is a movement founded by people in the USA who were accused of sexual abuse. It tries to provide proof that memories that arise out of dissociation are something patients imagine or their therapists suggest. The False Memory Syndrome Foundation also invented the concept of pseudo-memories.

Family board

A wooden board with various figures, animals, and so on, that allow scenes to be created showing inner processes and an inner map.

Fragmented memories

Split-off memories in parts that are no longer accessible as a complete narrative. Experiences are divided into individual parts, and various qualities of experience are not at all integrated.

Hippocampus

Part of the brain primarily responsible for the first spatial-temporal orientation during information processing. Broadly speaking this part of the brain makes sure that during the further processing of information neither the "when did it happen" nor the "where did it happen" is lost. If we know the time, we can place experiences and genuine memories in a temporal framework rather than thinking they are happening in the present moment. The hippocampus acts as a memory indexer by sending memories to the appropriate part of the cerebral cortex for long-term memory and retrieving them when necessary. It connects emotions and senses to the "story" aspect of memory.

In the public eye (the external stage)

The external reality, as opposed to the internal stage that contains the image of an inner reality. This means that, for example, because of the sadistic father in the outside world, on the inner stage a terrified child has arisen and possibly an inner part which simulates the sadism of the father. Imaginative work with the inner parts takes place on the inner stage.

Inner parts

The most neutral designation for speaking about various split-off parts of a person. You can also speak of inner parts existing within healthy, non-split-apart persons. Identification of parts is also helpful in order to construct a complete identity that consists of more than just fury or psychosis. In my book I have also used the word "inner parts" when I wanted to make it clear that not all the inner splits were really inner persons with a personality and a life of their own, but sometimes merely fragments.

Inner person

Designation for an inner split that develops a kind of personality.

Inner stage

Imaginative work with the inner reality and the inner experiences of the client.

Inner system

The structure of the inner reality of the split-off fragments and inner persons, the system.

Invalidation

In this case the primary attachment figure's devaluation of a child's own feelings, perceptions, and so on, as false.

Inverse

Reverse.

Janet, Pierre

Over a hundred years ago he described for the first time in great detail the symptoms that we today recognize as dissociative symptoms. There is nothing to add to his brilliant explanations. Nonetheless for eighty years clinical representations of PTSD and dissociation were absent from diagnostic manuals.

Limit of adaptation

The threshold at which an event overburdens our normal ability to adjust. Rather than reacting pathologically, we then have to dissociate, splitting off from the event. Overwhelming experiences, for example severe trauma, cross this threshold.

Live acts

"Customers" of sadistic violence are offered the chance to not only watch films but also to torture a victim in real time or to be present at her torture.

Man-made disaster

Violence by human beings towards human beings.

Mental efficiency

The capability for goal-directed, planned actions, for effective, thoughtful experimental actions, and for implementing complex plans effectively. Mental efficiency allows us to solve problems and to adjust plans according to our own skills and abilities. This requires a large degree of flexibility in our ways of thinking. People who are extremely split have less mental efficiency and energy in completing their actions because the mental energy and efficiency of their total system is not available to them.

Mind control

A focused kind of brainwashing that attempts to take control over many parts of a person's consciousness and make him controllable through external commands. Through infliction of pain, administration of drugs, and use of hypnosis, inner parts are deliberately created. It was originally developed within the framework of military research with the goal of creating spies who wouldn't have conscious knowledge of things and therefore couldn't be forced to reveal them under torture. MK Ultra was such a project in the USA and included many subprojects. Today perpetrators in the realm of organized violence make deliberate use of this knowledge for their own purposes.

Modulated on (superimposed upon)

Designation for a condition or a thought that doesn't originate from the self of the client, but was produced by an outside influence, deliberately set upon an existing structure or brain process (for example the alarm system or a mode of defense).

Narrative

A story that can be told completely, and in the correct chronological context. All elements are present: what happened, when, who was there, what it means for me, how I evaluate it, which feelings and which sensory perceptions are connected with it. Genuine narratives can be localized in space and time. We know what feelings we had in that situation, but no longer experience them in the present.

Phase model for trauma treatment

Before treating a pathological core there has to be a stabilization phase after which the person can confront the trauma, which then through integration of the various aspects of the traumatic experience can find its closure. For all practical purposes with complex trauma disorders we have a succession of many pathological cores that have to be dealt with.

Reality

Rather than there being a single reality, the experience of reality is a construct, and with respect to fundamental premises we have to agree among ourselves as to what should be valid. Things in the cultural space like boundaries and rules, meanings and meaningful distinctions have to be negotiated over and over again, even in a close relationship. Humberto Maturana said: "Explanations take place in the praxis of living of the observer, and they are experiences also. Yet explanations as experiences are second-order experiences in the sense that they are reflections of the observer in his or her praxis of living in language about his or her praxis of living. In this context, reality is not an experience, it is an argument in an explanation. In other words, reality arises as an explanatory proposition of our experience of operational coherences in our daily and technical life as we live our daily and technical life. Yet, in these circumstances, reality can arise as an explanatory argument or proposition of one kind or another according to whether the observer accepts or rejects the question about the biological origin of his or her properties as such." (see www.univie.ac.at/constructivism/papers/maturana/88-reality.html)

Skills

Proficiencies. Concept from dialectic behavior therapy (DBT) for treatment of borderline disorders. Participants are taught to develop various skills, in particular for regulating strong emotions that get out of control and become difficult to endure. These skills are an alternative to destructive methods of changing emotional states such as self-mutilation.

Structural coupling

In the context of neurobiology Humberto Maturana helped us look at human beings as structurally determined creatures. The human being has to connect with his surroundings—both structures (person and surroundings) affect each other—which changes each structure. It is the same with connecting to other people. With respect to therapy, this means that people are connected to and affected by each other in a relationship, and that the offer for the best possible connection for the client has to come from the therapist.

Systemic constellations versus family systems sculptures

Systemic constellations is a term used for a kind of role playing originally developed by Virginia Satir (2004), in which the client seeks out representatives for herself and her family, whom she then positions with respect to each other according to particular issues. It is a type of psychodrama that uses representatives to allow the client to depict concrete representations of both desired and actual conditions in her family. Satir and others practiced it in a respectful dialogue with clients. Hellinger (2010) adopted the basic idea of using substitutes for different important roles in the family or in a conflict, but did not mention at all that this was not his invention. The underlying system of values is very different between Satir and Hellinger. Since Hellinger has become so famous, many people use the term "systemic constellation" to refer to any role-playing work with representatives, unaware that Hellinger's contribution is not the method itself, but the way it is used, with "healing sentences" and other additions of Hellinger's. So I would prefer to only use the term "systemic constellation work" if I am referring to practicing Hellinger's own method.

Systems of motivation

According to attachment research, human development is governed by two central systems of motivation: the system of attachment and the system of curiosity. The system of attachment is of such central importance that only after secure relationships are present is it possible for people to confront the outside world.

Time loss

Designation for the result of an abrupt change among different inner persons. When person A starts watching a film, and after the first five minutes person B pushes itself to the forefront (and A moves to the back), and person A only comes to the forefront again at the end of the film (that is, the things happen in her consciousness), then person A experiences a time loss. Something must have happened in between, but she doesn't know anything about it.

Treatment setting

General conditions required for therapy work, and the designation for various constellations in which treatment can take place (individually, couples, family).

Trigger

Cue that sets into motion the inner parts with stored traumatic experiences.

Working model

Designation indicating that this is not a scholarly, proven model or concept, but instead a helpful invention for practical work.

Yes, yes, yes pattern

Fundamental description of how perception is constructed along the lines of what comes before; a mechanism sometimes used by therapists and hypnotherapists to make a yes answer more likely. For instance, answer the following questions: What color is snow? What color is paper? What does the cow drink? Many people answer the last question automatically with "milk".

NOTES

Chapter One

1. I have chosen the designation "so-called" advisedly. Some results of studies, when examined more closely, turn out to be mere claims, others consist of inadmissible generalities and transferring results of studies of everyday psychological feats of memory to traumatized human beings.
2. By levels of the system I mean the depth structure of the dissociation. That means, on the one hand, its distance to the consciousness of the client and on the other hand the distance to the core of its essence. For practical reasons I call them system levels one, two, and three.

Chapter Two

1. Research on attachment assumes two fundamental systems of attachment: attachment and curiosity. Attachment is so primary that if it is damaged, curiosity isn't possible; therefore there is no learning in the good sense and no discovering the world. Thus no unique individual view of the world develops.

Chapter Twelve

1. Almost 100 percent takes into account the circumstance that it was previously not possible for someone to control another human being 100 percent in all his inner parts—almost 100 percent has however absolutely happened.

REFERENCES

Agar, H. (1943). *A time for greatness*. London: Eyre & Spottiswoode.

Améry, J. (2008). *Hand an Sich Legen. Diskurs über den Freitod.* Stuttgart: Klett-Cotta.

Andersen, H. C. (2013). *Sämtliche Märchen.* Coburg: Artemis & Winkler.

Bateson, G. (2002). *Mind and Nature: A Necessary Unit (Advances in Systems Theory, Complexity, and the Human Sciences).* New York: Hampton Press.

Bock, T., Buck, D., & Esterer, I. (2000). *Es ist normal, verschieden zu sein. Psychose-Seminare—Hilfen zum Dialog.* Psychosoziale Arbeitshilfen 10. Bonn: Psychiatrie-Verlag.

Braun, B. G. (1988). The BASK model of dissociation. *Dissociation: Progress in the Dissociative Disorders, 1* (1): 4–23.

Breitenbach, G., & Requardt, H. (2001). *Psychotherapie mit entmutigten Klienten.* Kröning: Asanger.

Brisch, K. H. (2010). *Bindung und Trauma, Risiken und Schutzfaktoren für die Entwicklung von Kindern.* Stuttgart: Pfeiffer bei Klett-Cotta.

Buchholz, M. B., Lamott, F., & Mörtl, K. (2008). *Tat-Sachen. Narrative von Sexualstraftätern.* Gießen: Psychosozialverlag.

Confucius (2008). *The Analects.* Oxford: Oxford University Press.

Confucius (2014). *Konfuzius Says.* HORIZON Online. http://www.horizont. net/agenturen/nachrichten/Konfuzius-sagt--es-genuegt-nicht-zum-

Fluss-zu-kommen-mit-dem-Wunsch-Fische-zu-fangen.-Man-muss-auch-ein-Netz-mitbringen.-131429 [last accessed 21 November 2014].

Crowley, A. (1977). *The Book of the Law*. Newburyport, MA: Red Wheel/ Weiser.

Dickinson, E. (2007). *The Collected Poems of Emily Dickinson*. Fairford: Echo Library.

Faltin, T. (2008). *Im Angesicht des Todes: Das KZ-Außenlager Echterdingen 1944/45 und der Leidensweg der 600 Häftlinge*. Leinfelden-Echterdingen: Stadt Filderstadt.

Fricke, H. (2004). *Das hört nicht auf, Trauma, Literatur und Empathie*. Göttingen: Wallstein.

Giesbrecht, T., Lynn, S. J., Lilienfeld, S. O., & Merckelbach, H. (2008). Cognitive processes in dissociation: an analysis of core theoretical assumptions. *Psychological Bulletin, 134*: 617–647.

Hass, W. (2009). *Das Hellinger-Virus: Zu Risiken und Nebenwirkungen von Aufstellungen*. Kröning: Asanger.

Hellinger, B. (1995). *Finden was wirkt, Therapeutische Briefe*. Munich: Kösel.

Hellinger, B., Hohnen, H., Ulsamer, B. (2001). *Mit der Seele gehen*. Freiburg: Herder.

Henderson, D. J. (1975). Incest. In: A. M. Freedman, H. I. Kaplan, & B. J. Sadock (Eds.), *Comprehensive Textbook of Psychiatry* (2nd edn.) (pp. 1530–1539). Baltimore MD: Williams and Wilkins.

Hilgers, M. (2001). *Die Ordnung achten*. TAZ, 18 May. http://www.taz. de/1/archiv/?dig=2001/05/18/a0162 [last accessed 26 November 2014].

Hobbes, T. (2012). *Of Man, Being the First Part of Leviathan*. Vol. XXXIV, Part 5. The Harvard Classics. New York: P. F. Collier & Son, 1909–14; Bartleby. com, 2001. www.bartleby.com/34/5/ [last accessed 21 October 2014].

Kastner, H. (2011). *Väter als Täter am eigenen Kind*. Munich: Knaur.

Kernberg, O. F., & Schultz, H. (2009). *Borderline-Störungen und pathologischer Narzissmus*. Frankfurt: Suhrkamp.

Künzler, A., Böttcher, C., Hartmann, R., Nussbaum, M. -H. (2010). *Körperzentrierte Psychotherapie im Dialog—Grundlagen, Anwendungen, Integration*. Berlin: Springer.

LaVey, A. (2007). *Die Satanische Bibel*. Vienna: Index.

Maturana, H., & Varela, F. (1992). *The Tree of Knowledge: The Biological Roots of Human Understanding*. Boston MA: Shambhala Publications.

Miller, A. (2014). *Becoming Yourself: Overcoming Mind Control and Ritual Abuse*. London: Karnac.

Nijenhuis, E. R. S., & den Boer, J. (2009). Psychobiology of traumatization and trauma-related structural dissociation of the personality. In: P. F. Dell, & J. A. O'Neil (Eds.), *Dissociation and the Dissociative Disorders* (pp. 337–366). New York: Taylor & Francis.

Nijenhuis, E. R. S., & Reinders, A. A. T. S. (2012). Fantasy proneness in dissociative identity disorder. *PLoS ONE* 7(6), e39279. doi:10.1371/journal.pone.0039279. Supporting information S1.

Ophüls, M. (1988). *Hotel Terminus: The Life and Times of Klaus Barbie*. USA: Goldwyn.

Reddemann, L. (2001). *Imagination als heilsame Kraft*. Stuttgart: Pfeiffer bei Klett-Cotta.

Reinders, A. A. T. S., Nijenhuis, E. R. S., Paans, A. M., Korf, J., Willemsen, A. T., & Den Boer, J. A. (2003). One brain, two selves. *Neuroimage, 20*: 2119–2125.

Reinders, A. A. T. S., Nijenhuis, E. R. S., Quak, J., Korf, J., Haaksma, J., Paans, A. M., & den Boer, J. A. (2006). Psychobiological characteristics of dissociative identity disorder: a symptom provocation study. *Biological Psychiatry, 60*: 730–740.

Reinders, A. A. T. S., Willemsen, A. T. M., Vos, H. P. J., den Boer, J. A., & Nijenhuis, E. R. S. (2012). Fact or factitious? A psychobiological study of authentic and simulated dissociative identity states. *PLoS ONE, 7* (6): e39279. doi:10.1371/journal.pone.0039279.

Satir, V. (2004). *Kommunikation. Selbstwert. Kongruenz: Konzepte und Perspektiven familientherapeutischer Praxis*. Paderborn: Junfermann.

Schopenhauer, A. (1859). *Werkausgabe*. Leipzig: F. A. Brockhaus.

Studentischer Sprecherrat der Universität München (Ed.) (2005). *Niemand kann seinem Schicksal entgehen: Kritik an Weltbild und Methode des Bert Hellinger*. Munich: Alibri.

Vachss, A. (2004). *Merkt Euch Ihre Namen! "Bert" Hellinger, Therapeut der besonderen Art*. www.vachss.de/mission/berichterstattung/hellinger. html [last accessed 23 October 2014].

Van Derbur, M. (2003). *Miss America by Day*. Denver CO: Oak Hill.

van der Hart, O., Nijenhuis, E. R. S., & Steele, K. (2006). *The Haunted Self: Structural Dissociation and the Treatment of Chronic Traumatization*. New York: W. W. Norton.

van der Kolk, B. (1996). *Traumatic Stress*. New York: Guilford.

von Goethe, J. W. (1997). *Faust: Part 1 and 2*. London: Bloomsbury Academic.

Wheeler, C., & Springmeier, F. (2000). *The Illuminati Formula Used to Create an Undetectable Total Mind Controlled Slave*. www.theforbiddenknowledge. com/hardtruth/illuminati_formula_mind_control.htm [last accessed 26 November 2014].

Weber, G. (2010). *Zweierlei Glück: Das Familienstellen Bert Hellingers*. Heidelberg: Carl Auer.

World Health Organization (1992). *The ICD-10 Classification of Mental and Behavioural Disorders: Diagnostic Criteria for Research*. Geneva: WHO.

Zweig, S. (2003). *Castellio gegen Calvin oder Ein Gewissen gegen die Gewalt*. Frankfurt: Fischer.

FURTHER READING

Barlow, M. R., & Freyd, J. (2009). Adaptive dissociation: information processing and response to betrayal. In: P. F. Dell, & J. A. O'Neil (Eds.), *Dissociation and the Dissociative Disorders* (pp. 93–105). New York: Taylor & Francis.

Bower, T. (1987). *The Paperclip Conspiracy: The Hunt for the Nazi Scientists.* Boston, MA: Little Brown.

Bryant, N. (2009). *The Franklin Scandal: A Story of Powerbrokers, Child Abuse and Betrayal.* Walterville OR: Trine Day.

Camper, F. (1996). *The MK/Ultra Secret: An Account of CIA Deception.* Savannah GA: Christopher Scott.

Dell, P. F. (2006). The Multidimensional Inventory of Dissociation (MID): A comprehensive measure of pathological dissociation. *Journal of Trauma & Dissociation, 7* (2): 77–106.

Epstein, O. B., Schwartz, J., & Schwartz, R. W. (2011). *Ritual Abuse and Mind Control: The Manipulation of Attachment Needs.* London: Bowlby Centre/ Karnac.

Freyd, J. (1996). *Betrayal Trauma.* Cambridge, MA: Harvard University Press.

Herman, J. (1992). *Trauma and Recovery.* New York: Basic Books.

Hoffman, W. (2014). *The Enslaved Queen: A Memoir about Electricity and Mind Control.* London: Karnac.

215

Kluft, R. P. (1993). Basic principles in conducting the psychotherapy of multiple personality disorder. In: R. P. Kluft, & C. G. Fine, (Eds.) *Clinical Perspectives on Multiple Personality Disorder* (pp. 19–50). Washington, DC: American Psychiatric Press.

Kluft, R. P. (1997). On the treatment of the traumatic memories of DID patients: Always? Never? Sometimes? Now? Later? *Dissociation, 10* (2): 80–90.

Kluft, R. P. (2013). *Shelter from the Storm: Processing the Traumatic Memories of DID/DDNOS Patients with the Fractionated Abreaction Technique*. Online: CreateSpace Independent Publishing Platform.

Lifton, R. J. (1986). *The Nazi Doctors: Medical Killing and the Psychology of Genocide*. New York: Basic Books.

Miller, A. (2012). *Healing the Unimaginable: Treating Ritual Abuse and Mind Control*. London: Karnac.

Ross, C. A. (1997). *Dissociative Identity Disorder: Diagnosis, Clinical Features and Treatment of Multiple Personality* (2nd edn). New York: Wiley.

Ross, C. A. (2000). *Bluebird: Deliberate Creation of Multiple Personalities by Psychiatrists*. Richardson, TX: Manitou Communications.

Rutz, C. (2001). *A Nation Betrayed: The Chilling True Story of Secret Cold War Experiments Performed on Our Children and Other Innocent People*. Grass Lake, MI: Fidelity.

Rutz, C., Becker, T., Overkamp, B., & Karriker, W. (2008). Exploring commonalities reported by adult survivors of extreme abuse: preliminary empirical findings. In: R. Noblitt and P. Perskin Noblitt (Eds.), *Ritual Abuse in the Twenty-First Century* (pp. 31–84). Bandon, OR: Robert D. Reed.

van der Hart, O. & Nijenhuis, E. R. S. (1999). Bearing witness to uncorroborated trauma: the clinician's development of reflective belief. *Professional Psychology: Research and Practice, 30* (1): 37–44.

Woodsun, G. (1998). *The Ultimate Challenge: A Revolutionary, Sane and Sensible Response to Ritualistic and Cult-Related Abuse*. Laramie, WY: Action Resources International.

INDEX